Ancient Peoples and Places

THE ART OF
THE ROMANS

General Editor

DR GLYN DANIEL

Ancient Peoples and Places

THE ART OF THE
ROMANS

J. M. C. Toynbee

90 PHOTOGRAPHS

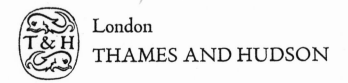

London
THAMES AND HUDSON

THIS IS VOLUME FORTY-THREE IN THE SERIES
Ancient Peoples and Places
GENERAL EDITOR: DR GLYN DANIEL

© J. M. C. TOYNBEE 1965
FIRST PUBLISHED 1965
PRINTED IN GREAT BRITAIN BY
WESTERN PRINTING SERVICES LTD, BRISTOL
NOT TO BE IMPORTED FOR SALE INTO THE U.S.A.

CONTENTS

6

ILLUSTRATIONS

In memoriam
Eugenie Strong

Preface

THIS BOOK IS INTENDED for the student and the general reader who are already well acquainted with the history and literature of ancient Rome, but have as yet no special knowledge of her archaeology and art. It is essentially an introduction, written in the hope that if such a reader is attracted by the subject of Roman art he will want to follow up the evidence on which the statements in the text are based, to investigate in greater detail the individual monuments and classes of monuments discussed and partly illustrated here, and to learn where he can find publications of the many works of art that are mentioned without any illustration. In the notes on the text an attempt has been made to provide the necessary aids to further study of this kind; and since these notes contain a good deal of detailed bibliographical matter, including references to some material not cited in the text, the Select Bibliography has for the most part been confined to general works on the art of the Romans as a whole that are larger or in some way more comprehensive than a book in this series could be, and to general monographs on various topics.

In a work of this limited compass Roman architecture—a subject demanding a volume to itself—could not be included. My volume is mainly concentrated on the other major arts of sculpture, painting, and mosaic; and there, rather than selecting certain monuments or some special viewpoint, I have tried to give the reader some idea of the range, in content, style, and geographical extent, of all the aspects involved. But inasmuch as sculpture has survived in far greater bulk and in more varieties than has any other major form of Roman art, more than two-thirds of my text and illustrations have been allotted to it. The so-called minor arts, which cover an enormous field, have had, it will be felt, a very mean share of my attention. On the other hand, had I attempted to deal with them on the same scale as the rest, I should have been obliged to neglect altogether a number of important categories of sculpture and painting. The best solution seemed to be to give in Chapter X a summary list of all the minor arts, to map, as it were, the complete territory for the reader's benefit, and to devote to them a longer and more detailed section of the bibliography and a few of the illustrations.

In recent times books on Roman art have been appearing in something of a spate that shows no sign of drying up. This fact proves that there is no longer any need to plead the cause of the subject as one full of interest and deserving of study in its own right. Nevertheless, within living memory such a need did exist; and in this field the foremost British pioneer was the late Eugenie (Mrs Arthur) Strong, whose books *Roman Art* (1900), *Roman Sculpture* (1907), *La scultura romana* (1923, 1926), and *Art in Ancient Rome* (1929) laid the foundations on which the researches of subsequent students have been built. My debts to fellow students of the art of the Romans are far too many to be listed here individually. But it is to Mrs Strong's inspiration and to the unstinted help that she gave me, when as a young graduate I decided to devote myself to Hellenistic and Roman history, archaeology, and art, that I owe the greatest debt of all. And it is to her memory that I dedicate, with respect and affection, this little work.

Finally, I wish to thank Dr Glyn Daniel and the publishers for their invitation to contribute to this series and for all their help and valuable suggestions.

J.M.C.T.

CHAPTER I

Introduction

ART IN THE ROMAN WORLD FROM THE SIXTH CENTURY BC TO THE END OF THE SECOND CENTURY BC

IN THIS BOOK the term 'Romans' is used in its widest sense, to denote not only the inhabitants of Rome, but also all those peoples of the ancient world who, from her first emergence as an expanding power down to the end of the fifth century AD, looked to her as the centre of the common life and culture that they shared in their varying degrees. Thus Roman art possesses a threefold meaning. It is, in the first place, the art of the city of Rome from the sixth century BC to its occupation by Teutonic conquerors in the late fifth century of our era. In the second place, it is the art of Italy as gradually absorbed by Rome and ultimately united under her hegemony. In the third place, it is the art of all the lands outside Italy that came, stage by stage, to be controlled by, or dependent on, Rome, the art of every province of her Empire and of every Romanised peripheral region, from southern Scotland to Mesopotamia, from the Sahara to beyond the Rhine and Danube. It is an art that is both regional and cosmopolitan in its almost infinitely varied manifestations. And its spirit and motifs were still alive and active far beyond the point of time at which we date, conventionally, the beginning of Byzantine and medieval history.

The Roman people in the narrow sense, that is, the original inhabitants of Rome and the stock directly descended from them, were not, it seems, naturally endowed with creative artistic genius. All the evidence suggests that for the sculptural and painted decoration of their earliest temples, notably the temple of Jupiter on the Capitol, they depended on Etruscan artists, who were themselves, as is of course well known, deeply indebted to the art of archaic Greece. Greek art reached Etruria partly through objects imported from the eastern Mediterranean world and partly through immigrant Greek artists, who came to work for patrons in Italy; and this was the first true art known to Rome, in her regal period of Etruscan domination during the sixth century. With the literary tradition that records the names and activities of Graeco-Etruscan craftsmen in Rome at this time the findings of archaeology are in full agreement. There are fragments of architectural terracotta figure sculptures, once brightly painted and bearing that peculiar local stamp that differentiates Etruscan products from those of Greek art proper. Such discoveries in Rome can, indeed, be closely paralleled in the contemporary sculpture and painting of all the chief central Italian cities of Etruria and Latium; and in the fifth century BC, when the Romans had expelled their kings and become an independent republic, terracottas were still being made in or for Rome (to judge from those unearthed on her site that can be dated to that century) which were derived from the same Etruscan source and were worked in the same archaic style. For Etruria, curiously, seems to have very largely missed the influence of the early- and mid-classical Greek development and her art passed almost straight from the archaic phase to the late-classical and Hellenistic phases of the fourth and third centuries.

For some time to come sculptors, using clay, stone, and bronze, and painters of Etruscan and Latin origin were to play a leading role in Rome's artistic life; and in the early fourth century cult-statues plundered from the temples at Veii and Praeneste found their way Romewards.[1] But the young Republic had in the meantime begun to make its own direct contacts with Hellenic art. We are told[2] that two Greek sculptor-painters, Damophilus and Gorgasus, came to Rome, most probably from Magna Graecia, to decorate the temple of Ceres, which is held by some to have been erected in the fifth century; and that a statue of a certain Hermodorus of Ephesus was set up in the Comitium.[3] It was, however, not until the closing years of the fourth, and the first half of the third, century, when the Samnite and Pyrrhic wars brought the Romans face to face with the culture of Campania and southern Italy, that they began to experience the full, and from then onwards, permanent effects of Greek artistic influence. We have, for instance, the record of statues erected in Rome by the citizens of Thurii.[4] These were doubtless imports from Magna Graecia, as were also almost certainly the statues of Pythagoras and Alcibiades placed in the Comitium.[5] This was also the period at which the late-classical and early-Hellenistic idealising 'portrait' made its first appearance in Rome in the form both of the bronze statues of contemporary leading citizens that litera-ture describes and of the imaginary 'portraits' of kings and early republican heroes, ascribed in the written sources to a much earlier time, but clearly products of the late fourth and early third centuries, when the Romans had begun to develop a historical self-consciousness.

It is, in fact, just the 'portrait' style of this age that we see reflected in the heads of kings and early republican notables on the obverses of Roman silver coins issued in the first century BC[6]—heads that are very likely to be copies of the then still surviving original bronze statues. Most of these coin 'portraits' are in the rich, plastic, fully Hellenic manner. But some show applied to this basically Greek style the drier, more linear, and more formal treatment of human features, hair, and beards which marks the bronze, stone, and terracotta heads found in central Italy, outside Rome, that date from the fourth and third centuries. It would seem that among the bronze 'portrait' statues set up in Rome a few, at least, were by the hands of Etrusco-Latin artists; and the impact made upon such artists by the new Greek 'portrait' is further evidenced by the two thousand statues, not of gods, but of human persons, that a Roman general is reported to have plundered from Volsinii in

264 BC.[7] Traces of this mid-Italian type of treatment can be seen re-appearing, here and there, throughout the history of Roman iconography. It was one of Etruria's lasting legacies to Rome: others—equally important—were the togate statue, the figures stretched in the sleep of death, or reclining at the funerary banquet, on the lids of sarcophagi, and the carved and painted scenes depicting those religious rites and secular spectacles that the Romans had borrowed from their neighbours.

Fabius Pictor, who is said[8]—and we have no grounds for doubting the tradition—to have painted, round about 300 BC, the walls of the temple of Salus in Rome, is the first painter with a Roman name known to us. We have no indication as to what his work was like or as to who were his masters in the art. This was the time at which an early-Hellenistic style of painting first appeared among the Etruscans. Fabius' inspiration may have come from them or directly from Magna Graecia; and to about the same period also belongs the well-known Ficeroni bronze casket engraved with a scene from Hellenic legend—from the story of the Argonauts—shown in a landscape setting.[9] This scene might have been based on an early-Hellenistic picture and the inscription—'Novios Plautios made me in Rome'— could refer to the maker of the casket, not to the engraver of its decoration. At any rate a Greek may well have been the author of the painting presenting his victories in Sicily that Manius Valerius Maximus Corvinus Messala exhibited in Rome in 264—the first example that has been recorded[10] in the long series of Roman triumphal pictures which were destined to continue far into imperial times. We know the names of two painters of such Roman scenes in Rome in the second century BC and both of them were Greeks—Metrodorus from Athens, who worked for Lucius Aemilius Paullus' Macedonian triumph in 168,[11] and the 'place-painter' Demetrius of Alexandria;[12] while of paintings of contemporary, or near-contemporary, events we have at least one early-Hellenistic example. This is the picture, mentioned by the Elder Pliny,[13] of the battle of Alexander and Darius executed by Philoxenos of Eretria for one of Alexander's generals, which, if the famous mosaic pavement from Pompeii[14] faithfully reflects it, was very circumstantial in its details. But whoever carried out the earliest of these triumphal paintings, they themselves were the first manifestations of a very special and enduring taste among the Romans for the factual, documentary rendering of scenes from recent and contemporary history; and their descendants were the great State reliefs of the early and middle Empire (Ch. IV). In Italy outside Rome a similar taste can be detected in such historical scenes, dating from the third century BC, as those in the paintings from the François Tomb at Vulci[15] and on the engraved bronze casket from Praeneste, where the triumph of a Roman general is represented.[16] The only significant surviving fragment of a historical painting of this period found in Rome comes from a tomb and shows in three superimposed registers scenes that include one of a surrender and another of a parley in which are involved the same two generals, one Roman, the other Italian.[17] Of the painter we know nothing; but he could, like Fabius Pictor, have been a Roman.

Of actual works of art belonging to the third century BC that have come down to us, coin types alone provide a continuous sequence of monuments whose development can be securely traced. In 269 Rome adopted for the first time coinage proper on the Greek model, striking both in silver, according to the precedent long established in Magna Graecia, and in heavy bronze (*aes grave*), which reflected the tradition of currency in the shape of large brick-like pieces (the so-called *aes signatum*), stamped with figures of animals, birds, and other objects, all rendered in a naturalistic, Hellenising style, which had come into circulation in central Italy about the beginning of the century. These initial issues of coins in the true sense, of which the silver was almost certainly intended for use in southern

Italy, carry types—heads of Greek and Roman deities, animals, etc.—that are definitely Greek in treatment; and there can be little doubt that south-Italian artists played a prominent part in their designing. This would seem to be particularly true of the finer types that appear on the silver, whereas the coarser bronze types might have been the work of the central-Italian pupils of the Greek masters. These issues lasted until about 222 BC; and the same general stylistic characteristics mark the second set of issues, which continued into the late third or early second century. The leading reverse types of the silver of this period are Jupiter driving a four-horse chariot towards the right (*quad-rigatus*) and Victory driving a four-horse chariot towards the left (*victoriatus*); but one type displays a scene from Roman military ritual—an oath-taking over the body of a pig. Both the reverse groups and the obverse heads of deities on these silver issues are extremely delicate and neat in their technique.

During the closing years of the third century BC the plunder-ing by victorious Roman generals of Syracuse, Capua, and Tarentum marked the beginning of the mass-importation into Rome of the art-treasures of the Hellenistic world. In the second century this process was extended eastwards across the Adriatic to Greece proper and Asia Minor. As from Magna Graecia, so from the east, a steady stream of Greek artists flowed north-wards and westwards, partly at the bidding of the generals and partly in search of new and wealthy patrons in the city by the Tiber that was now emerging as the mistress and cultural centre of much of the Mediterranean world.

From the second century, as from the third, relatively few original works of Roman art survive apart from coin types. Some numismatists hold that what was to become the standard Roman silver monetary unit, the *denarius*, was issued for the first time *c.* 212, others date its inauguration to *c.* 187. But whenever they began, the types of these *denarii* were, to start with, almost invariably the head of a helmeted goddess on the obverse and on the reverse the Dioscuri galloping side by side. Here again the style and the technique are very fine. After the middle of the century other divine figures—gods and personifications—appear on the reverses, together with a few scenes that allude to Roman legend and earlier history. Towards the close of the century the oath-taking scene recurs; and another Roman scene shows voting in the Comitium. The stage is now set for the rich variety of legendary and historical reverse types which give the *denarii* of the first century BC their unique interest both as State reliefs in miniature and as preludes to the essentially medallic types of the great imperial coin and medallion issues (Ch. X).

One unique Roman coin belongs to a series of works of art of the second century BC that were produced by Greek artists on Greek soil and in the full Hellenistic style, but in a Roman context and under Roman auspices. This was the gold piece struck by Titus Quinctius Flamininus in Greece to commemorate his victory over Philip V of Macedon in 197.[18] On the reverse is a Victory with the legend T QVINCTI, while the obverse shows a portrait of the victor with wind-tossed hair and upward-gazing eyes. Flamininus was an ardent philhellene and it must have pleased him to be portrayed in this 'baroque' guise, patently reminiscent of the heaven-inspired Alexander type, with a few individual facial traits superadded. Nearly thirty years later another Greek artist recorded in Greece a further Roman victory, that of Lucius Aemilius Paullus at Pydna over the Macedonians under Perseus. On the thanksgiving monument dedicated by Paullus at Delphi is a sculptured frieze depicting the battle—a somewhat academic rendering enlivened by bold foreshortening and the realistic representation of the national arms and armour of the combatants.[19] It seems not unlikely that the designer of this frieze was the Metrodorus from Athens whom, as we have seen, Paullus summoned to Rome to execute his triumphal paintings. If so, Metrodorus might have brought to Italy the cartoons that he had made for

Plate 1

the Delphic frieze; and it is noteworthy that a tomb in southern Italy, at Lecce, of about this date was adorned with a limestone relief[20] that resembles quite remarkably closely, both in its style and in its details, the frieze on Paullus' monument in Greece.

The masterpieces of sculpture which, from the second half of the third century until the middle of the second century, the kings of Pergamon commissioned both for Athens and for their own royal capital had established the latter's claim to be the most distinguished centre of artistic activity in the whole Hellenistic world. All this Rome inherited when in 133 BC Attalus III bequeathed his kingdom to her; and from the late first century BC down to the early third century AD we can follow the persistent influence exercised on Roman art by the Pergamene sculptural tradition as regards both the style and content of its figure subjects and the treatment of its decorative motifs. Meanwhile we can observe how the character of mid⁄ Hellenistic carving in general is mirrored in the few surviving works of monumental sculpture, dating from the late second century BC, that have come to light in Rome and were locally produced. Such are the large terracotta pedimental figures, executed mainly in the round, from a temple on the Caelian Hill. Particularly striking are the very naturalistically modelled torso of a sacrificial attendant and the highly pictorial, spirally twisted posture of a seated goddess.[21]

Plate 2

But the most important gift to Rome from second⁄ and early⁄ first⁄century Hellenistic art was the true portrait, that is, the realistic, unidealised likeness of a specific individual as he or she actually appeared. That such likenesses were being made in Greek and Hellenised lands as early as the third century, and achieved their full development in the second century, we know from the coin portraits of the kings of Pergamon, Pontus, Bac⁄ tria, etc.—a series of brilliant physiognomic studies, in which the subjects' unprepossessing, sometimes brutal, features and expressions are rendered with an almost ruthless fidelity.[22]

For examples of large-scale true portraits of this period we must turn again to the series of works made by Greeks on Greek soil under Roman aegis, this time to the portrait statues carved on the island of Delos mainly between the establishment there by Rome in 166 BC of a colony of Italian merchants and the destruction of that colony in 88 BC by Mithridates VI of Pontus. As inscriptions make plain, the well-to-do settlers from Italy and the landowners from Athens, whom Rome protected, patronised the arts and attracted to the island whole families of sculptors from a number of Hellenistic centres. The subjects of the Delian portraits were both Greeks and Italians; but the artists whose signatures have survived were consistently of Greek nationality. The bodies of the statues often show these person-ages nude, in heroic guise, and are always quite conventional, mere stands for the heads, which, when preserved, are seen to be intensely individualised, with all the racial traits, of the Italians in particular, vividly delineated. Among the Italians portrayed were Caius Billienus, a governor, and Caius Ofellius Ferus, an official; and in these is reflected a growing Roman taste for creating likenesses, not only of kings, poets, philo-sophers, and other famous characters, but also of ordinary and relatively unimportant persons.[23] That this taste was also shared by contemporary and later Greeks is clear both from the finds on Delos and from discoveries made elsewhere, in Athens, for instance, and in Egypt. Nevertheless, in Rome there appears to have been a quite particular passion for honorific portraits of undistinguished people, since the Elder Pliny records[24] that in 158 BC the Senate ordered the removal from the Forum of all statues of magistrates that had not been officially authorised. It is very probable that, as on Delos, so in Rome, these statues were the work of Greeks, perhaps with the collaboration, in Rome, of some Etruscan portraitists, who were themselves now strongly imbued with the spirit of the mid-Hellenistic realistic portrait. Indeed, some idea of what the Roman honorific statues of the second century BC were like may be gained from the famous bronze portrait statue known as the 'Arringatore'.[25] Found in Lake Trasimene and carrying inscriptions that give the names of the subject, the artist, and the person who com- missioned it, all Etruscans, it displays the early, skimpy style of toga and unmistakably individual features—a square head, an irregular mouth, and a rumpled brow. It dates from the second half of the second century.

At any rate, there was in Rome a special *milieu* that particularly favoured the development of true portraiture. It was the *milieu* of the old, aristocratic Roman families, the patrician *gentes*, who had possessed from early times the private, exclusive right of keeping in their homes masks, or *imagines*, of their ancestors, which were brought out and paraded, along with those of the recently deceased, at family funerals. No primitive masks of this kind have survived from Rome itself; but from primitive funerary masks found elsewhere, and from other types of early representations of the dead in Italy, we may infer that originally these *imagines* were of a very generalised and un- individualised character, certainly not to be equated (as has often been done) with death-masks proper cast directly from the faces of the deceased. Of that mechanical and somewhat sophisticated process there is no sign in Rome and Italy before quite late republican times. Neither Polybius[26] nor the Elder Pliny[27] give any hint of it when they describe in two well- known passages the display of masks at patrician funerals in Rome about the middle of the second century BC. But what Polybius in particular does show quite clearly is that by this period the old Roman *imago* had become an extremely in- dividualised and realistic likeness—just at the time when Rome had encountered the vivid realism and individualism of mid- Hellenistic portraiture. The Roman nobility had, in fact, acquired a taste for funerary masks that were truly portraits in this Hellenistic sense; and in Rome Greek craftsmen, together with their local pupils and imitators, had found a new scope for their skill in Roman aristocratic and religious practice.[28] *Imagines* made primarily for ceremonial use in terracotta, wood, or wax, could not by themselves, however realistic they might be, have created an art of portraiture as the Hellenistic Greeks understood it. But when this Roman funerary tradition had been thoroughly fused with the new second-century demand for honorific, non-funerary likenesses of individuals the time was ripe for the appearance, during the first century BC, of the Roman republican portrait as we know it from the great array of realistic heads, busts, and statues of Roman subjects, in stone, marble, and occasionally bronze, which have actually come down to us and which will be surveyed in Chapter II.

In tracing the story of Roman art from the opening of the first century BC onwards we shall have at our disposal a plentiful supply of original works of sculpture, painting, mosaic, and the minor crafts. We shall depend for our information much less heavily than we have done so far on literary references;[29] and coin types will no longer be our only abundant source of first-hand material. Henceforth we shall be studying our monuments chronologically class by class. But before we do that we must summarise the findings of the present chapter in so far as they bear upon the origins of art among the Romans—turning our backs, once and for all, on the controversy waged for so long between those who claim that these origins derive predominantly from Italy and those who would trace them solely to Greece. Central Italy (notably Etruria), Magna Graecia, mainland and Asiatic Greece all played their parts and made their contributions to the synthesis. On the one hand, there is much in the developed Roman art of the late Republic and Empire which would be unintelligible without some knowledge of Rome's Etruscan heritage. On the

other hand, there is an absolute continuity between that Roman
art and the art of the Hellenistic world that Rome absorbed.
From the literary and epigraphic evidence we cannot but con-
clude that, at any rate under the late Republic and early Empire,
the artistic output of the Roman world was, for the most part, in
the hands of Greek or at least east-Mediterranean masters, who
led the schools and directed the workshops in Rome and Italy
and, to a lesser extent, in some of the western provinces, as well
as in the eastern, Greek-speaking lands. Moreover, we can see in
Hellenistic times the first appearance of the very three art-forms
that were destined to express the Roman spirit most eloquently:
the climax of realistic portraiture; the continuous style and the
documentary method in narration; and the naturalistic, three-
dimensional rendering of space, depth, and atmosphere in
distant and complex views in painting and relief sculpture.
And we may venture to suggest that, if Rome had not become,
from the second century BC onwards, the guardian and ruler
of the homelands of Hellenistic art, she would never have
produced the great imperial art that she has bequeathed to us.
Nevertheless, the converse is also true. Rome had a very definite
role of her own to play in the evolution of ancient art; and again
we would suggest that, if Greek artists had not been provided by
the Romans with a new setting and centre, new subjects, new
patrons, a new purpose and dignity, and a new sense of art as a
service both in public and in private life,[30] Hellenistic art,
having achieved the apotheosis of technical perfection and
having run through the gamut of its fresh ideas, might have
perished from aimlessness and inanition by the end of the first
century BC. As it was, not only did external circumstances en-
able Roman-age artists to work out and exploit on a much
more extensive scale the new artistic movements which had
been initiated in the Hellenistic period, but the Roman State
itself became a great new patron of the arts and a new well-
spring of inspiration. Roman art is, then, the child of the

marriage of two traditions—one, the Hellenistic art tradition, and the sculptural branch of that tradition in particular; the other, the political, social, religious, and psychological tradition of Rome, on which she built a new historical framework for ancient civilisation.

Chapter II

Portrait Sculpture in the Round and in High Relief

Of all classes of sculpture associated with the Romans the best-known and the one generally held to be the most characteristically Roman is the portrait, whether in the form of a bust or of a full-length statue, in the round or in relief. As we have seen (*cf.* pp. 17, 22 ff.), both idealised and realistic likenesses of individuals, including the 'fancy' ones of persons in Roman legend or in the more remote historical periods, first appeared in Rome under late-classical Greek and Hellenistic influence; and until the second half of the second century AD there was always an antiquarian demand for copies of portraits of famous Greek personalities. But for the Romans, with their deeply rooted family sense, their emphasis on character, and their factual concern with individual achievement, the true sculptured portrait satisfied a special psychological and social need. It could serve as a biography and summarise a man's career. Hence the marked development under the late Republic of an iconographic interest already present in the art of Hellenistic lands—an interest in portraying old and elderly people as they were remembered at the close of their *cursus vitae*.

This commemorative aspect of the Roman portrait was, of course, intimately linked with Roman funerary practice. Busts of ancestors and more recently deceased relatives could furnish descendants and survivors with objects for domestic veneration or they could be ranged in family mausolea; and it is clear from archaeological evidence that by the end of the Republic and first century of the Empire busts were sometimes used instead of masks as *imagines* preserved in the home and displayed at funerals. For instance, a togate statue in Rome (New Capitoline Museum) shows a patrician presumably walking in a funeral procession as he bears in either hand an ancestral bust.[1] These busts would be translations into marble of wax or clay originals; and while the statue itself is of the late Augustan period, the busts are of different shapes and styles and reflect two first-century BC portrait types of different dates. Middle-class plebeian families had, as a rule, no *imagines* in the strict patrician meaning of the term. But in late republican and early imperial times the portraits of their dead appear as busts or full-length figures in the round, and as busts, or, less frequently, as full-length figures carved in high relief on vertical tombstones (*stelae*). In Rome and Italy the faces of these funerary representations, which continued to the end of the first century AD (when in the central Mediterranean areas the carved sarcophagus [Ch. VI] began to replace the tombstone) and occasionally later, are often highly individualised and suggest that they are actual portraits. But throughout the provinces, in some of which the grave relief and the funerary human figure in the round survived as art-forms until as late as the third century AD, the 'portraits' are normally stock or typical renderings, corresponding in each case only in a general way with the sex, age, profession, etc. of the person or persons to be commemorated. Yet even there, from Britain in the west to Palmyra in the east, the details of the features, dress, and attributes show a realistic and intimate, not seldom local, characterisation that provides a striking contrast to the unswerving idealism of Hellenic grave reliefs of the fifth and fourth centuries and of their humbler Hellenistic successors. The same is true of the *ex-voto* human 'portraits', in the round or in relief, found in provincial temples.

Plate 4

 The earliest surviving examples in the west of true portrait sculpture belong to Rome and her immediate neighbourhood. The art was to begin with essentially a Roman metropolitan one; and it was, moreover, so far as we can tell, a sudden

flowering not long after 100 BC.[2] Among the obverse heads on
denarii of the first century BC there are, as we have already noted,
imaginary 'portraits' of kings and early republican heroes.
There was also struck *c.* 91 BC a decidedly more portrait-like
head of Scipio Africanus Major, who died in 183 BC, still
recalling the 'baroque' inspired Alexander type. But it is not
until we come to the obverse heads depicting the outstanding
men of the early first century BC, Lucius Cornelius Sulla, who
retired from political life in 79, Aulus Postumius Albinus,
who died in 89, and Caius Coelius Caldus, whose *floruit* was
c. 85–75, that we get completely realistic likenesses, with all the
folds and creases in the face and the individual traits and expression faithfully rendered. These coin portraits were struck
several decades after their subjects' deaths, but we have no
reason to doubt that they were based on contemporary sculptured portraits; and around the coin portraits of the public
figures we can group the sculptured portraits of unknown
Romans that are closely related to them in style.

A slightly later coin portrait, that of Caius Antius Restio,
whose *floruit* was *c.* 75–65, carries with it a group of sculptured
likenesses in which Hellenistic realism reached under Roman
auspices that extreme point in its development to which the
label 'verism' has been applied. Here we find reflected the
current conception of the time-honoured 'old Roman' national
character and the starkest manifestation of the descriptive,
biographical, chronicling style that was inspired by patrician
family tradition. This style is very dry and linear, more akin,
in a way, to that of wood-carving than to that of sculpture, and
it displays a microscopic observation of such exterior details as
wrinkles, hollows, creases, and folds of skin, even warts and
moles—all reproduced with remorseless, almost photographic,
exactitude. 'Verism' is already visible in portraits made in east-
Mediterranean lands during the late second and early first
centuries BC; and we have every reason to believe that its final

Plate 3

evolution in the west was the work, for the most part, not of native Roman artists, but of immigrant Hellenistic sculptors responding to the taste of a special stratum of Roman aristo-cratic society. It is obvious that likenesses of this type, of which the veiled head in the Vatican (Museo Chiaramonti)[3] and a head in the Torlonia Museum in Rome[4] are superb examples, demanded long experience and a very high degree of skill in marble-carving—a technique in which the Romans and Etruscans had no tradition of their own, since it was not until the time of Augustus that the Luna (Carrara) marble quarries of north-west Italy were systematically exploited.

cf. Plate 5

The 'Restio' style of portrait (see above) survived for several decades in bourgeois funerary and commemorative art. But in high-class monumental marble sculpture it was rapidly superseded by styles that harked back to the 'baroque' and idealising tendencies of early- to mid-Hellenistic iconography. This was due to the emergence during the period of the civil wars of leading personalities of strong philhellenic interests—such personalities as Lucullus, Pompey, Cicero, and Julius Caesar. A rich pictorialism marks the portraits of Pompey the Great, the best known of them being the marble bust in the Ny Carlsberg Glyptotek in Copenhagen.[5] This, as its technique shows, is a copy made in imperial times of a republican original (republican portraits continued to be copied until as late as the mid second century AD); but its close resemblance to the coin portraits of Pompey issued ten years or so after his death shows it to be a very faithful copy both in features and in style. The face is unidealised and extremely individual, with its flabby cheeks, mean eyes, puckered, worried brow, and bulbous nose. But there is a strong element of picturesqueness in the wind-tossed hair and in the soft, fluid modelling of the flesh. The still more plastic and decidedly more idealising treatment of the likenesses of Cicero is illustrated by a head in the Capitoline Museum,[6] while in a portrait of the orator in the Uffizi in

Florence the plasticity is modified by a more 'veristic' rendering of the wrinkles, folds, and creases.[7] We note an even sharper contrast of styles in the portraits of Julius Caesar and his contemporaries. The 'Restio' style is very evident in some of Caesar's coin portraits.[8] But the inspiration of the splendid head of Caesar in the Campo Santo at Pisa[9] comes from very early Hellenistic iconography; and with pieces of this type we have drawn very near to the classicism of Augustan portrait sculpture.

Plate 6

None the less, until the late third century AD the effects of the 'veristic', descriptive style of portraiture were never wholly obscured. It was the style that produced in late republican times the death-mask type of likeness, based, to all appearances, on death-masks proper taken directly from the faces of the deceased, although we lack explicit literary evidence that such a practice did in fact obtain in ancient Rome. And the greater part of the story of Roman iconography throughout the imperial epoch is the story of the interaction of two complementary rather than opposed principles—on the one hand, classicism and idealism, sometimes combined with vividly pictorial elements, on the other, a factual, prosaic realism ultimately stemming from the 'Restio' tradition.

The earliest datable portraits of Augustus (63 BC–AD 14) are on gold and silver coins of eastern mintage struck between 31 and 29 BC. The obverses of these pieces show his likeness in 'baroque' guise, with an intense gaze and long, somewhat untidy, wind-tossed hair. And it may be to those years that we should assign the creation of his Hellenistic type of portrait in the round, a type well exemplified in a marble head in the Capitoline Museum in Rome, where the locks on the brow form a single fork above the left eye and a sweeping triple curve, topped by a leonine wave, above the right temple.[10] Portraits in a fully idealising style, based on fifth-century BC Greek models, such as the head at Boston, Massachusetts,[11] most probably belong to the years immediately preceding the battle of Actium, when Caesar's youthful heir was establishing his claim to mastery of the western Roman world. But more than half of Augustus' surviving portraits belong to a third main type, which reveals a splendid fusion of Hellenic idealism with the individual features—notably the three-pronged fork of locks above the centre of the brow and the confident, controlled expression—of Rome's first citizen. This was clearly intended to be the norm for all his official portraits; and the type may well have been connected with the events of 28 and 27 BC, when the main lines of the Princeps' powers and position were permanently defined. It is known as the 'Prima Porta' type because its most brilliant example is the famous statue in the Vatican found in Livia's villa at Prima Porta, a few miles north of Rome.[12] This presents Augustus as *imperator*, greeting or addressing some vast, unseen audience, which he holds by the magic of his will and personality, and wearing an elaborate cuirass on which the cosmic setting of his rule and his practical achievements—in chief, the recovery from Parthia in 20 BC of the lost Roman standards—are depicted in relief. But this actual piece cannot have been the model for all Augustus' portraits of this type, since its bare legs and feet show it to be posthumous. It must be a copy of an earlier original.

Plate 7

Throughout imperial history the labelled and often precisely dated coin portraits of emperors, empresses, and other members of the ruling dynasties provide a firm foundation on which the series of portraits in the round of each successive reign can be securely built. They record, in particular, changes in both male and female hair-styles in so far as the profile view displays them. It is, then, generally speaking, fairly easy to identify the sculptural likeness of an emperor or empress and to assign to a given reign that of a private individual, since court fashions in coiffure were swiftly adopted by private citizens throughout the Roman world. Problems are, however, posed when the portraits of one age are consciously modelled on those of a former period; or when a later hair-style closely resembles one that was in vogue many generations earlier. Of the fascinating story of Roman iconography from the first to the late fifth century AD only the barest outline can be traced here.

Among the portraits of members of Augustus' family those of his son-in-law, Agrippa, are distinguished by the deep-set eyes and occasionally rather scowling brows. A refined and plastic classicism marks the likenesses of the first Princeps' grandsons and intended heirs, Caius and Lucius Caesar, whose hair-style recalls that of the 'Prima Porta' Augustus type. Those of Tiberius[13] are cold, academic, and unadventurous, with the locks of hair above the brow combed evenly forward; those of Caligula and of his father, Germanicus, are, if somewhat more elegant, no less conservative. But with Claudius the true realistic portrait of Hellenistic tradition springs to life again. The treatment is plastic; but the features are those of the real individual, with his large ears, flabby cheeks, double chin, and stocky neck—all vividly rendered, even when the emperor is portrayed in the guise of Jupiter, as in the colossal statue of him in the Vatican.[14] Among the few mature portraits of Nero that are genuine (there are many forgeries) are the head from the Palatine[15] and that at Worcester, Massachusetts.[16] These show the rich, exuberant modelling of early-Hellenistic idealised portraits, combined with Nero's special hair-style, the two superimposed tiers of evenly curved locks above the brow, sometimes with his side-whiskers (much in evidence on his later coin portraits), and with the terrible expression of the matricide, maniac, and tyrant.

The portraits of Vespasian, founder of the Flavian House, reflect his essentially sane, down-to-earth, middle-class origin and outlook. The rendering of his square skull and homely, benign features, as illustrated by a fine head of him in Rome,[17] is naturalistic and realistic, recalling in some ways the por-

Plate 8

Plate 9

traiture of Claudius and even that of the Pompey-Cicero-
Caesar period. But the treatment of the hair is new, being
sketchy and impressionistic. The likenesses of Vespasian's
elder son, Titus, show the same square head and unidealised
face, but the expression is more openly genial and the hair
rather neater and more pictorial.[18] Of his hated younger
brother and successor, Domitian, few sculptured portraits
survived the execration of his memory; but one, in the New
Capitoline Museum, reveals his imitation of Nero as regards
both the hair-style and the generally idealised appearance.[19]
With Trajan's portraits we return, to some extent, to the prosaic,
matter-of-fact republican tradition, with some veristic details
and a dry, linear handling of the hair, which is combed over
the brow in lanky, striated locks.[20] On the other hand, there is
a wholly non-republican softness in the moulding of the flesh;
and when the portrait is a bust this is deeper than in any earlier
period, comprising all the shoulders and much of the chest.

Plate 11

While there were under the Empire, as in late republican
times, a number of highly realistic portraits of old and elderly
women belonging to the ordinary ranks of society,[21] empresses
and other female members of the imperial family were invariably idealised and never shown as past their prime. For
instance, a statue of Livia, Augustus' empress, found at
Paestum, must, in view of the circumstances in which it was
discovered, have been made when she was already a widow in
her seventies; but the face is that of a woman in her thirties.[22]
As for feminine hair-styles—from the reign of Augustus to that
of Trajan fashions changed more markedly and reached a
greater climax of extravagance than in any other period.
Portraits of the Younger Octavia, Augustus' sister, and the
earlier likenesses of Livia show the front hair worn in a puff
above the brow, carried in a braid across the head, and gathered
with the side hair into a bun on the nape of the neck.[23] On
Livia's later portraits, such as that from Paestum, the hair is

Plate 12

waved stiffly on either side of a central parting and probably (could we see beneath her veil) gathered at the back of the neck into a bun, rather than plaited, in a 'door-knocker', as in the portraits of Antonia II, Augustus' niece, of Agrippina I, the wife of Germanicus, and of Messalina and Agrippina II, Claudius' successive wives.[24] On all these portraits the hair is waved, and sometimes curled, on either side of a central parting either simply or more elaborately, with one or two strands or ringlets falling on to either shoulder in front and with a row of

cf. Plate 10   tiny curls framing the temples in the case of the last two ladies. Flavian women kept the 'door-knocker' behind, but in front their hair was piled high over a frame in a mass either of cork-

Plate 13   screw curls or of small round curls with drilled-out centres producing the effect of a honeycomb. These erections were almost certainly composed of alien hair, as were also those affected by Trajanic ladies, whose frames were covered with hair either minutely braided or dressed in tiers of vertical rolls or spirals, while the subjects' own hair was wound on the back of the head in a crown of plaits.[25] No wonder that the later portraits of Sabina, wife of Hadrian, show a sharp reaction to a simpler coiffure with a central parting based on classical Greek and Hellenistic models.[26]

With Hadrian (AD 76–138) there came into vogue a practice

Plate 14   that was destined to characterise nearly all male portraiture down to the time of Constantine the Great, namely the wearing of a beard, now short, now more luxuriant and flowing. Between *c.* 100 BC and AD 117 clean-shaven chins had been the normal rule for Romans, although Nero sometimes sported an in-cipient beard and on reliefs of Domitian's time non-imperial persons are occasionally bearded (*cf.* plate 37). From Hadrian to Septimius Severus beards were full and curly; and during the third century, when close-cropped, sheath-like beards were mainly favoured, longish curly beards sometimes recur, combined then, for the most part, with a skull-cap-like hair-style, whereas the fashion introduced by Hadrian of wear‑ing the hair more or less elaborately curled lasted until *c.* 217. On Hadrian's later portraits the plastic rendering of the eye, that is, the marking of the irises by lightly incised circles and of the pupils by single or double drill‑holes, sometimes in crescent‑shape depressions, made its first appearance in the west in monumental marble portrait sculpture.[27] The effect of these changes was a brilliantly colouristic pictorialism, gathering momentum as the running drill was used more and more lavishly to produce vivid contrasts of highlights and shadows. All this was associated throughout the second century with a Hellenising idealism that still leaves the individual features of imperial and other personalities readily recognisable. For example, Antoninus Pius can be generally identified by a triangle of hair growing low above the centre of the brow (*cf.* plate 4), Marcus Aurelius by his long, thin face, Lucius Verus by his mop‑like wig of hair. With Commodus and Septimius Severus the curls of both the hair and the beard are extra long and abundant; flesh‑surfaces on portraits of Commodus, in particular, are often finished with a satiny, brightly burnished polish; and on many of Septimius' likenesses we see the three, four, or more forelocks dangling vertically over the forehead, a style borrowed from his patron, the Graeco‑Egyptian god Serapis.[28] From the late second century onwards the portrait bust is virtually half a full‑length figure.

Faustina I, Antoninus Pius' empress, plaited her hair behind and gathered it up into a round coil saucily perched on the crown of her head (*cf.* plate 4). But with Faustina II, Lucilla, and Crispina, the respective wives of Marcus Aurelius, Lucius Verus, and Commodus, simpler coiffures returned. The hair was now waved fairly simply on either side of a central parting and gathered in a bun behind. Septimius Severus' empress, Julia Domna, also wore her hair parted in the centre, but she had it stiffly waved down either cheek, so as to cover the ears

Plate 15

Plate 16

cf. Plate 17

completely; behind, it was gathered together or plaited and then fastened in a spreading pad on to the back of the head.[29] Variations on this style, with the pad narrowing and climbing finally right over the crown of the head to meet the brow, endured throughout the third century, although the ears are left wholly or partially exposed on the portraits of most imperial ladies and their contemporaries after Julia Domna, Julia Maesa, and Julia Soaemias, the second and third of these women being the sister and niece of the first.[30]

Caracalla, Septimius Severus' elder son, abandoned the cascading locks of his predecessors and had his hair and beard dressed in short, neat curls. The ruthlessly realistic reproduction of his brutal features and expression, as seen, for instance, on a

Plate 19

bust in Berlin,[31] reminds us of the fearlessly unidealised royal portraits on the Hellenistic coinages (p. 22). Of his immediate successors, Macrinus appears on his coins with close-cropped hair combined with a long, flowing beard, Elegabalus on his with the same hair-style and either no beard or a short and curly one. But with the sculptural portraits of Severus Alexander a new treatment of the hair and beard emerges: both are close-cropped and indicated only by light, brisk, impressionistic chisel-strokes. Furthermore, as can be seen very clearly on a bust of him in the Vatican, the facial planes have been simplified and generalised. Here are the beginnings of another tension in Roman iconography, that between naturalism and schematisa-tion. Third-century portraits are in many ways the finest in the whole imperial series; and it is, to a large extent, just this tension that gives them their particular significance.

In portraits of Maximinus Thrax the skull-cap hair and sheath-like beard, summarily pecked in the surface of the marble, are coupled with a splendidly realistic individualisation of the features. The same holds good of Pupienus' likenesses, apart from his beard, which is long and plastically treated.

Plate 20

Schematisation predominates on Balbinus' portraits, with his

close-cropped hair and beard, and on those of the youthful
Gordian III, whose hair is close-cropped while his chin is
beardless. Likenesses of Philip I, Trajan Decius, and Trebonianus Gallus are basically the same in style as those of
Maximinus, although in the case of Trebonianus the veristic
details are themselves becoming slightly schematised. Such
details do, indeed, seem to be introduced in the portraits of this
period less for their own sake than to convey an atmosphere of
strain, stress, and fear.

A complete, if relatively ephemeral, return to Hadrianic and
Antonine idealism and to the 'baroque' emotionalism of some
Hellenistic ruler portraits appeared *c.* 260 in the iconography of
Gallienus, with his plastically rendered locks of hair, his short,
but very pictorial, curly beard, and his upward-gazing eyes.
The famous head, the so-called 'Christ', in the National
Museum in Athens, with the same treatment of the eyes, beard,
and features, but with a leonine 'wig' of hair superadded, is
to my mind a Gallienic work, although other critics date it as
Antonine.[32] Other private portraits of the time are modelled
with a similar fluidity. This Gallienic style persists in the coin
portraits of some of the Gallic emperors—Postumus, Laelianus,
Victorinus, and Tetricus I. The severe, schematic manner, with
the skull-cap hair and the sheath-like beard, appears on the coin
portraits of Claudius Gothicus, Aurelian, Florian, Probus,
Carus, Diocletian, Maximian, Constantius Chlorus, and
Licinius I, often combined with furrows slashed across the
brow to give a pseudo-realistic touch or with the rendering of
such individual traits as Diocletian's endearingly *retroussé* nose.
Somewhat fuller and richer beards and a rather softer modelling
of the features, coexisting with the skull-cap coiffure, mark the
coin likenesses of Tacitus and Carinus. As regards portrait
statues in the round, an ultra-schematic, almost cubist version
of the Tetrarchic style, suggesting a deliberate cult of brutality
and ugliness, is exemplified by the porphyry groups of a quartet of

Plate 18

Plate 21

Plate 22

emperors at Venice and in the Vatican and by a porphyry bust in Cairo.[33] In general, the portraits of the third century vividly mirror its character as an age of harsh, stern realities and express the provincial, peasant origin and soldierly background of many of those who wore the purple during the course of it.

With the portrait style of Constantine the Great created during the early decades of the fourth century the schematisation of the male countenance finally gained the day. The facial planes tended now to be ever flatter; the hair became rigidly formal; a clean-shaven upper lip and chin was normally the fashion; and the eyes, often gazing upwards, were unnaturally enlarged and isolated, as it were, from the other features, representing the channels through which the spirit behind them communicated with an outside power. The emperor's image was intended to display him as God's vicegerent in the secular order, as one whom the closed world of natural humanity could confine no longer.[34]

Among the most imposing illustrations in the west of this new Constantinian iconographic style are two colossal heads

Plate 23

in the Palazzo dei Conservatori in Rome, one in marble of Constantine himself, the other in bronze of one of his sons—which of them it would be hard to say, since from their time onwards imperial persons were frequently depicted with uniform, unindividualised features, as though it were the office, not the man, that counted. Constantine's likenesses in high relief on the 'tondi' of his Arch in Rome (p. 65) represent a recutting of the original heads of Hadrian and can be readily distinguished, by their lank locks of hair combed forward on to the brow, clean-shaven chin, and smooth flesh surfaces, from the other recut heads of Hadrian portraying either Constantius Chlorus or Licinius I, on which are still retained the late-third-

Plate 24

century skull-cap hair, sheath-like beard, and furrowed brow. These reconditioned heads are, in fact, some of the finest portraits of the early Constantinian age that survive. As the fourth century progressed the sculptured faces of the emperors grew ever more inscrutable and mask-like—a process that may be said to culminate in the colossal bronze portrait statue at Barletta, with its monotonously patterned hair, glaring eyes, flat cheeks each gashed with a rather unconvincing crease of flesh, stern mouth, and fixed, immovable expression. The figure was recovered from the harbour at Barletta, having probably been looted from Constantinople in the Middle Ages; and the emperor in question has been variously identified as Valentinian I (364–75), Theodosius I (378–95), and Marcianus (450–7). The only variation on this unchanging type of imperial likeness is in the portraits of the pagan emperors Julian (361–3) and Eugenius (392–4), where the straight, lanky hair above the brow is coupled with a long and pointed Greek philosopher's beard.

As regards the female hair-styles of this period, the plait carried up from the nape of the neck across the crown of the head to meet the brow—the normal third-century coiffure (*cf.* p. 38)—was in vogue throughout the fourth century and lasted on into the fifth. But the Constantinian ladies introduced, for a short while, other fashions, of which both the coin portraits and the portraits in the round furnish evidence. Helena and Constantia, Constantine's mother and sister, wound their hair round their heads in a thick circlet of plaits; Fausta, one of Constantine's empresses, returned at one time to the late-second-century habit of waving the hair stiffly on either side of a central parting and gathering it behind into a small neat bun (*cf.* p. 37). Yet another style shows a round coil of plaits perched on the crown of the head, that recalls Faustina I's coiffure (*cf.* p. 37). Not only are these hair-styles throw-backs, probably deliberate, to the age of the Antonines, but the faces of the Constantinian women are carved with a plastic and naturalistic sensitivity that is almost second-century in feeling and provides a striking contrast to the conscious denaturalisa-

tion of the features of their male relatives. A similar plasticity
and naturalism in the handling of the flesh are to be found in
some male portraits of private persons characterised as late-
antique by the large, wide-open eyes and broadly rendered
Plate 25 facial planes. Examples are the portrait statues of magistrates[35]
and the crowned heads of priests from the great sculptural school
at Aphrodisias in Caria[36] and from other centres in Asia
Minor,[37] where, as in Greece proper[38] and in the Aegean
islands, marble portrait sculpture of the Roman age is distinguished, throughout its history, from Italian and other western
work by its softer, more fluid, and more exuberant modelling.

The characteristics of the portraiture of non-imperial persons
during the fifth century are summarised in two outstanding
works. One is a colossal marble head found at Ostia, with
enormous, deep-set, far-seeing eyes that wholly dominate the
face. The back and the top of the head are unworked, while a
thick wreath of heavy, stylised curls overhangs the brow,
across which are cut three equally stylised furrows. The cheeks
are spare, the mouth is very small, and the tapering chin is
enveloped in a pointed, longish beard that runs up the cheeks
to meet the hair. The expression is rapt, as of one who has
little concern with this world.[39] The second head, also male
and of marble, found at Ephesus and now in Vienna, carries
this intense, other-worldly quality to still further lengths: it
may even have been carved after 500. Here the long, emaciated
face, with its square forehead, huge staring eyes beneath
markedly arched eyebrows, and thin-lipped, down-turned
mouth, is crowned by a thick cap of stiff, striated hair and
terminates in a short beard rendered by long, light chisel-
strokes. This is the likeness of a prophet or contemplative. As
we look at it we are transported right out of the world of ancient
humanism into that of medieval spirituality.[40]

CHAPTER III

Sculpture in the Round
other than Portraits

THE TYPES OF THE OLYMPIAN GODS and goddesses and other deities created by archaic, classical, and Hellenistic Greece had reached, by the first century before our era, a pitch of intellectual and technical perfection that left little room for fresh inventiveness. In Rome and in all those central Mediterranean areas in which the Greek sculptural influence was paramount, artists were largely content to repeat the traditional forms of those divinities in cult or votive statues. Again, the republican practice of raping from their original settings masterpieces of religious and athletic Greek sculpture transformed them from objects of devotion and veneration into *objets d'art*. Their new *raison d'être* was almost entirely decorative or antiquarian—to adorn the temples and other public buildings of the west or the homes and gardens of wealthy Roman and Italian connoisseurs. When originals were not available, reproductions of them had to be obtained; and from the early first century BC until the latter part of the second century AD the copying of statues was a regular industry, conducted on an enormous scale in the workshops of Greece, Asia Minor, Italy, northern Africa, southern Gaul, and Spain. These copies, many of which are reproductions in marble of bronze originals, are of very varying quality. Some are poor, but not a few are outstanding works of art in their own right; and it goes without saying that without them much more of Greek sculpture might have been lost to us. Rome robbed, but she also conserved.

Only once in the history of Roman sculpture did this copying of classical Greek statues result in a certain creativeness—in the

idealised statuary types of the emperor Hadrian's favourite, the
Plate 26
Bithynian youth Antinous. In the stance and proportions of
the body and in the treatment of the hair these types are more or
less faithful reproductions of the canons of fifth/ and fourth/
century BC sculpture. But in the facial features and in the
manipulation of the flesh surfaces they reveal a new emotional
content, a new sensitivity and sensuousness, a new pathos and
melancholy. From the old models a fresh divine figure had
emerged. For originality in Roman sculpture, which com/
prises works in marble, stone, and bronze including bronze and
some silver figurines, so far as the Olympians, River Deities,
and other traditional Graeco/Roman personifications are con/
cerned we have to turn to the Empire's peripheries, particu/
larly to the northern and western provinces where the hold
of Greece was weaker. There, in central and northern Gaul,
in Roman Germany, in Britain, and in northern Africa, a
fresh and vigorous native genius—whose products, it is true,
were sometimes naïve in conception and crude in execution—
breathed a new life into the old, accepted forms. In such
provincial art those forms were not only fused with local
features, but they also recovered something of their one/time
religious spirit, since the Graeco/Roman deities were identified
with native gods and goddesses whose cult was a living thing.[1]

It was in the provinces again, both in the east and in the west,
that the worship of originally local, non/Graeco/Roman
divinities made new contributions to the history of Roman
religious sculpture. From Egypt the cults of Isis, Serapis, and
Horus (Harpocrates) spread throughout the Roman world. If
the art types of these Egyptian deities (and of their priests and
priestesses) were basically Hellenistic, the Roman age witnessed
an immense increase in the number of their statuary representa/
tions and the invention of new features, such as Serapis'
dangling forelocks[2] and the Roman military dress of Horus.[3]
Also widespread were the statuary types of the Syrian Jupiter

Dolichenus and of his consort Juno Regina, the former dis- Plate 27
tinguished by his conical Syrian hat, double axe, and cuirass
and frequently poised on the back of a bull, just as the latter is
perched on the back of a doe or heifer.[4] The cult of the Persian
god Mithras, in the form in which it was diffused as a mystery
religion through the Roman Empire, appears to have come
from Asia Minor; and it was most probably there that the
statuary types of Mithras the Bull-Slayer and of his companions,
Cautes and Cautopates, originated. In most of these groups
the god wears oriental dress, a Phrygian cap and trousers; but one
large marble group found at Ostia and signed by Kriton of
Athens shows him, most exceptionally, in Greek costume.[5]
Statuary renderings of native gods and goddesses from the
Celtic orbit ultimately owe their plastic, three-dimensional
modelling to contact with Graeco-Roman sculpture. On the
other hand, their facial expressions, hair- and beard-styles,
characteristic attributes, etc., are often wholly original.[6]

In Italy, Greece, and the more thoroughly Graeco-
Romanised provincial centres there were created a number of
new sculptural types of purely Roman deities and of figures
from everyday life, such as Roman priests and priestesses,
Roman soldiers, gladiators, other men of action, musicians,
slaves, and, above all, children. The last three items in this list
had, of course, Hellenistic precursors. Probably the most
original works of sculpture from these areas consist of new
mythological and allegorical figures and groups, and of fresh
figures personifying geographical and other natural features,
political or local entities such as cities, States, or peoples, and
such abstract ideas as powers, virtues, qualities, and blessings.
It must, however, be remembered that subjects of this kind had
also been familiar themes with Hellenistic sculptors; and we
cannot, obviously, ever be sure that some of the Roman-age
pieces, of which no Hellenistic counterparts are known to
us, are not, in fact, copies or adaptations of lost originals. A

lively group, probably a tomb group, of Orpheus and the Beasts, found in the neighbourhood of Rome, carved in local stone ('peperino'), and dating from late-republican times, certainly reflects, in the musician's features, the Hellenistic pathetic manner.[7] The famous marble statue of the Nile in the Vatican[8] has been repeatedly asserted to be a copy of an Alexandrian work of the Hellenistic period. Its technique is, none the less, completely Roman; and the piece could well have been made in Rome at one of those moments in imperial history when political or personal events induced a vogue for things Egyptian—under Augustus, Vespasian, or Hadrian.

We can certainly reckon as Roman originals such ethnic types as the figure of a Germanic or Dacian woman in the Loggia dei Lanzi at Florence.[9] It probably dates from Trajan's time, as does a series of heads of Dacians in the Vatican.[10] But when we have several Roman-age versions of a mythological group or groups, then the chances are that some unknown Hellenistic prototype lies behind them. This is the case with two statues of Centaurs, one old, the other young, found in Hadrian's villa at Tivoli, worked in black marble to imitate bronze and signed by two Hadrianic Greek sculptors, Aristeas and Papias, members of a 'colony' of artists from Aphrodisias in Caria working in Italy.[11] More likely to be original are some mid-second-century Athenian works—two cuirassed female torsos in the National Museum in Athens, held to be personifications of the Iliad and the Odyssey, the latter signed by Jason of Athens;[12] and the great figures of Tritons and Giants applied to the columns of the portico which was added to the Odeion of Agrippa in the Agora.[13] Probably dating from the closing decades of the second century AD is the just more than life-size marble statue of a cloaked, but otherwise naked, barbarian, with tumbled, flame-like hair, an anguished expression, and a strained and tortured pose, running as though from a pursuer and carrying a child, which was found in the Graeco-Roman

Plate 29

Plate 28

cityof Philadelphia (Amman) in Transjordania.[14] Inthe exedra, in which the piece came to light, there was room for another figure; and we may have here an allegorical group depicting the victory of civilisation over barbarism. The statue is charac⁄ terised by deeply drilled⁄out hair and beard and very highly polished flesh⁄surfaces. Its marble is of the type that comes from the Aphrodisian quarries and the figure could well be the work of an Aphrodisian sculptor and imported into Philadelphia.

With Romano⁄Christian art of the third, fourth, and fifth centuries only one main type of sculpture in the round can be associated, that of a shepherd carrying a sheep upon his shoulders. These small unsophisticated marble figures have been generally described as representing the Good Shepherd, whether in the person of Christ Himself or of an Apostle or of any Christian, clerical or lay, who obeyed the Gospel precepts. The motif of the animal⁄bearer was in origin a pagan one, stemming from such figures as the Moschophorus (calf⁄bearer) and Hermes Kriophoros (ram⁄bearer) of archaic and classical Greek painting and sculpture; and in Hellenistic and Roman paintings and reliefs it occurs in personifications of the Seasons —Spring or Winter—or as a symbol of the pastoral paradise. Recently it has been suggested[15] that, unless the motif is found in unequivocally Christian contexts, on sarcophagi with biblical scenes, for instance, it should be assumed that it is not Christian, but depicts allegorically the pagan virtue of *philan⁄ thropia*. On the other hand, it is admitted that pagan literature provides no evidence of such a link between *philanthropia* and the animal⁄bearer; and although some of the smaller renderings in bronze, terracotta, or bone (knife⁄handles) could have had merely a *genre* significance as pastoral figures, there would seem to be no reason why the marble statuettes should not have had a Christian meaning, whatever the use to which they were put— votive, funerary, or domestic. Their simple, unpretentious style agrees with that of Christian catacomb painting and of the reliefs on most early Christian sarcophagi; and the Christians had, after all, a quite specific incentive for choosing the motif. No sculptures in the round of the Roman period are more successful than those representing animals and birds. Only the merest handful of examples from a great array of splendidly naturalistic studies can be cited here. From Italy we have the magnificent bronze horse of Marcus Aurelius' equestrian statue on the Capitol;[16] the two splendid gilt-bronze heads of horses from Cartoceto di Pergola, now in the Ancona Museum;[17] two marble groups of two lithe hounds, of which the dog playfully gnaws the bitch's ear;[18] a neat, sprinting bronze pig found at Pompeii.[19] An altar-shaped funerary monument in Athens carries on its upper surface a thickly cushioned seat, on which reposes an obviously pampered and over-fed dog, wearing a studded collar and bell and staring confidently with small, round, bulging eyes at the onlooker.[20] Renderings of beasts from the northern and western provinces often show a vivid intermingling of Graeco-Roman naturalism in the creature's general pose and build with the Celtic taste for patterning in the treatment of the coat. Instances are the bronze group from Muri in Switzerland of the goddess Artio with her shaggy bear, which displays a curious whirligig of hair on its right flank as it slinks up to its mistress with friendly if somewhat embarrassing forwardness;[21] and two bronze dogs, one running, from Moudon (Canton de Vaud) in Switzerland,[22] the other resting, again with whirligigs of hair on the hips and shoulders, from Lydney in Gloucestershire.[23] One of the most remarkable Roman-age studies of birds is the bronze eagle found in the Roman town at Silchester in Hampshire: it was certainly an import into Britain from some southern land, perhaps from Italy.[24] Any number of other pieces might have been chosen to illustrate the wealth of surviving evidence, drawn from almost every quarter of the Roman world, for an interest in portraying living creatures unrivalled in any other age of ancient sculpture.

Plate 30

Plate 31

Plate 32

CHAPTER IV

Historical Reliefs in Stone and Marble

THE TERM 'HISTORICAL' is used here to cover all those stone and marble reliefs of an official character which depict public events, past or present, legendary or actual, or which represent in narrative or in allegorical and symbolic form the political ideas and propaganda of those who sponsored their sculpting.

Real events from contemporary, or near-contemporary, history had formed the themes of classical Greek reliefs on buildings of the late fourth century BC, for example, on the Nereid Monument at Xanthos and on the Heroon at Gjölbaschi. But, generally speaking, Greek artists and their patrons preferred to commemorate events of this kind under the veil of myth, as in the Gigantomachy and Telephus friezes on the second-century BC altar of Zeus at Pergamon, which alluded to the victories of Pergamenes over Gauls in Asia Minor and exalted the heroic origins of the Attalid House. So strong was the influence of this Greek preference for the use of legend as an allegory of present happenings that historical art in Rome, in its initial stages, could not escape it, despite the Romans' marked taste for concrete, factual representation (cf. p. 19); and in State reliefs down to the beginning of the fourth century AD personifications and other figures and groups of a symbolic character never failed to find a place. The two realms, the real and ideal, the divine and human, the natural and super-natural, were always, to some extent, intermingled.

Symbols are completely in possession of the field on the earliest Roman State reliefs in the west that have survived, those

that form a frieze carved in grey limestone, which was found at
the foot of the Capitol and may well have belonged to a
triumphal monument celebrating Sulla's eastern victories.[1] Its
subjects are Victories, candelabra, round and oblong shields
with bold devices in high relief, trophies, cuirasses, greaves,
Plate 33 and a splendid horse-chamfron. There can be little doubt that
the artist of this frieze was a Greek. The individual motifs and
the style and technique in which they are carried out recall
Pergamene carving of the second century BC, although the
static, sober type of composition, with the objects clear-cut in
outline and well spaced-out against the background, has
nothing in common with that Asiatic school's 'baroque'
turbulence, but proclaims its kinship with Neo-Attic sculpture.

Nowhere is the juxtaposition of the factual and the allegorical more strikingly illustrated than in two pendant reliefs,
one in the Louvre, the other in the Munich Glyptothek, which,
despite the contrast between them in content and treatment, are
carved in the same Greek marble, correspond in their dimensions and in their terminating pilasters, and must have come
from one and the same monument.[2] The Louvre frieze displays
three continuous episodes from the Roman census ceremonies
circumstantially rendered in a straightforward and dignified, if
somewhat dry and prosaic style. The Munich frieze is a graceful,
typically Hellenistic piece and depicts the wedding procession
of Neptune and Amphitrite, with Tritons, Nereids, and
Cupids in attendance. Long believed, almost certainly
erroneously, to have come from an 'altar of Ahenobarbus', the
friezes have now been associated, much more plausibly, with
the temple of the Nymphs (with whom the Nereids were
equated), in which were stored the census archives.[3] This
temple was restored after its burning in 57 BC and there is
nothing in the style of these friezes to suggest that they could not
have been carved for that restoration. The sculptor of the
Munich scenes was certainly a Greek; so may have been the

carver of the Louvre frieze, trying his hand, somewhat awk, wardly, at a Roman theme that was new to his own tradition.

Very different in style from both the Louvre and the Munich friezes is the marble frieze from the Basilica Aemilia,[4] which stood on the northern extremity of the Roman Forum. Dis, covered in fragments, several of its scenes have been pieced together and have revealed that its subject is Roman—episodes from legendary history, among which can be recognised the death of Tarpeia, the rape of the Sabine women, battle scenes, and the building of the walls of some city in Italy while a standing goddess looks on. But the treatment is in the rich, plastic, Hellenistic manner, with high relief, vigorous move, ment, some bold foreshortening in the figures, and conventional landscape elements. The Basilica Aemilia was restored between 54 and 34 BC and the frieze could belong to that time. On the other hand, its content is much more in place in the reign of Augustus, whose political propaganda included the glorifica, tion of Roman origins; and there was actually another restora, tion of the building after a fire in 14 BC. From its close similarity in style to the little friezes on the inner table of sacrifice of the Ara Pacis Augustae (see below) we may also date as Augustan the small frieze, most precisely and delicately carved with scenes of a triumphal procession, from the temple of Apollo in the Campus Martius, although no restoration of that temple by Augustus has actually been recorded.[5]

On the Ara Pacis Augustae, founded in 13 BC and com, pleted and dedicated in 9 BC, were erected the earliest western reliefs that can be strictly described as documentary, that is, depicting a contemporary event in which specific, identifiable individuals are portrayed as taking part.[6] This altar, which stood in the Campus Martius on the western side of the Via Lata, consisted of a table of sacrifice within a precinct, the walls of which were pierced by entrances on the east and west. The outer sides of these walls are carved with two superimposed zones of relief work and all the sculptured portions of the monument are of Luna marble. In the upper zone on the south side is shown the procession of Augustus and members of his family, with flamens and lictors, to the site of the altar on the

Plate 34 day of its foundation, 4 July 13 BC. Here we can recognise Augustus himself, the consuls of the year, Tiberius and Varus, Agrippa and one of his little sons, possibly Livia, the emperor's wife, Julia, his daughter, his sister Octavia, his two nieces, the Antonias, with their husbands and children, and Iullus Antonius, who was praetor urbanus in that year. On the cor-responding north side is the parallel, converging procession of members of the Roman priestly colleges, magistrates,

Plate 35 senators, and representatives of the Roman people with their children. This large-scale procession is continued in miniature on the inner altar proper, where friezes show figures of Vestal Virgins, priests, sacrificial victims with their attendants, and parts of other figures. Both of the large processional scenes are typically Roman, slow, stately, and purposeful, yet with their casual and homely touches—a young couple chatting, officials with their attention wandering, one child obviously frightened, another child tired of walking and asking to be picked up. But the treatment of the main figures, with their rhythmic draperies and idealised hair and features, is thoroughly classical and there can be little doubt that the sculptors of the Ara were Greeks. Of the four scenes that adorned the outside of the east and west walls two survive—Tellus or Italia, seated amid children, animals, and plants and flanked by the spirits of ocean and the inland waters, and Aeneas offering the white sow as a sacrifice to the Penates (of the two other scenes, the Wolf and Twins and Dea Roma, only fragments remain); and these, while Roman in content, are conceived and executed in the full Hellenistic pictorial style. Moreover, the lovely

Plate 36 floral composition, alive with tiny beasts, birds, and insects, that occupies the lower zone on the outside of all four walls and the great naturalistic swags of fruit, leaves, corn-ears, etc. that Plate 38 decorate the upper zone on the inner side of the walls can be closely paralleled in carvings from second-century BC Pergamon and in some first-century BC work in Attica.

Just as the procession on the precinct walls and altar proper perpetuates the actual ceremony of consecration, so the rest of the reliefs are likely to allude to the same occasion. The reliefs on the east and west walls could represent painted panel-pictures fixed to the provisional wooden structure that the altar was destined to replace. The floral zone could be reckoned to be a translation into marble of a ceremonial carpet or hanging used at the altar's site on the foundation day. As for the swags—we know that it was customary in Rome to deck with fillets and garlands a site set apart for a new religious building;[7] and although the marble versions as we have them combine in one luxuriant medley the flowers and fruits of all four seasons to symbolize the blessings of Augustan peace and plenty, we can reasonably assume that they take the place of the real garlands that were slung between the posts of the temporary precinct walls on 4 July 13 BC.

The reliefs of the Ara Pacis offer a superb example of the interweaving of the actual present with the legendary past, of concrete fact with symbol and allegory, of classical dignity and poise in the human figures with an uninhibited delight in all the details of Nature in the decorative friezes. In their own kind they remained unsurpassed throughout the history of Roman sculpture.

From the Julio-Claudian period there has come down to us no public monument whose whole scheme of sculptural decoration is completely known to us, as in the case of the Ara Pacis. One of the best-preserved reliefs of this time is a long frieze ornamenting one side of what would appear to have been a large base or altar, the reliefs on its other sides being wholly lost, apart from tiny fragments indicating that they once existed.[8] It was found in Rome beneath the Papal Chancellery and shows a procession of city magistrates (*vicomagistri*) accompanied by ministers (*camilli*) holding statuettes of the imperial Genius and Lares, sacrificial victims with attendants, musicians, and other male figures. The men and animals are ranged side by side along the field with little overlapping. In parts of the frieze there is a second row of figures carved in low relief on the background and of these the chief stylistic interest lies in the fact that their heads are slightly raised above those of the figures in the foreground, as though the spectator were viewing the procession from a somewhat elevated point of vantage. This device of vertical perspective, which we shall meet with again many times in Roman historical sculpture, has often been hailed as essentially a feature of popular Italian folk‚ art, which wormed its way into works of public and official sculpture. But normally it is the lower types of art that borrow from the higher, not *vice versa*; the convention occasionally appears in official Hellenistic sculpture and was probably to be found in monumental Hellenistic paintings, to judge from their apparent reflections in western funerary reliefs of Greek content and in Roman historical scenes of a strongly pictorial character, such as the reliefs with battles of Romans and Gauls on the Tiberian Arch at Orange;[9] and when we find it occurring, as here, on an elegant, refined, not to say academic, piece of carving and on works of court inspiration such as the reliefs on Trajan's Column (*cf.* pp. 57–60), it is hard to believe in its *Volkskunst* origin. Its increasing vogue and development are to be more reasonably explained by the general Roman passion for factual detail, which naturally expressed itself in attempting to display all the participants in an action, including those in the second plane, as fully as possible. Again, the device was at times obviously demanded by aesthetic considerations, when in architectural reliefs such as the Orange panels and the spiral bands on Trajan's Column, the whole effect depended on filling the entire field with sculpture. There we sometimes find the complete figures of the persons in the second plane tiered above those in the foreground.

The other surviving reliefs which can be dated to the Julio Claudian epoch need not detain us long. A series of parts of processional and sacrificial scenes now built into the Villa Medici on the Pincian Hill, and some fragments with architec tural and decorative motifs found on the Via Lata and now in the New Capitoline Museum, may have belonged to the Ara Pietatis begun by Tiberius in AD 22, but completed under Claudius.[10] There is a group of figures, including those of Divus Augustus and Venus, and part of a procession of sacrificial beasts, at Ravenna, also possibly Claudian.[11] Most of these pieces strike us as cold, conventional, and unadventurous. If Nero's ambitious schemes for new imperial residences (e.g. the Golden House) and for replanning Rome after the fire of 64 left him time for sponsoring buildings with historical reliefs, none have come down to us. The next significant works of this kind date from the reign of the third Flavian emperor, Domitian.

The two relief panels one on either side of the passage way of the Arch of Titus, erected at the eastern end of the Roman Forum by his younger brother to commemorate his apotheosis after his death in 81, were long regarded as embodying *the* Flavian sculptural style, to which the term 'illusionistic' has been applied.[12] If we mean by 'illusionism' the attempt on the artist's part to create in the spectator the belief that he is looking at the actual thing that a work of art purports to portray, then we may say that both of these panels are legitimately described as 'illusionistic'. For both are such excerpts from a whole, long procession as an onlooker might have seen framed by the window from which he was watching the ceremony. In the imperial cortège scene the actual chariot carrying the emperor is shown frontally as emerging from the background towards the spectator, as are also the figures in the foreground to the right of it. But the four horses which are drawing it and most of the lictors in the left background behind them are in profile, and the two foreground figures on the left, although partly shown frontally, are moving in the same direction. The most important part of the procession has, in fact, been caught by the artist in the act of making a right-angle turn leftwards. Similarly the scene of the bearing of the Jewish spoils is shown as emerging from the background on the left, bowing out in a curve at the centre, and then receding again through an arch set obliquely to the background on the right. Both reliefs produce the highly pictorial illusion of steady, continuous movement. In the second scene all the actors are human. But in the first scene Victory, Honos, and Virtus, divine personifications, have joined the historical personages.

The notion of *a* Flavian style was, however, shattered in 1938 by the discovery near the Papal Chancellery of two Domitianic reliefs, which depict, in a very different style, Vespasian's arrival (*adventus*) in 70 in Rome, where the young Domitian as Caesar (heir to the Empire) had claimed to be in charge during his father's absence, and the setting out (*profectio*) of Domitian (whose features have been awkwardly recut to resemble those of Nerva) for one of his northern campaigns as emperor.[13] While the *profectio* scene implies, of its very nature, an unseen goal beyond it, its composition is relatively selfcontained, centralised, and static, as compared with that of the Arch of Titus panels, and the *adventus* scene forms a single unit, wholly complete in itself. In both scenes the figures are arranged in planes flush with the background and no illusion of depth or space is created. The whole effect is classical and unpictorial; and although the heads of Vespasian and the young Domitian in the *adventus* scene are vivid portraits, the other individual figures both of the men and of the gods and personifications, who in both reliefs mingle freely with the human actors, are

Plate 37

statuesque in type and idealised in facial features. There was, in fact, another, classicising Flavian style, which is also to be found in the figure frieze, alluding to Minerva and her Roman cult, on the precinct walls of the forum planned and begun by Domitian, but dedicated under Nerva.[14] And the same style appears again in the Louvre relief of an imperial *suove-taurilia* sacrifice, dated by some as Julio-Claudian,[15] but more probably depicting Domitian (the modern face takes the place of one that was smashed deliberately in ancient times), sacrificing at the twin altars of Divus Vespasianus and Divus Titus.

The designer of the spiral relief bands on the shaft of Trajan's Column in Rome[16] did not, as we have seen, invent the Roman documentary method of historical narration in art. Nor did he invent the continuous style of composition, according to which successive episodes in a story are unfolded in one unbroken series within a single field, with no lines of demarcation between them, while the hero is shown recurring in each or almost every scene. This style is found in a limited form on fifth-century BC Attic red-figure cups painted with the labours of Theseus, in the Telephus frieze from the altar of Zeus at Pergamon, and on Hellenistic ('Megarian') moulded terracotta bowls with the labours of Hercules or scenes from Homer in relief.[17] What the Trajanic artist did was to produce the most complete, extensive, and novel exemplar of both the documentary method and the continuous narrative style that had, so far as we know, yet appeared in the art of the ancient Greek and Roman world.

Trajan's Column, 100 Roman feet in height, constructed of Parian marble, and completed and dedicated by AD 113, has its shaft entwined with a winding ribbon, about a metre wide, of sculptured reliefs in 23 spirals recording visually the story of the emperor's two Dacian wars (AD 101–2 and 105–6). Columns with spiral relief bands filled with purely decorative motifs were already known in Roman art.[18] Horizontal bands of figures had occurred on the shafts of votive columns in Gaul and Germany.[19] But this combination of figure scenes and spiral bands was, so far as we can tell, completely new.

Plate 40

As a 'document' this series of reliefs presents the Dacian wars, from start to finish, in straightforward, factual 'prose'—the emperor, the Roman army, the Dacian foe all intent upon their tasks of war. Divine figures, gods and personifications, are found extremely rarely. Typical, routine happenings in army life—imperial addresses to the troops (*adlocutiones*), sacrifices in the field, the fortification of strong-points, marches, battles of all kinds, etc.—do, indeed, recur; and these could have taken place at any time and in any order. But there are also shown certain particular events and places in the Dacian campaigns that are outstanding and unique—the initial crossing of the Danube by the Roman army, the emperor's voyage up the Danube, the submission of the Dacians at the end of the first war, Trajan's embarkation at Ancona for the second war, the great sacrifice by the Danube bridge, the storming of the Dacian capital, the death of the Dacian king Decabalus, etc.; and these things must have happened, for the most part, in the particular order in which they are recorded on the Column. We have, then, in the reliefs a sequence of events which is generally, but not, as it were, photographically true to history, not a literally exact chronological and topographical account of the campaigns, but a faithful outline of the story combined with a most minute and circumstantial description of the sort of problems that the Roman troops had to face in Dacia. The accuracy of the rendering on the Column of Roman military details and of Dacian physiognomy, arms, dress, fortifications, etc. can be established from other archaeological material; and there can be little doubt that behind these reliefs lie sketches made at the 'front' by eyewitnesses, namely army draftsmen who accom-panied the troops to war. It is likely that such sketches would have been originally made for the imperial archives, without the

Column in view. But when it was decided that the Dacian wars should be depicted in relief on its shaft, a master artist, commissioned to prepare measured drawings or cartoons for the sculptors, would have made a selection from the army draftsmen's work, elaborated their sketches, and fused them together within a single framework, using vertical perspective so as to fill each band from top to bottom with an 'all-over', tapestry-like design and to display the maximum amount of detail (*cf.* p. 54). A striking instance of this urge to omit nothing and to present everything in its greatest extent is the scene of a legionary wading a river and carrying his shield, piled with his equipment, on his head. Here vertical perspective for the river, which is shown spread out as on a map, is illogically combined with the horizontal viewpoint for the man, who is seen from behind. This combination of viewpoints must have been a deliberate part of the design, not just due to naïvety on the part of the carver, whose modelling of the soldier's back and arms reveals him as a very skilful artist. Similarly, the illogical disproportion in scale, throughout the reliefs, between the human figures and the architectural and landscape accessories was due, not to childishness, but to the necessity of making the human actors, whose activities were, after all, of primary importance, stand out and be distinguishable from a distance.

Plate 39

If it be urged that we have no direct evidence for the existence of army artists' sketches, the same applies to Trajanic illustrated scrolls relating the history of the Dacian wars, which are sometimes thought to have been the models of the Column frieze. And on what but war-time drawings could such scroll illustrations themselves have been based? The famous late-antique Joshua Rotulus in the Vatican provides no parallel to the Column band, since it shows, not an uninterrupted flow of interlocking scenes, but a lining-up in frieze form of separate, self-contained scenes, each with its appropriate text in a low column of writing beneath it.

Who designed the cartoons for the relief bands has not been recorded. We know that Trajan's Syrian-Greek architect, Apollodorus of Damascus, was responsible for the whole complex of forum, basilica, and Greek and Latin libraries, of which the Column was the central and dominating feature; and if he did not draw the cartoons himself, he must have supervised and approved them. But whoever he was, this master draftsman is agreed to have produced the classic example of the developed continuous narrative style in Roman sculpture, converting what had probably been isolated pictures into a single, unified, running frieze of closely interlocking scenes—a space-time continuum. Here the figure of the hero, Trajan himself, constantly recurs, seen, as in a film, passing rapidly from place to place against an unfolding landscape and architec-tural background. For in this great historical panorama, as the different incidents succeed one another (and often these in-cidents can have been separated only by a very short, if any, interval of time), the scene shifts by smooth transitions from river to camp, from camp to forest, from forest to town, and from town to open country. As we stand facing one side of the Column and watch the frieze appearing, disappearing, and re-appearing round the shaft as it climbs slowly, but resolutely, upwards to its goal, to victory, symbolised first by an imperial eagle and then by the statue of the emperor on the summit, we cannot but be stirred and awed at finding ourselves in the presence of this great dramatic action—so vast and so distant that we can only apprehend parts of it. If the language of these reliefs is prose, the ideas and the imagination that the language expresses have an epic quality.

Nothing else so exciting as the frieze on the Column has sur-vived from Trajan's reign. The nearest thing to it in content and style—so near, in fact, that it must have been designed by the same hand or in the same workshop—is a large, long frieze on a flat, straight surface, four substantial portions of which are re⁄used on the walls of the central passage⁄way and on the east and west attics of the Arch of Constantine in Rome, while a number of much smaller fragments once belonging to it can be recognised in various museums in Rome and elsewhere.[20] When casts were taken of each of the four sections on the Arch, it was found that all fitted together. On the left is an imperial *adventus* moving leftwards. Trajan is conducted home in triumph by Virtus, crowned by Victory, and accompanied by soldiers and lictors. Emerging rightwards out of the first scene, without a break, is one of a cavalry charge against Dacians, in which the emperor himself takes part on horseback. Meeting this battle scene in a leftward direction is a group of Roman soldiers presenting to the charging emperor Dacian prisoners and the severed heads of dead Dacians (a very similar presenta⁄ tion of severed heads to the emperor appears on the Column); and further to the right is a group of Roman horsemen charging over the prostrate bodies of fallen foes. Thus, whereas on the Column the main stream of the story flows consecutively from left to right, here, at least in the portions that we have, it ebbs and flows alternately to left and right and the scenes are grouped together with a total disregard of spatial and temporal logic. Moreover, whereas on the Column the emperor is never involved in the actual conflict and the Roman troops wear battle⁄dress, here Trajan leads the charge and the soldiers wear 'parade' uniforms with plumed and decorated helmets. These are, in fact, scenes of 'ideal' or dramatised war, such as we find on battle sarcophagi of later periods (*cf.* pp. 101–2); and it is not impossible that this great Trajanic frieze was designed after Trajan's death to adorn the temple dedicated by Hadrian to his adoptive parents and erected to the north⁄west of the forum and basilica that bore Trajan's name. The triumph of the emperor on this frieze is not terrestrial only, but also celestial—his victory over death by apotheosis. As compared with that on the Column, the relief on the frieze is high and the main figures have a relatively statuesque and richly plastic quality. Landscape accessories are very few; but there is the same urge here as there to fill the whole field by means of the more restrained use of vertical perspective that the scheme of the design allowed.

The well-known Arch of Trajan at Beneventum in southern Italy bears the date AD 114 and was certainly decreed by the Senate, possibly already built and dedicated as a structure, before the emperor's death.[21] Its fourteen large, rectangular reliefs, one on either side of its single passage-way and six on either face (attics and pylons), present an epitome of Trajan's achievements at home and abroad—his recruiting of troops, his founding of colonies in Italy and in the provinces, his establish-ment of new ports in Italy, his social policy, his pacification of the Danube lands (in the person of their patron deities), his friendly relations with Spanish and Germanic tribesmen, and his eastern conquests. One of the most appealing of these sculptured pictures is the passage-way relief that depicts the *alimenta*, the emperor's charitable foundation for the poor children of Italy, who appear in person to receive his bounty, along with their fathers and personifications of their native cities. All these reliefs form isolated, self-contained pictures, apart from the two in the lower tiers of the pylons on the side of the Arch that faces Beneventum, which constitute the single scene of Trajan's solemn welcome by the citizens of Rome in the Roman Forum, and those on the attic on the same side, again forming a single scene in which Trajan is greeted on the Capitol by the Triad and other divinities and receives from Jupiter the latter's thunderbolt, the symbol of his vocation to govern the world as the god's vicegerent. In this picture Hadrian is shown in imperial dress next to the emperor, while Italia lays a hand upon his shoulder as though to point him out as Trajan's heir. On the other side of the Arch, in the relief that records Trajan's eastern conquests, Hadrian is again indicated by the hand of an official laid upon his shoulder, while another

Plate 41

official rests his hand on the emperor's arm, as though to restrain him from that annexation to the Empire of Meso/potamia which Hadrian, once on the throne, immediately abandoned. It would seem to be certain that the carving of the Arch was not completed until after Hadrian's accession. The treatment of these sculptures is not only wholly different from that of the Column reliefs, but also carries much further the stylistic divergencies between those reliefs and the other frieze. The compositions are crowded, but the main monumental figures stand out boldly in even higher relief against the massed company behind them. Background architectural and land/scape elements are either absent or reduced to a minimum; and the use of vertical perspective is very limited. Gods, personi/fications, and human beings mingle freely. Some of the heads are badly weathered; but there still remain several striking likenesses of Trajan, and in the emperor's entourage are persons with arresting, portrait/like features.

The contrast between the principate of Hadrian, scholar, philhellene, pacifier, and traveller, and that of his martial and more practical/minded predecessor can be gauged from the absence under the former of a series of great commemorative monuments carved with scenes of the reigning emperor's victories and other spectacular achievements. The Hadrianic sculptures that approximate most closely to Trajanic work and probably date from the early years of the new regime are two modest reliefs cut on what would appear to have been two sections of a balustrade round a statue of Marsyas in the Roman Forum, since each scene terminates at one end in a figure of him on a pedestal and the splendidly rendered sacrificial beasts on the back of each slab could refer to a ceremonial restoration and rededication of that statue.[22] One scene relates to Hadrian's continuation and extension of Trajan's alimentary foundation: on the left the emperor with his suite stands on the rostra before the temple of the deified Julius Caesar and addresses representa/

tives of the grateful people, while further to the right is a statuary group on a base—Trajan seated and Italia with her children standing before him to thank him for his charity. The second scene records Hadrian's magnanimous cancelling, by the public burning of the debt-registers, of debts owed to the State. In the background of each scene is a reproduction in low relief of buildings in the Forum in their precise topographical order; and from these can be reasonably inferred (assuming that the onlooker was meant to find in the sculptures representations of the buildings that he actually saw above and beyond the slabs) the exact position and orientation of the balustrades, the site of the Marsyas statue being known from literary sources. The figures are less crowded than in Trajanic work; but the architectural details fill the whole background and the heads and shoulders of the figures in the second plane are raised above those in the foreground.

A still wider spacing of the figures characterises a frag-mentary relief, again of the cancelling of public debts, now in Chatsworth House, Derbyshire, on which the actors wear the short Hadrianic beard;[23] and a wholly classicising style marks three large, rectangular reliefs in the Palazzo dei Conservatori on the Capitol which clearly belonged to a sculptured arch of Hadrian's time.[24] For although the imperial heads on these reliefs are mostly restorations, the hair- and beard-styles of the other figures are of that period. One scene shows the goddess Roma handing a globe to the emperor on his arrival in the capital soon after his accession. Another depicts a dead empress—Plotina or Sabina—carried heavenwards on the back of the winged, torch-bearing, female figure of Aeternitas, while Hadrian sits watching and a male figure, personifying the Campus Martius, reclines beside the funeral pyre. In the third picture, which seems to be the pendant of the second, the emperor, mounted on a high platform, delivers an oration, probably in honour of the same dead empress, before the Genius of the Roman People and other listeners. These cold, correct, academic set-pieces, with their tracts of empty background and their calm, static actors, excite in us much less interest than do the eight roundels, re-used on the Arch of Constantine, which are sculptured with picturesque and graceful scenes of hunting, instinct with vivid movement, and of sacrifices on the hunting-field.[25] All the imperial heads were, as we have seen (*cf.* p. 40), re-cut in the early fourth century. But there can be no doubt that the original heads were those of Hadrian, whose passion for the chase was proverbial, whose youthful favourite, Antinous, can be recognised in several of the scenes, and among whose bronze medallion types are designs that are very close to some of the sculptured hunting episodes. For what Hadrianic monument these roundels were carved we do not know. We can only describe them as historical in so far as the emperor and some of the members of his suite whom they portrayed were public figures.

It is, however, very probable that we should ascribe to the last year of Hadrian the only series of State reliefs dating from before the late-antique period that have so far come to light in an east-Mediterranean land. These reliefs, found at Ephesus and now in Vienna,[26] have often been assigned to the joint reign of Marcus Aurelius and Lucius Verus. But one slab shows a group of four imperial persons, two of whom—and those the important—can be readily identified as Hadrian and Antoninus Pius standing side by side with a sceptre between them in a manner that can only be explained as an allusion to the former's adoption of the latter as his colleague, heir, and successor in February 138. The other two figures in the group, a youth and a small boy, must be Marcus Aurelius and Lucius Verus, adopted as his sons by Pius on the same occasion at the respective ages of seventeen and seven years. Pius had been popular in Asia when he served there as proconsul; and the whole monument could have been erected in Ephesus as a

Plate 42

compliment to the dynasty of which he was now a member. A striking scene presents an emperor, whose head is unfortunately lost, wearing military dress and riding, above the reclining form of Tellus, in the Sun God's chariot, with Victory holding the horses' reins and the Sun himself leading them.[27] This could be Pius' adoptive grandfather, the deified Trajan, imagined as the new Sol and as the pendant of Luna, who, on another slab, rides above the recumbent figure of Thalassa in a chariot drawn by stags, while Hesperus acts as charioteer and Nox leads the animals. The scenes depicting battles, sacrifices, groups of personifications of localities, etc. could then allude to those oriental victories of Trajan that shed lustre on his immediate successors, although they themselves did not emulate his martial programme. If the battles, etc. on this monument represented Lucius Verus' Parthian campaigns of 162–4, it would be difficult to see what warlike, divinised emperor would be relevant to such a context and why the adoption in 138 of Pius, in which the child Verus played but a minor part, should feature so prominently. The style and content of the Sol and Luna scenes, with their figures plastically modelled in very high relief, their paratactic arrangement of the actors, and preponderance of divine over human personages, are in the full Hellenistic sculptural tradition. But the presumably east-Greek carvers of these and of the other slabs were equally at home in the bold foreshortening of figures emerging from the background, in the rendering of depth in several receding planes, and in the use of vertical perspective in crowded groupings which we have so often found in western relief work. Noteworthy, too, in this east-Greek setting are the almost completely frontal poses of the family quartet.

Of Antoninus Pius' peaceful activities no records in relief have survived. But his predecessor's paramount interest in the provinces and his lengthy tours abroad were commemorated on the temple of Divus Hadrianus, dedicated in the Campus

Martius in 145, by a series of fine, statuesque, female figures carved in high relief and personifying countries and peoples of the Roman world, of which, however, only a few can be identified with any certainty.[28] After Pius' death a column was set up, also in the Campus Martius, to commemorate his consecration. The shaft, which was plain, to judge by the coin types that represent it, has vanished; but its large base, now in the Vatican, has an inscription on one side and its three other sides sculptured. The relief on the principal face, composed of large, classicised figures, is as cold, correct, and academic as the three Hadrianic panels now in the Conservatori and resembles one of them very closely in composition and content (*cf.* p. 64). Pius and his empress, Faustina I, are carried heavenwards, attended by eagles, on the back of a winged male Genius who holds a celestial globe, while their flight is watched by Roma seated on the right and the personification of the Campus Martius reclining on the left.[29] Since the whole monument was court-inspired, we can hardly dismiss as 'popular' and con-sciously anti-classical the very differently treated scene of diminutive figures that appears on each of the lateral faces of the base. This is a *decursio* or parade of foot-soldiers and horse-men, presumably one of the spectacles held at the emperor's funeral, in which cavalry were made to ride round a central, relatively static group of infantry.[30] But in order not to obscure any of the participants and to fill the field in a manner satisfying to the eye, the horsemen have been turned by the sculptor into a kind of wreath encircling the foot-soldiers, those in front of the latter (from the onlooker's standpoint) being placed below them and those behind them, above them. Given the limited space at the artist's disposal, the figures, particularly those of the infantry, could not be other than short and stocky. But this very dumpiness serves to produce a sense of sturdy strength; and the carving of the individual men and horses is careful and natural-istic. The ledges, on which the upper and central figures rest,

Plate 43

hold them down to earth and dispel any uncomfortable sug-
gestion that they are floating in mid-air.

The extreme type of vertical or bird's-eye perspective found
in these scenes on Pius' column-base is decoratively very
effective and in view of the topic set and the field to be adorned
its use was unavoidable. In the eleven large, rectangular panels
that have come down to us from some triumphal monument,
or monuments, of Marcus Aurelius' reign—three in the
Conservatori and eight re-used on the attic of the Arch of
Constantine—the subjects are such that the scenes could all be
drawn in logical, horizontal perspective, as seen from the
ordinary spectator's level.[31] Only in one very crowded scene of
sacrifice are the heads in the second and third planes raised
above those in the foreground. Human activity is, for the most
part, confined to the lower half of the picture, and buildings,
trees, spears, banners, and standards occupy the upper portion of
the field, sometimes crowding it, at other times leaving empty
tracts of background, but always providing a sufficient filling.
In one scene, that of an imperial largesse, the emperor and his
suite, being raised on a very high platform, are in possession of
the upper portion of the panel, while the recipients, men,
women, and children, stand at ground level in the lower
portion. Generally such scenes of largesse are viewed by the
spectator from the side. But here the imperial group directly
faces him and the citizens either move towards him or turn their
backs on him; and in this case logic in perspective is combined
with the full presentation of almost every actor. Despite the
theatrical gestures and intense glances that appear in these
reliefs here and there, our impression is that the monumental,
generally well-proportioned figures are playing their parts with
a stately, quiet dignity. The processions advance slowly; the
crowds do not jostle unduly; the sacrifices are unhurried; the
imperial speeches and audiences, whether to Roman troops,
a suppliant barbarian chieftain, or a group of prisoners, are

unimpassioned; and on the faces of the conquered there is little
trace of anguish. The Antonine calm still prevails. Meanwhile,
the richness of the background details and the lavish drilling of
hair, beards, folds of drapery, arms, and armour lend a high
degree of picturesqueness to the whole series.

The column in the Campus Martius known as the Antonine
or Marcus' Column is of Luna marble, stands 100 feet high,
and carries on its shaft a band of sculptured reliefs in 20 spirals.[32]
These reliefs tell the story of two of Marcus Aurelius' campaigns
against the northern barbarians, separated by the figure of a
Victory as are the scenes from the two Dacian wars on Trajan's
Column. The two campaigns have been variously identified as
those of 169–72 and 174–5, those of 172–3 and 174–5, or those
of 172–5 and 177–80. If the last set of dates were correct (and
the case for it has been strongly argued), this column would be
one of the *columnae* voted to Marcus after his death. Otherwise
it could have been begun as a victory monument, as was
Trajan's Column, during his lifetime. The carving of the relief
band must anyhow have been continued well into the reign of
Commodus at least; but the detection of different hands and
styles is complicated by the fact that the sculptures were much
restored under Pope Sixtus V in 1589. An inscription set up
by one Adrastus, Procurator of the Column under Septimius
Severus, quotes from an official letter of 193 which authorised
him to use for the building of his own house ten planks from
the scaffolding 'that had to be erected' on the Column. This
suggests that work was still being done on the sculptures up to
that date; and the style of some of the reliefs in the band near the
top is certainly close to that of Severan carving. One or two of
these scenes look like replacements of earlier pictures.

Trajan's Column was, of course, the model for that of
Marcus. Here, as there, the story begins with a crossing of the
Danube by the Roman troops, there are the same recurring
episodes, and scene succeeds scene continuously without a

break. Vertical perspective is no less freely used than on the earlier monument, the figures in the second plane being often raised quite clear of those in the foreground: rivers appear as on maps, while the boat-loads of men crossing are seen from the horizontal, human viewpoint. On the other hand, there are several marked stylistic and technical divergencies between the two friezes. Here there is little interlocking of adjacent scenes and we miss the Trajanic artist's skill in fusing together by subtle transitions incidents of different content. The total effect is less that of a moving film than of a series of juxtaposed still-pictures. Many of the scenes tend to break up into two parallel, horizontal, superimposed zones, so that the band loses its tapestry-like unity of design. Monotonous rows of figures in virtually identical poses now confront us. The relief is much higher than on Trajan's Column. Limbs, heads, and even bodies are worked wholly or almost in the round, as if free-standing statuettes had been flattened at the back and applied to the wall of the shaft. The result is brighter highlights and darker pools of shade. The artist of Marcus' Column dis-plays, on the whole, rather less interest in the landscape and architectural background. But buildings, army tents, the straw huts of the enemy, etc. are carefully delineated; and again the 'local colour' and the circumstantial military details suggest that the sketches of eyewitnesses were the basis of the frieze. As on the base of Pius' Column (*cf.* p. 67) the squatness of the figures serves to express the toughness and dogged determina-tion of the combatants.

More important still is the contrast in attitude and atmosphere between the two relief bands. On Trajan's Column the emperor and his men are comrades, with whom he is in full *rapport* when he addresses them, rendered in profile and as completely unconcerned with the spectator of the frieze. In scenes of *adlocutio* on Marcus' Column the emperor is reared on a lofty *podium* or ledge of rock high above, and isolated from, his audience, and gazes full-face over their heads—at us. The *princeps* had become a *dominus*, independent of the human conflict and looking for our homage. The reliefs of Trajan's Column portray war as productive of peace, security, and order: the success and permanence of Graeco-Roman civilisation are there unquestioned; and the vanquished are the objects of a kindly, if realistic, humanitarian outlook. Here the Roman army faces an unknown world, full of fear, as the strained expressions of the soldiers show. Security has broken down and man is oppressed by the horror and tragedy of war for Romans and barbarians alike. Above the tortured bodies and agonised faces of the conquered and the rigid forms of the soldiers mechanically carrying out their orders broods the spectre of the Rain God, with water streaming from his hair, beard, wings, arms, and finger-tips, perhaps the most haunting and imaginative figure that a Roman artist ever created.

Plate 44

The earliest historical reliefs of the Severan period known to us are those on the Arch with three passage-ways that stands in the north-west corner of the Roman Forum and was erected in 203 in honour of Septimius' eastern victories and in celebration of his first ten years of rule (*decennalia*).[33] On either face of the Arch, above the side passage-ways, are panels with episodes from the Parthian war—sieges of cities, Roman troops on the march, imperial *adlocutiones*, etc. The panels are carved with masses of small, crowded figures in laterally spreading scenes that are composed in superimposed registers. In some ways, particularly in the zone arrangement, in the frontal presentation of the emperor in the *adlocutiones*, in the dumpy proportions of the men, and in the use of the bird's-eye-view perspective for rivers and for cities, down into which we look as from the sky, these carvings are close to those on the Column of Marcus. But here the relief is much lower, the individual figures are less clear-cut and well-rounded, and the whole effect is more niggling. The scenes are, in fact, more like paintings than

Plate 45

sculptures, recalling the pictorial techniques of map-making and topographical painting (*cf.* pp. 18 f.); and one cannot but suspect that they had some connection with the 'public paint- ings', or triumphal pictures, of the Parthian campaigns which, according to Herodian,[34] Septimius exhibited in Rome. There is no reason to suppose that in these scenes the designer was breaking deliberately with classical tradition. For the groups of soldiers and captives in the panels on the bases of the eight engaged columns are treated in a monumental, plastic manner; and the four flying Victories, each with a child personifying a Season below her feet, in the spandrels flanking the central passage-way were obviously modelled on those of the spandrels of the Arch of Titus and of Trajan's Arch at Beneventum. Also plastic and monumental in their style are the figures in the Palazzo Sacchetti relief in Rome, which depicts Septimius, shown almost in profile, on a platform with his sons receiving a group of togate personages.[35]

The growing interest in frontality which we have already noted in Aurelian and Severan *adlocutiones* is illustrated again on the two main panels of the little Arch that clings to the western wall of the portico of the church of San Giorgio in Velabro, between the Palatine and the Tiber. It is known as the Porta Argentariorum, since its inscription states that it was dedicated to Septimius and his family in 204 by the bankers (*argentarii*) in collaboration with the wholesale cattle-dealers (*negotiantes boarii*).[36] These two reliefs as we see them now are incomplete, for after the murders of Caracalla's father-in-law Plautianus in 205, of his wife Plautilla in 211, and of his brother Geta in 212, the portraits of the victims were removed. One panel now shows Caracalla by himself, sacrificing at a tripod and virtually full-face, although his head is inclined slightly towards the spectator's left. In the other panel Septimius and his empress are also sacrificing at a tripod. Here Julia Domna is completely, Septimius very nearly, frontal and both of them display no interest in one another or in the rite that they profess to be performing, but gaze straight before them into the distance as though to scan the faces, and accept the homage, of the onlookers. Noteworthy, too, is the flat, two-dimensional technique in which the figures are rendered.

It is, however, a provincial monument, the great four-way Arch at Lepcis Magna in Tripolitania, that provides the fullest and most exciting document of Severan historical sculpture.[37] For the date of the erection of this Arch we have not a shred of epigraphic evidence. But there can be little doubt that its sculptured scenes are of local significance and refer to specific ceremonies enacted at Lepcis on the occasion of the visit of the imperial family to Septimius' native city *c.* 203(?). These ceremonies seem to have been staged with two ends in view—first, to stress the glory won by Septimius through his victories in the east, and, secondly, while enhancing the whole imperial family's prestige, to exhibit Caracalla in particular as the emperor's elder son, colleague, and destined successor. The deities and personifications depicted in the reliefs could all be local, or locally worshipped, ones, here shown as participating in, or witnessing, the ceremonies.

Of the four historical friezes that ran round the attic of the Arch three are reasonably well preserved. The most important of them presents the triumphal entry of Septimius into Lepcis. The procession advances from left to right and both a group of horsemen on the left, rendered in vertical perspective, and a group of foot-soldiers on the right, carrying a *ferculum* (bier) with captives, move rightwards. So do the horses of the emperor's chariot. But the front of the chariot and Septimius and his two sons standing in it are completely full-face, as are also the personages walking at the horses' heads and the repetitive figures of bearded men, who, ranged in a serried row and reared above the foreground figures, watch the procession from the background as it passes by. These spectators are, of course, logically so posed. But the imperial group has been deliberately pulled round to a frontal view in order to give it a hieratic aspect and rivet our attention upon it. The pharos of Lepcis in the background of the scene and the relief of the Tyche of Lepcis between its patron deities, Hercules and Bacchus, on the front of the chariot make the local setting of the triumph evident.

Plate 46

In another attic frieze, a scene of sacrifice in Julia Domna's honour, we find the same monotonous row of tiered, frontal onlookers in the background, while the figures in the fore/ ground, if not all rigidly full/face, are basically frontal, being turned only very slightly towards the central act which they are supposed to be witnessing. In the third more or less complete frieze, the so/called *dextrarum iunctio*, in which Septimius, clasping the hand of Caracalla, presents him to Lepcis (again symbolised by the Tyche, Hercules, and Bacchus in the back/ ground) as his fellow Augustus, the posing of the figures is more varied and there is a more naturalistic concentration of the actors on the ceremony. Characteristic of all three friezes is the exten/ sive use of drilling in the drapery and the almost wholly two/ dimensional carving of the figures in the second plane.

On the inner faces of each of the piers of the Lepcis Arch are three superimposed panels carved with historical scenes or groups of divinities. Sometimes there are three quite separate scenes, one above the other; other scenes occupy two tiers. In these we observe a wide variety of treatment. In the scene of Septimius' presentation of his elder son to the three Tychai of Tripolitania all the figures are almost completely frontal. In a scene of sacrifice, on the other hand, the lateral figures are almost completely in profile, turned centrewards. In the group of the local Capitoline Triad, with Septimius in the guise of Jupiter and Julia Domna in that of Juno, frontality again prevails. A group of deities, including Apollo and Diana, all in easy, three/quarter poses, is a purely Hellenistic, naturalistic piece. One pier relief, recomposed from many fragments, which

occupied all three tiers, is a superb bird's-eye view of a be-
leagured city in the style of the reliefs on Marcus' Column
and on the Severan Arch in the Roman Forum: the defenders
are at the top and the attackers are shown below the walls in a
series of mounting registers. This scene could well have been
based on a triumphal painting, displayed at Lepcis, of an
incident in the eastern campaigns. The flying Victories in the
spandrels of the Lepcis Arch, despite their anatomical distor-
tions, follow the models that we first encounter on Titus' Arch
in Rome. But a new element is introduced in the unrealis-
tically elongated figures of captives in the narrow panels at the
corners of the Lepcis Arch.

The material of this Arch is marble imported from Asia
Minor; and it would seem to be virtually certain that with the
marble came Asiatic sculptors to carve it, so close are the
affinities of the decorative elements on the Arch and other
Severan buildings at Lepcis with second-century decorative
work discovered at Aphrodisias in Caria.[38] Here, then, would
be east-Greek artists producing in a Latin-speaking province
sculptures that partly reflect Hellenistic, naturalistic tradition,
partly offer counterparts of the pictorial narrative styles of State
reliefs in Rome, and partly present in a developed form features
with which western artists were as yet only experimenting—
the extreme form of drill technique, with its highly patterned,
black-and-white effects, and an insistence on frontality that
recalls the 'Parthian' art of Palmyra, Dura-Europos, and
Hatra. All this makes us wonder to what extent the sculptural
methods that we think of as specifically Roman, because we
normally meet them first on western monuments, were originally
devised by east-Mediterranean masters and found their way
gradually from the east to the capital.

As its many fine portraits (*cf.* pp. 38–40) and carved sarcophagi (*cf.* pp. 102–3) prove, the third century in Rome was far
from being barren in sculpture. But a stormy, troubled period,

with one emperor not infrequently succeeding another with lightning rapidity, was not calculated to inspire the erection of a continuous series of great victory monuments carved with State reliefs. We do, in fact, know of only two such monuments in the capital dating from between the Severan Arches and that of Constantine, namely the Arch, or triple gate, of Gallienus, put up in 262, as its inscription records, on the site of the former Porta Esquilina, and an Arch of Diocletian (Arcus Novus) which spanned the Via Lata. Of the former only the central passage/way is left and no reliefs survive.[39] From the site of the latter were recovered in the sixteenth century a piece (now in the Villa Medici in Rome) with two fragmentary figures and an inscribed date, that could refer to Diocletian's twentieth year of rule in 303–4, and two column bases (now in the Boboli Gardens in Florence) each carved on three of its sides with reliefs of Victories, captives, and the Dioscuri.[40] The monumental, plastically worked, and naturalistic figures on the piece and on the bases are so superior in style and treatment to those on the corresponding panels on the Arch of Constantine (*cf.* p. 79), which was erected only twelve years later, and to those on the contemporary (303) column base of Diocletian in the Roman Forum, that it seems to be not unlikely that they were originally carved for an earlier Arch, perhaps a second, unrecorded Arch of the 'baroque' Gallienic period.[41] On the Diocletianic column base, worked on all four sides with processional and sacrificial scenes and a date/bearing shield upheld by Victories, the relief is flat, the poses of the figures are mainly frontal, and the non/plastic, linear folds of the drapery are rendered by deeply drilled/out grooves.[42]

For the fullest and most informative series of State reliefs of the Tetrarchic period we turn again to a provincial monument, to what was once the triple Arch of Galerius at Salonika, where the surviving sculptures are arranged in four narrow registers on each of three sides of the two inner piers.[43] Since

Plate 47

in one scene two Augusti and two Caesars appear to be represented, the Arch probably dates from between 296, the year of Galerius' Persian victory, and 305, the year of the abdication of Diocletian and Maximian. The small scale of the figures and the general effect of the self-contained, super-imposed friezes suggest the possibility that they were designed by a person or persons whose *métier* had been the decoration of sarcophagi. Two main types of composition are employed. There is the static, centralised type, in which the imperial figures appear at the centre of the scene in hieratic frontality, while the surrounding persons are placed symmetrically in balancing groups on either side. Such are the emperor's *adlocutio*, in which the speaker is on a much larger scale than the members of his audience, the imperial sacrifice, and the imperial 'epiphany', which shows the two Augusti seated and the two Caesars standing amid a galaxy of gods and personifications. The second type of composition is used for processional and battle scenes moving now briskly, now more slowly, in one main direction in a lively and naturalistic manner. The artist's choice between these types was obviously determined by the nature of the subject to be represented. A bird's-eye view of the background figures occurs in several scenes; and the outlines of some of the figures and objects in the second and third planes are incised on the background—a pictorial device found long before on Trajan's Column (*cf.* pp. 57–60), on the Arch at Orange (*cf.* p. 54), and on the panels of the Julii Monument, dating from Augustan times, at St Remy in Provence (*cf.* p. 91).

Much the same niggling 'sarcophagus style' and the same combination of the static, centralised type of composition with the laterally-moving type occur in the six narrow friezes which were carved for the Arch of Constantine in Rome[44] and of which two appear on each of the main, and one on each of the short, façades. These reliefs represent six episodes in Constantine's campaign against Maxentius which ended in his mastery of

Rome. Four of them are of the second type of scene—Constantine's departure from Milan, his siege of Verona, his victory at the Milvian Bridge, and his triumphal entry into the capital. In the siege scene there is a disproportion between the human figures and the city walls little greater than on the Columns of Trajan and Marcus: neither here nor in the other three military friezes do the tiering of the background personages or the dumpy, repetitive figures of the Roman soldiers present anything new; and the rendering here of the emperor on a much larger scale than the rest is paralleled on the Salonika Arch. The two remaining friezes, which depict Constantine's address and largesse to the citizens of Rome after the city had passed into his hands, are in the centralised, symmetrical, hieratic style. In the former the emperor stands fullface on a dais and gazes straight at us, not at the crowd that is massed on either side: his proportions are only slightly larger than those of

Plate 48

his entourage and of the crowd. But in the scene of largesse the emperor, seated on a lofty platform, rigidly frontal, is noticeably larger than his attendants and much larger still than the little figures of recipients grouped to right and left at ground level and than the figures of officials who distribute cash from a series of upper balconies. This difference in scale and the lack of variation in the posing of the citizens was clearly deliberate, to emphasise the distance that separates God's vicegerent from the common run of undistinguished humanity. The methods used to express ideas of this kind are basically the same in these Roman friezes and in those of the Salonika Arch; and both these methods and these ideas are the logical denouement of things at which the artists of late Antonine and Severan times were aiming. We need not suppose that the designers of either series of earlyfourthcentury reliefs were in conscious revolt against classical standards.

Indeed, the artist who planned the Constantinian carving on the Roman Arch was definitely not anticlassical in taste. The two reliefs of Sol and Luna in their chariots in the roundels on the short sides are obviously modelled on the eight Hadrianic roundels and are, if technically inferior to the latter, vigorously drawn and skilfully adapted to their circular fields. In the flying Victories with Seasons at their feet in the spandrels of the central passage/way, in the Water Deities in those of the lateral passage/ways, and in the groups of Victories and cap/ tives on the column bases he followed the long/established traditions of Roman and Italian sculptured Arches. These more monumental figures are the least successful of all the Con/ stantinian carvings on the Arch. Apart from the Seasons, which are as good as many on contemporary Seasons sarco/ phagi (*cf.* p. 103), those in the spandrels are ungainly and dis/ torted, while those on the bases, in particular the Victories, are bodiless and two/dimensional, with drapery folds that fashion decorative linear patterns but bear little or no relation to the forms beneath them. Here we must admit a falling/off from, not a rejection of, the classical ideal.

For the final stage in the story of frontality in Roman historical sculpture we pass to New Rome, to the reliefs on the base of the obelisk set up by Theodosius in AD 390 in the hippodrome in Constantinople.[45] Here the emperor and his family, seated or standing in strictly frontal poses and accompanied by officials, soldiers, and monotonous rows of repetitive spectators in two superimposed tiers, watch performances in the hippodrome— chariot races, dancing displays, and the actual erection of the obelisk. The late/fourth/century Columns of Theodosius and Arcadius, both of which were drawn before they were des/ troyed, bore on their shafts spiral relief bands obviously modelled on those of the Roman Columns. Of the Column of Arcadius with scenes from the Gothic wars we have an especially fine set of drawings made by a German artist in the sixteenth century:[46] these indicate that the band contained both scenes of the static, ceremonial, frontal type and scenes of vivid

Plate 49

action. Thus these reliefs carry on, to the eve of the Byzantine epoch, the documentary, narrative style of historical sculpture that the Ara Pacis Augustae had inaugurated. Meanwhile the centralised composition, with the imperial group as the focal point of interest, was destined to play a long and significant role in the art of the Christian Church, with Christ and His heavenly court replacing the emperor and his entourage as the central, dominating theme.

CHAPTER V

Miscellaneous Reliefs in Stone and Marble

WE HAVE EXAMINED IN SOME DETAIL the his׳ torical reliefs of the Roman world from late׳repub׳ lican to late׳imperial times because they form a relatively small series of official works, characteristically Roman, in which we can trace the development of style and of politico׳religious artistic concepts as evolved by the leading sculptors of each successive period. The reliefs of miscellaneous kinds to which we now turn, whether carved in Rome and Italy or in the provinces, are mostly found in very great quantities, are very varied in their quality, and are often difficult to date. All that can be done here is to indicate the principal classes into which they fall, discuss briefly their general characteristics and purpose, and cite a few typical samples.

PICTORIAL RELIEFS

The smallest class of these reliefs consists of those which appear to have had a mainly decorative function in public and in private contexts. They are rectangular marble panels with sub׳ jects drawn chiefly from mythology, legend, daily life, or the realm of Nature. The well׳known relief in the New Capi׳ toline Museum of Mettius Curtius leaping fully armed and on horseback into the chasm in the Roman Forum may have adorned a balustrade round the Lacus Curtius.[1] Its somewhat homely style suggests that it may be a late׳antique copy of a republican original. To the early Empire (first to early second century AD) probably belong a number of sophisticated pieces elegantly carved with scenes from Greek mythology. Examples from Rome are the Hermaphrodite in the Palazzo Colonna, the Aesculapius and the Nymph, both in the Lateran Museum, the Perseus and Andromeda and the Endymion, both in the Capitoline Museum, the Bellerophon and the Amphion and Zethus, both in the Palazzo Spada.² One could imagine these as wall decorations in wealthy people's houses; and this could conceivably also have been the purpose of two famous reliefs of Antinous, both now in Rome, one in the Villa Albani, where he appears as Vertumnus, half-draped and crowned with fruit and flowers, the other in the Istituto dei Fondi Rustici, which is signed in Greek by Antonianos of Aphrodisias and presents him as a young and slim Silvanus³—unless these were votive pieces associated with the posthumous cult of Hadrian's favourite.

Obviously pendants and illustrative of the same Roman-age delight in natural history that lay behind the figures in the round of animals and birds (*cf.* p. 48) are the two so-called Grimani reliefs now in the Kunsthistorisches Museum in Vienna.⁴ Both show a mother suckling her young in a rocky cave—a lioness with a pair of cubs and a ewe with her lamb— amid a setting of trees, rustic shrines, and altars. These are typical *genre* pictures, rich in the delicately rendered landscape and architectural details that are found in painting and stucco work of the Augustan and Julio-Claudian periods.

A most remarkable relief found in the Lago Fucino was possibly one of a series connected with the draining of the lake by Claudius and affixed to the walls of some public or private lakeside building. It displays an extremely realistic prospect of a walled town with streets of houses two storeys high, a large gate, extramural villas, groves, and gardens, and a broad high- road or river running past it.⁵ The houses are depicted in tiers and might be thought to be rising up a hillside. But the features outside the walls cannot be explained in that way;

and the whole scene must be regarded as an outstanding instance of the use in pictorial sculpture of the bird's-eye-view perspective—a landscape painting in marble.

FIGURED RELIGIOUS RELIEFS ON ALTARS, VOTIVE TABLETS AND TEMPLES

We considered in the last chapter monumental public altars with historical reliefs such as the Ara Pacis, the Ara Pietatis, and that from the Chancellery with part of a long sacrificial procession on one of its sides (*cf.* pp. 51–4). Here we are concerned with the small altars of a semi-official or private character relating to the imperial cult (emperor worship) and to gods and goddesses and personifications of every kind— Graeco-Roman, oriental, and local provincial.

Three early-imperial altars from Rome belong to the cult of the Lares of Augustus.[6] All carry statuesque figures of the Lares and two show scenes of sacrifice in which the sculptors have been quite successful in producing the three-dimensional effect of a group of persons standing in a circle round an altar. Probably associated with a private cult of the Gens Augusta is a fine piece found at Carthage and sculptured like the Roman altars on all four sides.[7] The subjects are the Dea Roma seated on a pile of arms, holding a Victory, and accompanied by symbols of the world-wide Augustan peace; Apollo seated beside the Delphic tripod; Aeneas escaping from Troy with Anchises and Ascanius; and Augustus himself sacrificing in honour of his legendary ancestors and of the divine protectors of his House. The large single figures of Roma and Apollo are better carved than are the Aeneas and Augustus groups; two different hands may have been at work on this altar.

A Hadrianic altar found at Ostia and precisely dated by its inscription to the year 124 was dedicated by a freedman with the authorisation of the town councillors.[8] Here the leading deity is

Mars, shown on one side standing with Venus and a little figure who may be Hymenaeus. Two sides display attractive groups of Cupids sporting with the god's arms and chariot, while the fourth side alludes to one of the god's amours: Romulus and Remus, suckled by the She-wolf, are watched over by the Tiber God and found by shepherds. The style of all four reliefs, including that of the Roman scene, is completely Hellenistic.

The surviving altars and votive tablets with figures of the deities and personifications in whose honour they were dedicated or with scenes of sacrifice to them, are found in every corner of the Graeco-Roman world and run into thousands. As with statuary in the round (Ch. III), so with reliefs, the most interesting and original types are those that illustrate oriental and provincial cults. On a marble panel in the Vatican two priests and two priestesses of Isis, carved by an accomplished hand, walk in solemn procession, wearing their distinctive robes and head-dresses and carrying their ritual implements and other symbols of Egyptian worship.[9] From the shrine of Jupiter Dolichenus on the Aventine comes a set of fine reliefs portraying the god and his consort, Juno Regina, poised on the back of a bull and a doe respectively and accompanied by attendant deities.[10] For the cult of Mithras we have, chiefly from the northern and western frontier regions, but also from Rome, the great reredos slabs presenting normally his bull-slaying exploit, occasionally other episodes in his saga, together with countless minor tablets and altars showing figures of the god and his associates or scenes from the Mithraic cycle.[11] Reliefs featuring the local Palmyrene deities, wearing costumes that are largely Graeco-Roman, but posed in the rigidly frontal attitudes that are the hall-mark of art in the 'Parthian' orbit, come from Palmyra itself and from the surrounding districts.[12] Undistinguished aesthetically, but novel in content, are the Rider God votive slabs from Danubian countries.[13] Among the most varied

Plate 50

and pleasing of the new religious subjects on altars and tablets dedicated in provincial shrines are those that portray the local gods and goddesses of Celtic lands. Only a few outstanding examples can be noted here—the Matronae Aufaniae at Bonn, Plate 51 with their curious, tea-cosy-like headgear and graceful, enveloping mantles; the horned god Cernunnos at Reims, squatting cross-legged on a bench in the centre of the scene and pouring coins from a bag, while the classical gods, Apollo and Mercury, stand respectfully in attendance on either side of him; Epona, the patroness of donkeys, mules, and horses, either riding side-saddle on a horse or enthroned between two of her protégés.[14] In order to appreciate the wealth and attractiveness of this material and to realise how creative could be the impact of classical tradition on the religious life of unsophisticated native populations, one must be prepared to spend time in studying the local collections of Roman France, Germany, and Britain.

Temple pediments in Rome with figures of deities in high relief are known from representations of them on historical reliefs with architectural backgrounds—the temples of Quirinus, Mars Ultor, Fortuna Redux, etc.[15] That the new Capitolium built by Vespasian had pedimental sculpture is recorded by his coin types;[16] and part of the actual figured pediment of a small shrine, probably that of the African Dea Caelestis, survives in the Capitoline Museum. For other actual sculptured pediments with figures in relief we must turn to the provinces—to the temple at Oea (Tripoli), with the city Tyche, Apollo, Minerva, and a Dioscurus, to the small temple of Mercurius Augustus at Cologne,[17] and, above all, to the temple of Sulis Minerva, goddess of the healing springs, at Bath.[18] The design of the last is purely classical—a central shield upheld by a pair of flying Victories, with a Triton in each angle. But the mask on the shield, a male Medusa, with head-wings, snakes writhing in the hair and beard and knotted below the chin, a moustache, and the flapping hair and sinuous beard of a Water God, is a Celtic conception matched by the flat, two-dimensional technique, which is in many ways more akin to drawing than to carving.

FIGURED CAPITALS AND COLUMNS

Pilaster and column capitals with figures in relief of animals or human beings form a class of architectural sculpture inherited by Rome from the Hellenistic world. The repertoire comprises human heads, busts (sometimes on shields), half-figures, and whole figures, and the heads or foreparts of beasts and complete animals. Examples dating from before our era are plentiful in Greek lands east of the Adriatic and in Hellenised Etruria and southern Italy; and both these and the Roman imperial series are the subject of a recent and exhaustive analysis and study.[19] Pieces carved with complete human figures or with half-human figures have come to light in substantial numbers in Rome and Italy and on many provincial sites. They clearly appealed to the taste of the times; and the figures do indeed provide a very attractive kind of surprise as they emerge or step from the acanthus foliage. The most elaborate instances in Rome are the single capital from the Baths of Alexander Severus and the four in the Baths of Caracalla. All of these show complete figures of gods and men richly carved in very high relief.[20] Once again, the pre-eminent provincial instance is from Britain, the great capital found at Corinium (Cirencester) in Gloucestershire, with the bust of an unidentified Celtic divinity on each of its four faces.[21]

Plate 52

The majority of columns with figures in relief on their rounded shafts and rectangular bases come from Roman Germany. These are the so-called Jupiter columns, which generally carry series of standing, classically conceived figures of Graeco-Roman divinities arranged in superimposed tiers on the shafts and in panels on the bases. Occasionally the column takes the form of a rectangular pilaster with tiers of panels, each with its deity, on three or four of its sides.[22] Here, as on the Reims relief (*cf.* p. 85), the Graeco-Roman gods are subordinated to a Celtic divinity, in this case the native Jupiter, whose figure on horseback, borne on the shoulders of a snakelegged monster, normally surmounted each of these columns or pilasters.

RELIEFS WITH FLORAL MOTIFS

The lovely swags of flowers, fruit, and corn-ears and the great acanthus dado of the Ara Pacis Augustae were, as we have seen (*cf.* p. 53), most probably inspired by a Hellenistic school at Pergamon whose members had a special taste for the naturalistic rendering of plant forms. A similar naturalism sometimes appears in decorative work in Magna Graecia and in such central-Italian ornamentation as was produced under southItalian influence. In other Hellenistic centres, particularly in those that were dominated by the Neo-Attic style, floral motifs were much more formal and conventionalised, as on the large marble vessels and articles of marble furniture that were imported during the first century BC from Attic workshops into Rome and Italy. There the effects of this stylised manner can be traced, for example, in architectural friezes carved in local stones with running floral scrolls. But in the Augustan age it was the naturalistic style that prevailed, not only on official monuments such as the Ara Pacis, but on many minor works of sculpture; and it owed its popularity to the fact that it could satisfy the particular delight taken by the Romans and Italians of the time in trees, plants, flowers, and gardens, whether real or counterfeited in works of art of all kinds. Examples in unofficial sculpture are a circular base in the Lateran Museum, which is girdled by swags of fruit and flowers linking lyres;[23] an altar in the Museo Nazionale Romano with sprays of plane leaves;[24] and a little altar in the Museo Nazionale in Naples with a garland of fruit and flowers very close in treat-ment to the garlands of the Ara Pacis.[25] The taste for this naturalistic style endured throughout the first century AD into late Flavian times, to which period belong the carvings in relief, now in the Lateran Museum, from the tomb of the Roman family of the Haterii. Among these are two candelabra veiled in rose sprays,[26] a panel covered all over with sprays of lemon and quince, and a pilaster adorned with two vine-stems rising from an acanthus calyx and interlacing so as to form a series of medallions, in each of which a Bacchic figure stands.[27]

This pilaster is a good example of the so-called 'peopled scroll', now vertical, now horizontal, harbouring in its medal-lions or spirals whole or half human figures and whole or half figures of animals.[28] A conceit inherited from Hellenistic sculpture, mosaic work, and metal work, the 'peopled scroll' enjoyed an immense popularity with Roman imperial sculptors (and painters and mosaicists), not only in Rome and Italy, but throughout the provinces and lands on the outskirts of the Empire, both in east and west, and right on into the late-antique period. From the Severan age onwards, with the gradual substitution of two-dimensional for three-dimensional effects in carving, the rendering of plant forms became less plastic and naturalistic, so that the floral pattern and its in-habiting figures tended to look like a flat, 'all-over', lace-like design standing out in brilliant light against a black back-ground. The great vine and acanthus-scroll pilasters, with Bacchic and Herculean, etc. figures, in the Severan basilica at Lepcis Magna are superb examples of this manner. But to the very end these sculptured scrolls are evidence of pleasure in the natural world both for its own sake and for its decorative potentialities and of a lively sense of fun and fantasy in making men and beasts burst from the hearts of flowers, stand poised on slender stalks, or dart in and out through curling tendrils.

Plate 53

CHAPTER VI

Funerary Reliefs

GRAVESTONES

Of the two methods of disposing of the dead normally practised by the ancient Greeks and Romans, cremation and inhumation, the former was almost universal in Rome from *c.* 400 BC, at the latest, until the turn of the first and second centuries AD. No Roman vertical gravestones (*stelae*), associated with cremation burials, that are carved with reliefs have survived from before the second half of the first century BC. Nearly all the late-republican Roman and Italian pieces of this type, and many of those that date from the early Empire, carry portrait busts or portrait figures of the dead; and these, together with the 'portrait' *stelae* in the provinces, have been briefly reviewed in Chapter II. Some *stelae* of imperial times, both military and civilian, usually taller than they are broad and carved on one side only, show portraits combined with scenes of a religious, mythological, professional, or daily-life character; and it is with scenes of that kind, in most cases not combined with portraits, that we are concerned now. Once again, the mass of the material is so enormous that only a very general survey of the subjects represented throughout the Roman world can be attempted here and only a few outstanding individual instances can be quoted. The artistic quality of these unofficial and often humble sculptures is seldom very high: their interest lies chiefly in their very varied content.

Most of the surviving *stelae* probably stood above cremation burials. But in the period of transition from cremation to inhumation, and in certain conservative circles, some may have marked inhumations.

Scenes on *stelae* of a soldier on foot or horseback charging a foe or of a huntsman attacking a wild animal are not necessarily to be thought of as portraying the deceased, but could be allusions to the soul's victory over death and evil. Racing chariots may likewise designate victory in the next world or the race of life in this world. A groom leading a horse or horses on a soldier's gravestone obviously refers to his calling as a cavalry, man; and on civilian *stelae* business scenes of all kinds abound. These subjects would be partly retrospective, recording the mundane avocations of the dead, and partly looking forward to the immortality won by honest toil in this life. Other *stelae* carry scenes from daily life or *genre* groups used allegorically; or religious scenes such as the celestial banquet or the heads and figures of deities connected with death and the life beyond the grave; or mythological groups and figures, such as Satyrs, Maenads, Sileni, and Centaurs, emblems of the Bacchic paradise, Tritons and Nereids, alluding to the journey of the soul across the ocean to Islands of the Blessed, Cupids, symbols of the souls themselves. Some provincial *stelae*, probably asso, ciated with cremation burials and dating, in some cases, from as late as the early third century AD, take the form of lofty pillars. Examples are the stone at Pettau in Austria, much broader than it is thick, but carved both on the front and on the short sides, its main relief on the front showing Orpheus and the Beasts, an allegory of the charming of the soul in paradise;[1] and the famous Igel Monument near Trier belonging to the Secundini family of wealthy cloth-merchants, square in section and carved on all four sides with intimate and vivid scenes from the owners' business life and with such appropriate episodes from mythology as Hercules' reception into heaven by Minerva.[2] The workmanship of both these sets of reliefs is of a high stan, dard; and the same is true of the funerary reliefs of second, and third-century date from Neumagen on the Mosel, which were found built into the walls of the fort erected on the site in Constantinian times. These show, *inter alia*, a lively school scene, a lady at her toilet, a family group at table, the convey,

Plate 54

ance of barrels of wine by water, and a scene with a group of men and a large pile of cash, probably rent collecting.[3] These Neumagen reliefs could have come from pillars of the Igel type or from mausolea.

The Igel Monument does, in fact, form a link between the *stelae* or gravestones proper and the funerary structures, carved with reliefs, which outrival it in size or height and in architectural elaboration and which are grouped together here under the somewhat loose heading of mausolea. The earliest of these structures certainly marked cremation burials. The laterepublican or earlyAugustan tomb of the masterbaker, Marcus Vergilius Eurysaces, which represents a colossal oven and stands just outside the Porta Maggiore in Rome, has a sprightly frieze of smallscale figures depicting the various stages of breadmaking.[4] The earlyAugustan Monument of the Julii at St Remy in Provence, a tall pillarlike building, comprises a large square basis with a panel of relief work on each of its four sides.[5] These present battle and hunting scenes rendered in a highly pictorial style, showing vertical perspective, bold foreshortening, the outlining of figures by grooves to make them stand out more clearly, and the incising instead of carving of background details—all perhaps derived from lost Hellenistic paintings. That the hunts and combats are largely allegorical (the overcoming of evil and death) is clear from the fact that one of the battle scenes includes a group consisting of the figures of the dead members of the Julii family, a Victory, and a small winged figure with a tablet or scroll, who may be Death himself. A mausoleum of JulioClaudian date, that of Caius Lusius Sorax, found at Amiternum near Chieti and now reconstructed in the Museo Nazionale Romano, takes the form of a temple with a pediment and frieze above an open portico of columns. In the pediment a magistrate, seated frontally in the centre of a group of frontally posed seated and standing spectators and flanked by two groups of musicians, watches the gladiatorial display that is depicted in the frieze immediately below.[6] A similar temple-mausoleum, with a columned portico and gabled roof and reliefs covering every inch of its façade, side walls, and the sides of its *podium*, is shown on one of the

Plate 55

reliefs in the Lateran Museum from the tomb of the Haterii;[7] and it seems very likely that some of the square or rectangular marble reliefs from Rome and Italy of the first century AD featuring business scenes came from the façades or side walls of temple-mausolea. Examples are the two panels with cutlers' shops in the Vatican Museum and the two with upholsterers' shops in the Uffizi Gallery in Florence.[8] All these early-imperial mausolea would have housed cremation burials. But of the house-tombs of the second century AD, with vaulted roofs and plain façades without columns, such as those found in rows beneath St Peter's in Rome[9] and at Isola Sacra to the north of Ostia,[10] some contained cremation and inhumation burials side by side, others only inhumations. Some of the Isola Sacra mausolea have on their façades terracotta panels carrying scenes from the trades and professions of the occupants—a tool-merchant, a butcher, a boatman, a miller, a water-seller, a doctor (an accouchement scene), and so forth. Other reliefs, of marble, with professional representations from Isola Sacra and Ostia itself adorned the insides or outsides of tombs. It is probable that a number of the Gallo-Roman grave reliefs with business and daily-life scenes, those, for example, in the rich and varied series from Sens and Arlon,[11] were not parts of *stelae* but decorated mausolea, for cremation or inhumation burials, that have long since disappeared.

Two provincial groups of mausolea with reliefs of the types that concern us here merit special mention. One is a series of tall rectangular monuments found in fragments at the site of the ancient Celeia, now in Jugoslavia, and re-erected.[12] Some of these are elaborate, two-storeyed structures consisting either of two solid altar-like elements piled one upon the other or of a solid base topped by an *aedicula*, that is, a niche flat behind and flanked in front by two free-standing colonnettes, from the capitals of which springs an arch, the whole being topped by a pedimented roof. On the upper altar-like element or in the niche are portrait figures or portrait busts, worked in high relief, of members of the families to whom the tombs belonged— the Vindoni, the Ennii, and the Prisciani. But in both types of structure the lower solid portion carries on its front and sides mythological episodes and figures used as allegories of death and the after-life—Hercules bringing back Alcestis from the grave, incidents in the story of Iphigenia in Aulis and in Tauris, Ganymede borne aloft by the eagle, the Rape of Europa, the Dioscuri, Satyrs, Maenads, Cupids, griffins, and marine monsters. The portrait figures and busts are stiff and hieratic; but the other reliefs are carved with a plasticity, naturalism, and grace of movement that place them in the first rank of provincial sculptures. Their style suggests the second century; and since in the provinces cremation persisted alongside of inhumation well on into the third century, these monuments may have marked cremation burials.

The other set of provincial mausolea, with reliefs that are much cruder than those at Celeia and probably later in date (third and fourth centuries), are at Ghirza in Tripolitania, on the borders of the desert.[13] They are elaborate temple-mausolea in two storeys, the lower one being a lofty *podium*, while the upper one sometimes consists of an inner 'shrine' surrounded by a colonnade. From our present point of view the most interest-ing of these are those whose column capitals carry arches with an entablature above. There the spandrels of the arches and the frieze surmounting them are naïvely, but vividly, carved in flat, two-dimensional relief with pictures from local life, renderings of the fauna of the area, episodes from classical mythology, and scenes and symbols relating to the other world. A number of the sculptures are still *in situ* on the tombs; others found scattered in the cemetery must have come from mausolea of the same types. The subjects include hunting, the reaping and threshing of corn, the winnowing of grain, ploughing with camels, processions of birds and animals, the Labours of Hercules, the celestial banquet, fish (the souls of the departed), and rosettes (emblems of life): one slab shows a central rosette surrounded by a group of eight fish, four of which are nibbling at it. It is quite probable that the burials in these mausolea were inhumations.

ALTARS AND ASH-CHESTS

From archaic to late-Hellenistic times Etruscan ash-chests of terracotta or Volterra alabaster, often with reclining figures of the dead on their lids, had been decorated on their sides with reliefs drawn principally from Greek mythology, sometimes from Italian saga or from local ceremonial life. Probably under the influence of this tradition there were produced in Rome and Italy during the first century of our era a number of marble altar-shaped, rectangular ash-chests carved, often very elegantly, in relief with scenes, figures, and symbols relating to death and the life beyond the grave. An altar of this type, now in the Louvre, made for Amemptus, a freedman of the deified Livia and therefore likely to be of Tiberian date, bears sculptured garlands, flaming torches, an eagle of apotheosis, and Cupid and Psyche each mounted on a music-making Centaur, the last groups being emblems of bliss in paradise.[14] A Flavian piece in the Uffizi Gallery in Florence, worked for one Junia Procula (whose bust with the characteristic Flavian coiffure is inset in a panel on the front), carries masks of Jupiter Ammon (a protector of the dead), garlands, eagles, and two small figure groups, one of a beast eating fruit from an overturned basket under the eyes of a Cupid, the other of a griffin despatching a bull.[15] The reliefs on another first⁄century altar, probably of Julio⁄Claudian date and now in the Museo Nazionale Romano, convey the idea of the mystic marriage of the souls of the deceased in paradise. Beside the usual floral sprays and garlands we are shown a bride and bridegroom clasping hands, the carrying of objects for a sacrifice, and two ecstatic dancing Maenads.[16] A first⁄century altar in the Aquileia museum bearing the name of Maia Severa, has a *genre* scene that was perhaps intended as a portrait of the dead—a girl seated in a high⁄backed chair with her feet on a footstool, holding a mirror in one hand and with her other petting a bird, which nestles in her lap.[17]

Plate 58

Marble ash⁄chests in the strict sense, circular or octagonal in shape and equipped with a lid, date from the first or early second century. An example at Aquileia shows the celestial banquet on its wall; another Aquileia piece, in the form of a round wicker basket, carries on its lid a very realistically portrayed sleeping dog worked in high relief.[18] A particularly pleasing octagonal example in the Capitoline Museum, pro⁄bably of early Hadrianic date, that held the ashes of one Lucius Lucilius Felix, is carved on each of seven of its faces with an exquisite, 'Donatellesque' figure of a dancing or music⁄making Cupid.[19]

SARCOPHAGI

The burial rites of cremation and inhumation had both been practised by the classical and Hellenistic Greeks; and, as regards the latter, very wealthy people had been laid to rest in expensive sarcophagi of marble, elaborately carved and richly painted. Famous examples dating from the mid and late fourth century BC are the group found at Sidon and now in the

Istanbul Museum[20]—the so-called Mourning Women, Alexander, Lycian, and Satrap sarcophagi, the second of which
still retains much of its vivid colouring (and at this point the
reader may be reminded that most, if not all, Greek and Roman
sculptures, whether in the round or in relief, were once brightly
painted). Carved on all four sides, either with rows of single
figures each flanked by colonnettes or with continuous scenes,
and equipped with mouldings, sometimes heavy and complex, above and below the figure work and with gabled lids,
these and other pieces of the same periods and types set the
pattern for the series later produced in the eastern Roman
provinces and known as 'Greek' sarcophagi in contrast to the
western or 'Roman' sarcophagi.

Meanwhile, in Etruria, where cremation and inhumation
were likewise both in use, from archaic to late-Hellenistic
times, members of the richer levels of society had been buried in
sarcophagi of terracotta, alabaster, or stone. Of these the stone
pieces prevalent from the fifth to the first century BC are as a
rule carved in relief on one long side only and carry on their lids
figures of the dead, worked partly in the round and partly in
very high relief, either lying flat on their backs or with the head
and shoulders slightly tilted up or reclining with the head and
shoulders erect.[21] And it was the latest Etruscan stone sarcophagi that furnished the makers of marble funerary effigies and
sarcophagi in Rome and Italy and in other western Mediterranean lands with their prototypes. Recumbent figures are
never found on the lids of pre-imperial Greek sarcophagi; and
when they occur on lids in the imperial Greek series we must
probably attribute their presence to Italian influence.

In Rome from the end of the fifth century BC to the turn of
the first and second centuries AD cremation was, as we have
seen (*cf*. pp. 29, 89), the general rule; and only a very few
carved sarcophagi for the inhumation of special people have
survived from that epoch. The earliest of these is the sarco-

phagus of Lucius Cornelius Scipio Barbatus, consul in 298 BC, which was found in the tomb of the Scipios on the Via Appia just south of Rome. It is made of local stone and bears on its principal face a simple architectural design consisting of a frieze of triglyphs and metopes (each containing a rosette) below a row of dentils.[22] A second, much later, piece, the marble 'Caffarelli' sarcophagus, now in Berlin, is 'Greek' in the sense that it is carved on all four sides; it may once have had a gabled lid.[23] On the two long sides are garlands of fruit, flowers, and corn/ears slung between ox/skulls, while each short side bears a candelabrum flanked by two olive trees. The style of the garlands is a shade less naturalistic than those of the Ara Pacis (*cf.* p. 53) and may point to a Tiberian date.

In the first century AD the Etruscan tradition of 'gisants' figures on the lids of sarcophagi was continued in a series of funerary monuments mostly from Rome and her neighbour/hood. These, which show the recumbent figure of the dead lying on a couch on his or her back or side or partly propped on a pillow, have often been described as the lids of sarcophagi. But, apart from the facts that none have been found resting on sarcophagi and that cremation is known to have been the normal rite in Rome until the early years of the second century, it is clear from a number of funerary reliefs, mostly of Flavian date—for instance, two from the Haterii tomb,[24] one in the Capitoline Museum,[25] and another in the Lateran Museum[26]— that the couches on which these 'gisants' are lying are not sarcophagus lids, but representations of independent funerary biers, whose now vanished legs would have rested on the ground or on a platform. Examples are the figure of a Julio/ Claudian boy in the Museo Nazionale Romano[27] and that of a Flavian lady in the Vatican Museum.[28] Such effigies lying on couches were sometimes made in the second century after inhumation in sarcophagi had become the general custom in Rome; in the Vatican Museum is the figure, on a couch resting

Plate 56

on short legs, of a woman with Faustina I's hair-style;[29] and
there is the figure of a priest of Cybele, of third-century date,
also lying on a couch which does not seem to have been the lid
of a sarcophagus, from a tomb at Isola Sacra.[30] But effigies do
not appear on the lids of imperial sarcophagi either in the east
or in the west until the mid second century.

From the time of Trajan onwards in Rome, Italy, and other
central Mediterranean areas inhumation increasingly superseded cremation as the general method of burial and had by the
second half of the third century spread to the more distant
provinces. This change of rite cannot be explained by a change
in pagan eschatological doctrine, such as the advent of belief in
a bodily resurrection to take place at the end of time. It may,
however, possibly reflect the growth of a more personal and
individual notion of the life after death, a greater interest in the
fate of the individual soul, and hence a greater reverence for the
relics of the body that had been the soul's dwelling-place. But
whatever cause lay behind it, the change itself was destined to
play a major role in the history of Roman art. For the carved
sarcophagi that were its product form an unbroken series of
mainly private, unofficial monuments illustrating the development of style and technique in sculptural relief work right down
to the end of the pagan Empire under Constantine and in the
Christian art of the third, fourth, and fifth centuries. As with
the votive altars and tablets dedicated to the gods and with the
funerary *stelae*, so with the sarcophagi the output of the workshops, although mainly concentrated in the central Mediterranean lands (Italy, Greece, Asia Minor, southern Gaul, and
Spain), was on an immense scale. Once again, only the outline
of a very long and important story can be sketched here.

The 'Roman' or western sarcophagus was carved on the
front and short sides, but left plain behind, since it was normally
placed inside a tomb, in an alcove, or backed against a wall.
It had a lid that was either flat or sloped up slightly from the

back towards the front, where it was edged by a narrow, vertical, carved panel running along the whole length of the front and generally terminating in a mask at either end. Often, but not always, the subject of the sculpture on the lid was closely connected with that on the front and sides and was carved with the same care as that on the front, although its relief was lower and its figures were on a smaller scale. In general, not however universally, on the coffin's short sides, which were less visible, not only was the relief lower than on the front, but the work-manship was much more summary. In the third century sarcophagi with rounded ends, sometimes with the figure of a lion carved in high relief on the front side of the rounded surface, came into fashion. And for the rectangular sarcophagi there was also introduced in the third century a scheme of design in which two fluted panels separated a central from two lateral figured panels, the central panel sometimes containing in a roundel a portrait bust of the deceased person. Portrait busts of men and women also occasionally appear in this period on panels on the lid.

The subject-matter of the western sarcophagus reliefs falls into two main categories. One category comprises narrative scenes drawn from mythology or from public and private life, such scenes being used as allegories of death, of the after-life, and of the cultural activities, tasks, and ordeals of this world as a preparation for the next. Thus, besides the episodes from legend, the relevance of which in a funerary context is usually obvious, we have Dionysiac revels and processions, sportive Cupids   Plate 57
(souls in paradise), personifications of the Seasons as symbols of the fruitfulness of heaven, marine personages and creatures, allud-ing to the deceased's voyage across the ocean to the Blessed Isles, pastoral scenes (paradise again), a 'mystic' marriage (sometimes with reference to the married pair that occupied the sarco-phagus), battles, hunts, incidents in a public man's career, philosophers teaching their pupils, musicians making music,

scenes of the training of children (sometimes chosen for a child's coffin).

The second main category is that of the garland sarcophagus, on which the front bears two or three swags, while the short sides carry each one swag, of fruit, flowers, and leaves slung from the shoulders of three or four standing figures, which are usually those of Cupids, although Satyrs, Nymphs, and Victories sometimes take the Cupids' place. Each of the semi/circular spaces above the swags is occupied either by a mask or by a miniature figure scene drawn from mythology or religious ritual or, in the third century, by a portrait bust. The swags represent the actual garlands offered to the dead on the day of burial and on anniversaries, besides being symbols of other/worldly fertility, and the figures supporting them are emblems of the after/life. This general scheme of composition remained fairly constant on garland sarcophagi throughout the second and third centuries. But the style of the garlands grew progres/sively flatter and, with the increasing use of the drill, more lace/like; and the Cupids were gradually transformed from chubby babies into heavy boys.

It is the style of the garlands on the examples of this second category that is one of the strongest proofs that the Roman sarcophagus series did not start before the early second century AD. Apart from the quite exceptional Caffarelli piece, none show either the naturalistic manner of the swags on Augustan and Julio/Claudian altars and other monuments or the pictorial, black/and/white effects of Flavian wreaths. The earliest examples that can be approximately dated—one in the Campo Santo at Pisa, which bears the name of Caius Bellicus Tebanianus, probably the man who was consul in AD 87,[31] and one, now in the Lateran Museum, that was found near the Porta Viminalis in Rome in a tomb which had brick/stamps of the years 132 and 134[32]—carry much more stylised swags composed of a stiff, compact, solid mass of large, heavy fruits and conventional flowers, indicating that return to the classical and normal Hellenistic (Pergamon apart: *cf.* p. 87) types of floral ornament which is the hall-mark of early-second-century AD decorative work. And it was in the same Hadrianic tomb that the earliest narrative sarcophagi which can be dated by external evidence came to light, two with mythological reliefs depicting respectively the story of Orestes and the slaughter of the Niobids.[33]

These two mythological Hadrianic pieces illustrate the two main methods of composition employed in the treatment of narrative figure scenes by sarcophagus carvers of the second and third centuries AD. On the piece that presents three successive episodes, each containing a figure of the hero, in the story of Orestes' revenge all the figures are on one level, as seen from the ordinary human viewpoint. Other examples of the same scheme show the myth of Orestes again, of the marriage of Peleus and Thetis, of Bacchus and Ariadne, of the Giganto-machy, of the Rape of the Leucippides, of Medea, of Alcestis, etc.[34] Some pieces with scenes from public life are treated in the same way.[35] On the Lateran Niobid sarcophagus, on the other hand, the front of which gives a higher field, the back-ground figures are raised in vertical perspective above those in the foreground. And raised still higher, on the lid, are small-scale figures of Apollo and Diana shooting at their victims.

This second method of composition represents the same urge to decorate all the available space, leaving no blank areas, and to show the maximum amount of detail that we have already noted on historical reliefs from Trajan's Column onwards. The result is a similar, at times more intensified, tapestry-like effect, particularly on the pieces with battles between Romans and barbarians, which often display a wild, confused mêlée of overlapping figures, writhing this way and that in every possible attitude and climbing, as it were, tier above tier, up the coffin's front.[36] The higher the field, the greater the scope for

Plate 60

designs of this kind, the supreme examples being an exceptionally high late-Antonine sarcophagus, now in the Museo
Nazionale Romano, from the Via Tiburtina[37] and the great
Ludovisi sarcophagus also housed there, on which a portrait of
the emperor Hostilianus (AD 251) has been identified in the
central figure and which may therefore be one of the few
emperors' sarcophagi that have come down to us.[38] Both of
these scenes suggest extremely complicated patterns on woven
textiles rather than carvings in marble. The eye of the spectator,
baffled in any attempt to analyse the whole complexity, fastens
in each case on the central horseman and, in the case of the Via
Tiburtina piece, on the statuesque lateral groups of trophies
and captives, and is content to enjoy the rest simply as ornament. The same tapestry style appears on an early-third-
century sarcophagus in the Vatican Museum showing a
mythological battle between Greeks and Amazons dominated
by the central figures of Achilles and Penthesilea;[39] and the
same extreme use of vertical perspective is found on another
piece with a scene from mythology, the late-Antonine sarcophagus in the Villa Medici with the Judgment of Paris.[40]

Other third-century sarcophagi, often equipped with lids on
which the figures of the dead recline on couches, are carved in
a style that presents the greatest possible contrast to the restless,
intricate, all-over manner just described. These show either
continuous scenes from mythology composed of large-scale,
clear-cut, statuesque, and plastic figures, as on the piece in the
Capitoline Museum with Achilles among the daughters of
Lycomedes,[41] or rows of figures, mostly frontally posed and
even more statuesque, of real or mythological persons, as on the
remarkable fragment from Acilia, near Rome, now in the
Museo Nazionale Romano, with a boy and a group of heavily
bearded men, and the large sarcophagus that may be that of the
emperor Balbinus, still in the Praetextatus Catacomb, where it
came to light.[42] A mixture of the two styles, the statuesque and

Plate 59

the tapestry, is to be found on the early/third/century former
Badminton sarcophagus, where large/scale, static figures of
Bacchus on a panther and the Seasons occupy the foreground,
while the spaces between them and the background are choked
with tiers of tiny subsidiary beings.[43] This revival on western
sarcophagi of a calm, classical, truly sculptural style—a style
which survived into the fourth century on Seasons sarcophagi[44]
—is probably to be explained partly by the influence of the two
main groups of 'Greek' or eastern sarcophagus workshops, the
products of which had, from the middle of the second century,
been arriving in Italy, as well as in southern Gaul, Cyrenaica,
and Syria. To these we must now turn.

Plate 61

The sarcophagi known as Attic originated in Greece proper
and are found in considerable numbers on the Greek mainland
and on some of the islands, the largest concentrations being
those in the museums of Athens and Salonika. A few of these
are garland sarcophagi;[45] some show on their troughs portrait
busts or portrait figures of the dead.[46] But the majority are
mythological, with scenes from legend[47] or with groups of
sportive or revelling Cupids. Of the pieces with Cupids the
Athens Museum has a particularly attractive series.[48] All Attic
sarcophagi are carved on all four sides and many still retain their
lids, which are either gabled or take the form of couches on
which the figures of the dead (sometimes unfinished) are
reclining. Of the Attic pieces found in the west and in east/
Mediterranean lands outside Greece itself, some, it seems, were
prepared in their preliminary stages in Attica and then shipped
abroad, with their reliefs only roughly blocked out, along with
Attic craftsmen who completed their carving at their places of
destination. This would explain why such pieces of western
provenance as the Hippolytus sarcophagi at Trinquetaille near
Arles and at Agrigento are fully worked only on the front, since
there they were to be placed against walls, instead of being, as in
Greece, free/standing.[49] Other Attic sarcophagi of non/Greek

provenance would have been the products of local workshops staffed partly by immigrant Attic sculptors and partly by their local pupils and imitators.[50]

The second main group of 'Greek' sarcophagi are those that were produced in the ateliers of Asia Minor, again both for home and for foreign markets. Although frequently found in the west, their Asiatic and eastern origin is attested by the large number of examples unearthed on Anatolian sites and by their being carved on all four sides.[51] The fact that those discovered in Italy are generally fully worked on the back and sides, as well as on the front, suggests either that the method of production of the pieces designed for foreign clients was somewhat different from that of their Attic counterparts or that most of the Asiatic craftsmen who completed them in the west refused to leave more than half of their handiwork unfinished. The lids, when preserved, generally represent funerary couches, on which the effigies of the departed are shown as either lying flat upon their backs or reclining with their heads and shoulders erect. The trough of the coffin is an elaborate architectural structure representing the tomb itself. On the great majority of pieces both the long and the short sides are carved with a series of *aediculae* with rounded or gabled tops supported on pairs of colonnettes; the door of the tomb is sometimes rendered on one of the short sides. The treatment of the details of the column-capitals and arches is two-dimensional and colouristic. But in each niche and often in each of the spaces between the niches stands or sits a statuesque, classical figure worked in very high relief and depicting either the deceased or members of his or her family or deities and mythological personages appropriate to an other-worldly context. Poets and Apollo and the Muses, emblems either of immortality won through cultural pursuits or of celestial wisdom and harmony, not infrequently appear. Among the most notable examples found in Asia Minor are the sarcophagus from Sardis of Claudia Antonia Sabina, dated by the hair-style of her effigy to *c.* AD 200,[52] and the Selefkeh and Sidamara pieces, both in the Istanbul Museum.[53] The Selefkeh sarcophagus has on one of its short sides, that from Sidamara on one of its short sides and on its back, no architectural features, but an undivided hunting scene with well-spaced-out figures, and there are a few pieces on which all four sides bear continuous, likewise uncrowded pictures, with pilasters only at the corners.[54] Of the architectural, columned type a considerable series is now to be seen in the public and private collections of Rome; and although the find-spots of some of these are unrecorded, all are likely to have come from the cemeteries of the capital. With the Roman clients of the Asiatic workshops Apollo and the Muses and the Labours of Hercules seem to have been favourite subjects.[55] Of the other imports into Italy the most imposing is the great sarcophagus found near Melfi and now in the Palazzo Pubblico of the town.[56] The hair-style of the woman lying on her back on the lid dates this piece to *c.* 170. Local Roman imitations of the Asiatic imports are exemplified by a piece with a tomb door at the centre of its front, now in the Palazzo Riccardi in Florence, a perhaps Hadrianic piece from Velletri with a gabled lid and two zones of figure scenes, and a second-century piece from a site on the Via Cassia, about eight miles north of Rome, with the Labours of Hercules.[57]

Plate 62

A third and less important group of 'Greek' sarcophagi, again originating in Asia Minor, comprises those carved in marble from the quarries of Proconnesus near the southern entrance to the sea of Marmara and chiefly manufactured for markets in Asia Minor, Syria, and Egypt. These are generally decorated on all four sides with floral swags, from each of which a bunch of grapes often dangles.[58]

Christian sarcophagi of the third, fourth, and fifth centuries have already had a place in another volume in this series.[59] But since they form an integral part of late-antique Roman sculpture, they cannot be omitted here.[60] The style of the third-century Christian pieces is, in general, the same as that of their simpler pagan contemporaries.[61] Biblical subjects, such as the story of Jonah, sometimes appear. Other sarcophagi show pastoral scenes or teachers instructing pupils; and these can only be distinguished from pagan pastoral and 'philosopher' sarcophagi by the presence of those 'Orans' and 'Good Shepherd' figures which are generally, but not universally, recognised as being at this period specifically Christian motifs (*cf.* p. 47). With the advent of the Christian Empire under Constantine biblical scenes and other groups and figures of a definitely Christian character are universal. In one main series, that of the so-called frieze sarcophagi, the Christian counter-parts of the earlier pagan narrative sarcophagi, the aim of the carvers seems to have been to get in as much as they possibly could. The front of the trough is crammed with as many episodes from the Old and New Testaments as it can hold. The figures are small and often ungainly and squat; and all aesthetic principles in composition have been sacrificed to wealth of content. But a fresh and lively spirit animates the scenes. Pieces with a very high trough are made to carry two superimposed friezes of this kind, often interrupted at the centre by a roundel containing a bust, or a pair of busts, of the departed. The second main fourth-century class, that of the so-called column sarcophagi, was clearly influenced by the pagan Asiatic pieces. Here between each pair of colonnettes is a single figure or a group of figures or a scene worked in higher relief and much more statuesque in treatment than are the figures on the frieze sarcophagi. Very rarely do column sarcophagi show two superimposed tiers.

Christian sarcophagi of the fifth century are well represented at Ravenna;[62] and these display a real revival of classical tradition in their clear-cut, naturalistic, and plastically carved figures, widely spaced along the trough, and in their symmetrical or at any rate carefully balanced schemes of composition, whether they display continuous scenes or single figures and groups flanked by colonnettes or purely symbolic designs. 'Greek' influence is also evident in their emphatically architectural structure, with rich classical mouldings and heavy, roof-like gabled or vaulted lids. These last examples of Roman monu-mental relief work, the last within the time-limits that we have assigned to the term Roman, do indeed bear striking testimony to the strength and persistence, right to the very end, of the principles of Hellenistic art.

CHAPTER VII

Wall and Ceiling Painting   ·

THE HISTORY OF ROMAN MURAL PAINTING in its late-republican and early-imperial phases is known to us chiefly from the ruins of the Campanian cities destroyed by the eruption of Vesuvius in AD 79—Pompeii, Herculaneum, and Stabiae—and from discoveries made in Rome from Renaissance to modern times. The bulk of these finds come from private houses, some from public buildings, including the palaces of emperors, some from tombs. In every instance there are two main aspects to be studied: the general decorative scheme of composition with which a wall was covered and the panel pictures or friezes of pictures, which, although in a sense self-contained units or groups, are essentially part of the whole ornamental design in which they were included. The bad, old practice of gouging out these pictures from their walls and displaying them in a museum gallery has now been almost entirely abandoned. It is often in the combination and order of the pictures as we see them round the walls of a room that is found the key to the ideas which determined their selection.

The four main schemes of wall designs running from the second century BC to the last quarter of the first century AD are known conventionally as the 'Four Pompeian Styles'. Of these the First Style is undoubtedly the earliest. But the Second, Third, and Fouth Styles are not strictly successive in time. The later phases of the Second Style overlap with the Third; and a number of Third and Fourth Style painted walls can be shown to be contemporaneous. We have also to reckon with deliberate harkings back to Second Style models by painters who belonged to Third and Fourth Style *milieux*.

Of these Four Styles the only one for which definite fore-runners in the Hellenistic world survive is the First. It is known as the 'Incrustation' or, more properly, the 'Masonry' Style, since its earliest examples, in private houses of the late-third and early-second centuries on the island of Delos consist of imita- tions in stucco of white marble masonry blocks with bevelled edges.[1] Some Delian walls counterfeit in paint veneers of coloured marbles; and it was these polychrome effects that were taken over by the wall decorators who worked at Pompeii from the second half of the second century to *c.* 80 BC. The scheme of design, well illustrated in the 'House of Sallust' and the 'House of the Faun',[2] shows a threefold horizontal division of the wall—a dado below, then the main central area with the 'incrustations', and a space above the cornice on top; and generally also a vertical division of the wall by means of pilasters cutting across the horizontal divisions, which seems to have been an Italian refinement. In the 'House of the Griffins' on the Palatine in Rome the central zones on the walls of its barrel- vaulted chambers consist of a series of flat, vertical panels of painted imitation marble, veined and mottled, separated from one another by narrow flat pilasters or rounded columns, also painted.[3]

No wall paintings of the First Style in Italy include figure scenes or other representational motifs; and the general effect is that of rooms confined by solid walls. But the rounded columns of one of the rooms in the 'House of the Griffins' stand on *podia* and are so painted as to seem to project in front of the lower dado; and their realistically rendered, three-dimensional shafts and capitals already belong to what is one favourite feature of the Second Style in most of its complex manifestations, namely a light, but logical, screen or grille standing out in the front plane against a background in the second plane. Some- times that background is still a solid wall of painted panels, but now enlivened with decorative figures, small pictures, and other representational subjects. One room in the House of Augustus (often called the House of Livia) on the Palatine shows swags of fruit and flowers, as naturalistic as those on the precinct walls of the Ara Pacis Augustae (*cf.* p. 53), slung on the lower portion of the background wall behind the projecting columns; a narrow frieze of landscape scenes topping the main vertical panels of the background; and above that another series of panels, each of which is filled with a group of the fantastic little human and animal figures—poised on, or bursting from the hearts of, flowers or composed from the waist downwards of slender leaves and tendrils—which characterise both the later phases of the Second Style and the Third, or Ornamental, Style.[4]

Meanwhile, the earlier stages of the Second Style had intro-duced a novel element, of which in the Hellenistic Masonry Style there are only small and scanty adumbrations, namely the opening-up of the background wall behind the architectural screen by means of elaborate figure and landscape pictures. One of the most remarkable instances of this is the famous frieze in what is usually described as the *triclinium* of the 'Villa of the Mysteries', which stands a short way outside the Herculaneum gate of Pompeii.[5] The frieze formed part of the redecoration, perhaps about the middle of the first century BC, of a house originally built and then enlarged at earlier periods, and it consists of a series of scenes with almost life-size figures taking part in a ritual over which Dionysus presides. The ritual is, in my opinion, best interpreted as successive episodes in the mystic pre-nuptial initiation and ordeal of a bride; it includes a lekanomancy (divination by reflection in wine), the mystic marriage of Dionysus and Ariadne, the covering up, after an unveiling, of a phallus, and the flagellation of the bride-to-be to induce fertility. Here the screen or colonnade in the fore-ground has actually been dispensed with and the action is carried out on a low, narrow stage which has the effect of pushing back the walls of the room and thus enlarging it. In this instance the walls consist of a series of flat scarlet panels divided from one another by mainly purple vertical strips. The

Plate 63

figures cut across these strips and thus the scenes run on continuously, except where the corners of the room and its doors
and windows intervene.

The masterly drawing and modelling of these statuesque
figures of human, divine, and mythological personages in the
'Villa of the Mysteries' frieze reveal the hand of a highly
skilled, probably Greek, painter; and we ask ourselves, If his
subject-matter was dictated by some piece of pre-nuptial ritual
in part, at least, actually performed, were his painted figures and
groups and his organisation of the sequence of events into an
artistic composition his own creations? This question brings
us up against the whole vexed problem that concerns all the
pictures, whether religious, mythological, historical, or landscape, which appear on walls of the Second, Third, and Fourth
Styles on Italian sites, pictures that can sometimes reveal a
power in the handling of human forms and a range of emotions
in the presentation of human faces that few works of ancient art
in other media can surpass—namely, To what extent were they
original and to what extent derived from classical Greek and
Hellenistic models and prototypes? According to a view still
prevalent these pictures, the great mass of which are certainly
Greek in content and whose inscriptions, where these are
provided, are normally in Greek, were copies or adaptations of
lost Greek masterpieces produced in Greece proper, Asia
Minor, or Hellenised Syria and Egypt. If so, we must enquire,
How would these mural decorators in Italy have known those
masterpieces? Wall painters working in Rome could have seen
and studied such easel pictures as had been looted from the
east in late-republican times and placed in public buildings.
But extant wall paintings in Rome cannot easily be linked with
pictures known to have reached the capital in this way; and the
Campanian artists could only have worked from copy-books
based on Greek originals. That copy-books were in circulation
among the Pompeian and other wall decorators would seem to

be proved by the fact that in Campanian pictures in general and in the 'Villa of the Mysteries' frieze in particular there are a number of figures and groups which have their counterparts in works of art earlier in date and in other media. But this need not imply that the pictures as a whole, in their conception and in their composition, were taken straight from copy-books and were not original. We have a few literary descriptions of pictures by famous classical Greek and Hellenistic painters, but with such descriptions the Campanian pictures that represent the same subjects seldom, if ever, tally closely enough to demon- strate that they were copies of those masterpieces. Apart from a few painted tombs and *stelae* no monumental paintings of pre- imperial times have survived in lands east of Italy; and although some Campanian pictures may, like such Roman-age reliefs as those on the Monument of the Julii in Provence (*cf.* p. 91), have been indirectly based on lost Greek paintings, it is surely unwise to quote and reproduce (as has often been done) the works of Pompeian and other artists in Italy as examples of fourth-century and Hellenistic Greek painting. The hypo- thetical model of the 'Villa of the Mysteries' frieze has, for instance, been assigned to Pergamon and variously dated to the fourth and second centuries BC. But such attributions are guess- work; and this frieze and all Roman and Italian paintings of the late-republican and early-imperial periods, even if they could be copies, are best studied on their own intrinsic merits, as reflections of the taste and standards of their age.

In the frieze of the 'Villa of the Mysteries' the background wall is, as we have seen, pushed slightly back and enlivened with a vivid action that almost obscures its solidity. In other paintings of the Second Style that solidity is completely denied by substituting for a panelled or marbled background vast windows, as it were, thrown open on to the world outside. In one most striking instance, that of the barrel-vaulted room with landscape paintings, now reconstructed in the Museo

Nazionale Romano, from the empress Livia's villa at Prima Porta, north of Rome, the architectural screen in the foreground is again dispensed with.[6] As we stand in this room, which is, indeed, all 'windows', we seem to be looking in all four directions from an open terrace on to a great park or garden, only separated from us by a pair of low fences between which runs a grassy path. The uninterrupted prospect is one of thickly planted trees of all descriptions—firs, pines, palms, cypresses, and heavily laden fruit trees, swaying in the breeze: beneath is a rich undergrowth of flowering plants and shrubs; and above are the fowls of the air, fluttering hither and thither and perching on the branches. This lovely world recedes as far as the eye can see; and it is a world of fantasy, for although the actual details are highly realistic and naturalistic, the whole is a paradise of the imagination in which the flowers and fruits of all the seasons bloom and ripen at one and the same time.

Plate 64

In some Second Style paintings that deny the solid wall surfaces no less effectively the characteristic architectural screen of uprights and horizontal architrave is present, but is so arranged that the columns or pilasters resting on their dadoes merely serve as unobtrusive lines of demarcation between the window vistas. In the so-called *cubiculum* of the Villa of Fannius Sinistor (sometimes known as the Villa of Lucius Herennius Florus) at Boscoreale near Pompeii was a series of self-contained pictures (now in the Metropolitan Museum of Art, New York)[7] divided off from one another by slender columns and showing vistas of columned halls, streets and houses, and rural landscapes, which seem to have been influenced, to some extent at any rate, by painted stage scenery, since they very closely correspond respectively with the tragic, comic, and satyric 'sets' described by the Augustan architect Vitruvius.[8] But by far the most remarkable example of this opening-up of the solid walls in Second Style painting and, indeed, of landscape painting in the whole of extant ancient art are the famous pictures in the

Plate 66

Vatican with scenes from the Odyssey found on the upper part, it seems, of the wall of a long room in a house, dating from about the middle of the first century BC, on the Esquiline in Rome.[9] Behind a double colonnade of scarlet pilasters in the immediate foreground is unrolled as in a film a continuous series of episodes from Odysseus' adventures seen by the spectator standing in the room as from an open verandah. The pilasters are, in fact, so placed as to come between, not cut across, the various scenes. But we are meant to think of the landscape as passing behind the pilasters; and when some of the pictures were recently cleaned and the modern over-painting that masked their true colours was removed, it became clear that the scenes had first been painted continuously and that the pilasters, through which landscape features sometimes show, had, if planned from the first, been added at a later stage. The natural features—mountains, rocks, trees, and sea—are im-pressionistically executed, with the human figures wholly sub-ordinated to them; and we have the full effect of a panoramic landscape setting which contains the figures and is seen from a distance in bird's-eye view. The inscriptions that identify the figures are in Greek. Does this mean that the painter was Greek-speaking and working for a cultured Roman patron acquainted with Greek? Were these figures taken, complete with their names, from some Hellenistic copy-book? If the wall-painter's figures were borrowed, could the composition and the landscapes as a whole have been his own original idea? Certain inconsistencies in the scenic continuity and in the use of perspec-tive, and the fact that the inscriptions would have been illegible and certain significant details of the scenes invisible to the eyes of the spectator standing at ground-level, have been held to imply that this Roman frieze was a copy or adaptation of some famous Hellenistic Odyssey landscape frieze intended for the central, not for the upper, section of a wall. On the other hand, it is obvious that larger inscriptions would anyhow have spoilt the general effect, which was doubtless regarded as of more importance than the visibility of details; and the errors in composition could have been due to this being perhaps the painter's first experiment in landscape work of this kind. There is no inherent reason why such landscapes should not have been invented by Hellenistic artists; yet in no extant earlier works of art in east-Mediterranean lands, whether in relief or in painting, do we find outdoor atmosphere, distance, space, and light rendered anything like as convincingly as here. Mythological panel pictures of the Third Style show landscapes with the same high viewpoint, similar effects of perspective, depth, and light, the same impressionistic treatment of rocks and vegetation, and much the same subordination of the human and animal forms to their setting (cf. p. 118). There are, more-over, some small, narrow friezes with continuous landscape scenes and tiny figures, as in the room already mentioned in the House of Augustus on the Palatine (cf. pp. 109–10).[10] But in their aspect as a monumental frieze of uninterrupted landscape through which the viewer travels as he moves from scene to scene the Vatican Odyssey pictures have as yet no surviving counterparts in the whole history of ancient painting.

Friezes of continuous figure scenes with landscape and architectural features strictly secondary to the figures, illustrating myth or legendary history, are not uncommon in painting of this time in both domestic and funerary buildings. Good examples are the frieze depicting the origins of Rome, now in the Museo Nazionale Romano, found in the tomb of the Statilii on the Esquiline[11] and the frieze in the same collection, with figures shown against a black background and illustrating an Egyptian legend, found in the Villa Farnesina Roman house on the right bank of the Tiber.[12]

The more usual form of Second Style mural decoration is that in which the wall as a solid surface is partially denied by piercing through it large 'french windows' that admit a vision of an imagined world outside the house. Here the architectural screen in the foreground is much more elaborate than in the Odyssey paintings and in the *cubiculum* of the Villa of Fannius Sinistor; and both the 'windows' and the flat tracts of back, ground between them are adorned with imitation pediments, architraves, friezes, columns, and other architectural details. The scheme of the design is generally tripartite, both horizon, tally, with a dado, a main architectural area, and a space above the pediments, etc., and vertically, with a large central 'window' forming a species of *aedicula* and smaller lateral ones, one on either side of it. The views seen through these 'windows' on a single wall are not necessarily all linked in content. For example, in the House of Augustus on the Palatine one wall carries in the centre a scene from mythology, Io watched by Argus and Hermes, the latter's name being inscribed beside him in Greek; while one of the lateral scenes (the other has been destroyed) shows a realistic view of a street of houses several storeys high.[13] A painting, now in the Museo Nazionale Romano, from the Villa Farnesina Roman house has only one, central 'window', through which we see a Nymph suckling the infant Dionysus against a background of buildings, trees, and other human figures. The two lateral panels do not seem to be views pierced through the wall, but framed pictures, in each case of women making music, upheld against its solid surface on the raised hands of creatures that are partly human, partly bird— probably Sirens.[14] The mainly mythological 'window' pictures in this type of Second Style painting can, to some extent, be studied as independent units, although if they are divorced from their setting their function as vistas is obviously lost.

The Third Style represents a complete reversal of the three, dimensional effects and opening, up process which are the hall, mark of the Second Style. The walls regain their confining solidity, an almost wholly two, dimensional flatness prevails, and the columns, architraves, and other architectural elements

Plate 65

are reduced to functionless, unsubstantial ornaments. A fore-taste of this is, indeed, to be found in the black-ground paintings of a later phase of the Second Style in the Villa Farnesina house. There the dado no longer projects, the columns, between which hang swags of foliage, have dwindled into reeds plastered against the surface of the wall, and the light-coloured landscape scenes between these reeds, although drawn naturalis-tically in vertical perspective and peopled with tiny figures, as in the Odyssey pictures, are lacking in light and atmosphere.[15] In the Third Style scheme, well exemplified in the House of Marcus Lucretius Fronto at Pompeii,[16] the tripartite horizontal and vertical divisions of the wall remain and the central vertical compartment is still in the form of an *aedicula*. But the excessively thin uprights which flank the *aedicula* and the meaningless horizontal slab that tops it serve merely as a frame for the central screen or curtain, on which is displayed a relatively small mythological panel picture obviously not thought of as a 'window' opening on to the world outside. In the paintings of this particular house the two small colonnades rendered in perspective one on either side of the so-called *aedicula* do not persuade us that the screen or curtain with its inserted picture really masks part of a semicircular *exedra* extending behind it; and the fantastic, airy-fairy structures, also drawn in perspective, which occupy the topmost horizontal section of the wall are no less unconvincing, particularly when a small aquarium is oddly intruded among them. In Fronto's house, again, the two lateral panels in the main central horizon-tal zone carry each a candelabrum, shown against a dark background, to the stem of which is affixed a small panel picture of a waterside or country mansion. The lower portion of the dado is painted charmingly, if somewhat illogically, with a prim, fenced flower-garden. Both in their treatment and in their content the Third Style walls lack all organic coherence. Their attraction lies in their gay display of clear, bright, empty tracts

Plate 67

of contrasting colours, in the dainty drawing of the decorative details, and in the beauty of their mythological panel pictures, particularly those in which mythology and landscape are combined. That the later phases of the Second Style and the Third Style paintings overlapped in time seems to be clear from the fact that Vitruvius included both the fanciful figures mainly of the former and the unreal architecture mainly of the latter in one and the same sweeping condemnation.[17]

The mythological landscape paintings of Third Style walls have formed the subject of a special study.[18] In these, as has already been said (*cf.* p. 115), the treatment of the natural features and the subordination to those features of the human and animal figures, found in the Vatican Odyssey frieze, are transferred to self-contained, isolated panel pictures. One such picture, indeed, presents the episode of Odysseus and the Sirens, with Odysseus' ship in the foreground, the Sirens in the middle distance perched on rocks, and the sea stretching away in vertical perspective to the top of the picture.[19] A painting of Paris on Mount Ida shows the sketchy trees and impressionistic rocks, and the luminous effect of atmosphere that we noted on the great Second Style frieze.[20] Similar characteristics mark a scene of rustic sacrifice in a mountainous setting.[21] A favourite subject is the story of Daedalus and Icarus. One rendering of this episode offers a good example of continuous or simultaneous representation within a single framework.[22] Above we see the chariot of the Sun and Icarus hurtling from the sky as the wax with which his wings were attached melts in the heat. Below them Daedalus, who has been more cautious, flies along unaware of the disaster (only the tip of one of his wings is now preserved); and in the foreground Icarus appears again, drowned in the sea into which he has fallen headlong. In the middle distance is the bird's-eye view of a seaside town and ships on the water; while in the foreground on the left are two girls witnessing the tragedy. Perspectival diminution is here most successfully

Plate 69

achieved. But if this could be managed by painters of the late Republic and early Empire (working in the Second, Third, and Fourth Styles), they did not, with a very few exceptions, master the principles of a single vanishing-point, to which all receding lines converge, and of the illumination of a picture by light from a single quarter. They did, in fact, use several vanishing-points[23] and light generally falls on their pictures from more than one direction.

Of all the styles of mural painting the one most frequently found at Pompeii is the Fourth Style, since it was in this that were redecorated the many houses damaged by the earthquake of AD 63. This style has many variations, but one of its outstanding characteristics is the denial once again of the wall's solidity. In the House of the Vettii the general scheme is much the same as that which we associate with the Third Style. In the main horizontal zone of decoration the centre of the wall is occupied by a species of *aedicula* flanked by reed-like posts and framing a mythological panel picture; and architectural features fill the space above. But, while on the walls of some Fourth Style houses the central pictures are relatively small and still resemble panels attached to screens or woven on tapestries, here these pictures tend to be larger than those of the Third Style and could, indeed, be imagined as views seen through windows, particularly as the lateral panels on either side are opened-up by receding architectural vistas.[24] Furthermore, the structures depicted in the upper zones on the House of the Vettii walls are, for the most part, much more convincing than their Third Style counterparts and give a realistic effect of depth, since the colours are, in some cases, skilfully graded from the dark seated or standing figures in the immediate foreground to the pale tints of the most distant architectural elements. Similar figures backed by receding structures are found on the upper parts of some walls in Nero's Golden House in Rome. The House of the Vettii painters also revived the Second Style use

Plate 68

of a black background for small polychrome figured friezes, as in the well-known scenes of Cupids vintaging and plying trades and industries.[25]

In other Fourth Style paintings, such as those in a room in the House of Pinarius Cerialis at Pompeii, the whole wall has virtually vanished and its place is taken by a *scaenae frons* or stage-building of a Roman theatre, with solider and more functional, if still fanciful, columns and architraves, against which a play is acted, here Euripides' *Iphigenia in Tauris*.[26]

Another type of mural painting of the second half of the first century AD is exemplified in Rome, namely that in which the predominant feature is a flat, white background. Small figure scenes in white-ground panels framed by dainty arabesques are found in Nero's Domus Transitoria on the Palatine[27] and in the Golden House, alongside of other panels showing light-coloured figures on a dark ground.[28] In the Golden House there are also larger expanses of white-ground walls and vaults covered with a light and widely spaced-out network of painted panels framed either by thin, plain lines or by orna- mental borders, the centres of these panels being occupied sometimes by small square or rectangular pictures, sometimes by tiny free-standing figures or groups of birds, animals, grotesques, etc.[29] The emergence under Nero of this white- ground network scheme of painting is of no small importance, inasmuch as it became from then onwards, down to the late fourth century, the prevailing style in the west of decoration for the walls and vaulted ceilings of sepulchral chambers of all kinds, examples of which may be found in some of the second- century mausolea under St Peter's in Rome,[30] in the third- century hypogeum of the Aurelii in Rome, and among the Christian Roman catacombs.[31] The panels in these networks are squares, rectangles, circles, half-circles, or other shapes.

The walls and ceilings of other tombs, for instance of some of the second- and third-century mausolea at Isola Sacra north of

Ostia, show larger and more substantially framed panels, which contain boldly painted, statuesque figures on a brightly coloured ground.[32] Other funerary places display on their walls or in lunettes at the ends of vaulted chambers large and complicated scenes, sometimes involving several or many figures and even architectural and landscape features. Examples are the row of the Apostles, the 'Sermon on the Mount', the Ithaca and Paradise scenes in the hypogeum of the Aurelii,[33] and some of the biblical scenes in the new catacomb on the Via Latina[34]— to quote a few from among the many pictures of this kind to be found both in pagan tombs and in the Christian catacombs. Of tomb paintings from the Roman world outside Italy the most interesting are those from the south-eastern provinces and from the Empire's eastern outskirts. A mid-third-century vaulted hypogeum at Palmyra has in one of its lunettes the scene of Achilles among the daughters of Lycomedes and on its walls repetitive motifs consisting of Victories holding up medallion portraits of the dead—all shown in the strict frontality that marks the art of this 'Parthian' orbit;[35] as it does also the scene of a funerary banquet in a tomb at El Abian in Cyrenaica.[36] A very elaborately painted fourth-century tomb at Ghirgaresh (Gargàresc) in Tripolitania has at the back of its principal burial niche a medallion portrait of the deceased upheld by two girls, while on the wall surrounding the niche are, above, two Victories supporting an inscription in a wreath, below, a circus race of four-horse chariots, and on either side, a richly robed man grasping a lighted candle.[37] Wholly different in their naturalistic treatment are the complex paintings of mid-second-century date found in temple-tombs at Hermoupolis in Egypt and depicting episodes from Hellenic legend—the Trojan Horse, the history of Oedipus, the story of Agamemnon.[38] Further north and west, in what is now Bulgaria, we have at Silistra, the ancient Durostorum, a late painted chamber tomb, on the walls of which the occupants, a married pair,

Plate 70

and a series of attendants are portrayed in simply framed panels, above which project counterfeited beam-ends; pairs of con-fronted peacocks fill the two lunettes, and the barrel-vaulted ceiling is covered with an 'all-over' pattern of octagons and roundels.[39] The tomb paintings of the Roman Empire were, indeed, extremely varied; and although a few general principles of design can be detected in them, they do not lend themselves, as do the house paintings of the first centuries BC and AD, to definite classification.

Two paintings of the first half of the second century AD, one an idyllic seaside or lakeside landscape from the Hadrianic Villa of the Quintilii south of Rome, the other a harbour scene in what may have been a funerary guild room under the church of San Sebastiano on the Via Appia, carry on the landscape tradition of the Second Style, with its feeling for space, atmosphere, light, and receding distance.[40]

Middle-class domestic wall decoration of the second and early third centuries AD is best represented at Ostia, a site which, like the overwhelmed Campanian cities, has remained unoccupied since the Roman period.[41] Most of the surviving paintings are in the large, several-storeyed apartment blocks that were going up at Ostia from the reign of Hadrian onwards; and, as with the tombs of the Roman world, so here there is a far less clearly marked differentiation of styles than at Pompeii and Hercula-neum. There is also much less elaboration of ornamental detail. The dominant feature of the horizontal zones into which the wall spaces are divided is the colouring of bright, mainly red and yellow panels—a feature tending to distract the eye from the relatively small single figures or small groups of figures, mostly mythological in character, that are painted in white, green, violet, etc. in the panels of the central zones.[42] More conspicuous are the small framed pictures, occasionally flanked by receding architectural vistas that recall the Third Pompeian Style, which sometimes appear in the panels at the middle of

the walls.[43] Among the most attractive of the small non-
mythological figure scenes are the racing chariots, the panther,
and the horseman-and-stag group in the 'Insula of the
Charioteers'[44] and the seated figures of the Seven Sages, each
with his name written in Greek beside him, in a wine-shop that
later formed part of a set of baths near the insula just cited.[45]
Somewhat reminiscent of the Golden House white-ground
style are the paintings on the walls of the House of Lucretius
Menander, into which a Mithraeum was afterwards inserted.
These show a row of large, square panels framed by coloured
bands and each containing a tiny scene in the centre of a flat
white field.[46]

Two Ostian wall paintings of the Severan period, one of
Venus at her bath ('Baths of the Seven Sages'), the other of
Europa on the bull ('Pharos Baths'), are large, spreading, un-
framed pictures, both of them more successful in their colouring than in their draftsmanship.[47] A contemporary painting in
Rome of similar type is the great mythological scene of uncertain significance (possibly representing Peleus and Thetis)
on a wall in the Roman house below the church of SS. John
and Paul on the Caelian. On a flat rock surrounded by water,
on which Cupids are boating, are two reclining women, one
half-draped and throwing back her veil, and a standing male
figure who greets them.[48] Assigned to the same Severan date
are the paintings in another room of this house, the so-called
'Aula degli Efebi', where along the upper portion of the walls
is a row of standing youths, naked save for cloaks hanging
down behind them, linked at shoulder-height with one another
by swags of fruit and flowers, and with a large and a small bird
between each pair of them. Over the barrel-vaulted ceiling are
spreading vine scrolls amid which small naked Genii are
vintaging, while birds feast on the grapes or perch among the
tendrils.[49] Roughly contemporary again, but very different in
character, is another row of figures, this time from the 'House of

the Palace Heralds' in the Via dei Cerchi at the foot of the Palatine. Here men wearing white tunics with purple stripes are seen against an elaborate architectural background.[50]

Of non-domestic secular painting of the middle Empire remarkable examples are the sea or river scenes strewn with boats and fishes of all descriptions that cover the walls and barrel-vaulted ceilings of two chambers with brick-stamps of the year 123, which came to light at Pietra Papa (Porto Fluviale di S. Paolo) just south of the Roma Trastevere railway station.[51] Of secular painting of the later Empire, domestic and non-domestic, only a few specimens can be quoted here. The two great friezes with hunting scenes that run along the tops of the north and south walls of the *frigidarium* of the 'Hunting Baths' at Lepcis Magna in Tripolitania are difficult to date, since the building itself could have been erected at any time between the early third century and the first half of the fourth century and the style of the paintings offers no sure chronological criteria.[52] Of the scene on the north side, a lion hunt, only scanty traces remain. But the pendant picture on the south wall, a leopard hunt, is almost completely preserved and presents ten hunters engaging six leopards, the names of some of the men and beasts being inscribed beside them. The whole scene throbs with life and movement and the leopards' skins, skilfully shaded and showing orange, brown, mauve, and grey spots on a buff ground, are realistically rendered, as are also the beasts' varying expressions of rage, determination, or pain. The background has no landscape or architectural features, but a deep cream-to-sandy wash represents the arena in which the episode is taking place and throws the figures into strong relief. This is a fine example of the standard to which provincial painters were sometimes able to attain. Certainly late (fourth-century) in style is another Tripolitanian painting, a panel picture from a private house at Sabratha, of which the subject is Ariadne found by Dionysus.[53] The flat

Plate 71

corporeal forms, the large eyes, the stylised tree, and the striped decoration on Ariadne's couch all smack of the late antique age. The same is true of the two dimensional bodies, enlarged eyes, and illogically frontal postures of Perseus and Andromeda in a painting from a house on the slope of the Capitol in Rome.[54]

Plate 72

Among painted places of worship in Rome, other than those specifically designed for the burial and cult of the pagan dead, is the hypogeum on the Via Livenza on the north east side of the city. Its most important element is a wall with a central niche, flanked on one side by a picture of Diana hunting, on the other of a Nymph accompanied by a hound. In front of the niche is a basin of water. On another wall is a painted scene of Cupids boating, swimming, and fishing below a fragmentary mosaic of Moses striking the rock and bringing forth living water. Yet despite this biblical scene and the discovery in the building of two brick stamps with the Chi Rho monogram, the hypogeum would appear to have been the site, not of a Christian baptistery, but of some pagan water cult, for which a borrowing was made from Christian iconography. The date of the building must, in view of these features, be not earlier than the fourth century, for which time the drawing and model ling of the painted figures is extremely free and naturalistic.[55]

The siege and capture by the Sassanian Persians in *c.* AD 257 of the Romano Parthian city of Dura Europos on the Euphrates, and the steps taken on that occasion by the citizens to strengthen their defences, have incidentally resulted in the preservation of a most important series of religious mural paintings—pagan, Jewish, and Christian. From the temple of the Palmyrene gods are two scenes, two dimensionally rendered, of sacrifice at a tripod. The sacrificants are, in the one case, the priest Konon and two fellow priests, all of whom are rigidly frontal and wear white coats of local cut and special white caps, in the other case, two private persons, who stand in the same frontal poses but wear tunics and cloaks of Roman type.[56] In the first half of the third century there was added to this temple a picture in which the Roman tribune Julius Terentius, accompanied by a priest, a standard-bearer, and a mass of soldiers, sacrifices to the three Palmyrene gods, shown as present, while the Tychai (personifications) of Palmyra and Dura are seated in the foreground.[57] Here again all the figures are two-dimensional and strictly frontal. In the cella of another temple, that of Zeus Theos, the god himself is represented in colossal proportions, wholly full-face, with a nimbus, wearing local military dress, and standing beside his chariot, while two Victories hold wreaths above his head. On the side walls are rows of priests and worshippers, also rigidly frontal and arranged in three superimposed tiers.[58] These paintings are typical examples of the 'Parthian' style.

The walls of a Christian baptistery that was installed in a small Duran house, when it was converted during the first half of the third century from a domestic residence into a house-church, are painted with naïve, but vivid, scriptural scenes which illustrate the theme of the neophyte's spiritual rebirth and resurrection—the Good Shepherd, Adam and Eve, two miracles of Christ, the Holy Women at the Sepulchre, David and Goliath, the Samaritan woman at the well.[59] But by far the most impressive of all the Duran religious paintings are those, dating from the first half of the third century, in the house-synagogue, the walls of which were completely covered, virtually from floor to ceiling, with three tiers of closely juxta-posed, rectangular panel pictures of varying widths illustrating portions of the Old Testament. All the pictures are extremely detailed and elaborate and are carried out in brilliant poly-chrome.[60] The question of the prototypes (if any) of these scenes is a burning one. The miniatures of hypothetical illus-trated bibles, produced by Hellenised Jews of the Diaspora in such Hellenistic centres as Antioch on the Orontes and

Alexandria, have been suggested as the models. But while it is true that the pictures show a number of elements derived from Graeco-Roman sources, their painters must have been, to some extent at least, independent of such influences, since the un-compromisingly illogical frontality of the figures and the Parthian dress and coiffure that many of them affect are local Mesopotamian, completely non-Hellenistic, features. The ar-tists of the synagogue could have worked directly from the sacred texts as selected by their patrons; and copy-books, rather than costly manuscripts, most probably supplied them with the details that are based on Greek and Roman motifs.

Dura-Europos also possessed a Mithraeum, the decoration of which was partly in relief work, and partly painted.[61] Sur-rounding the main bull-slaying slab (*cf.* p. 84) in the niche at the end of the temple are small painted panels each with an episode from Mithras' saga, while on either jamb of the niche a Mithraic sage is depicted. On each of the side walls adjacent to the niche is a scene of Mithras as a mounted hunter, accom-panied by a friendly snake and aiming with his bow at a group of wild beasts which flee before him. Four Mithraea with painted Mithraic subjects have been found in Italy—in the gardens of the Palazzo Barberini in Rome,[62] at Santa Maria di Capua Vetera near Naples,[63] at Marino in the Alban Hills,[64] and under the church of Santa Prisca on the Aventine in Rome.[65] The first three all have painted versions of the bull-slaying episode with subsidiary scenes or figures surrounding it. The Capua Mithraeum has in addition scenes of Mithraic ritual on the side benches in its 'nave'. The Santa Prisca Mithraeum has no painted bull-slaying, but carries on its side walls processional scenes and scenes of ritual banquets ex-cellently painted in the style of the early third century. These three brilliantly coloured bull-slaying pictures give us some idea of what the corresponding reliefs must have looked like when they still retained their paint.

Plate 73

Some barrel-vaulted ceilings with paintings have been already mentioned in the foregoing pages. On the vaulted ceiling of the tomb of the Pancratii by the Via Latina, just south of Rome, painting and white stucco relief work are combined.[66] The painting partly takes the form of delicate panel pictures of landscapes, birds, flowers, etc., partly of coloured backgrounds to white stucco panels or to white painted figures imitating stucco. Remains of flat painted ceilings with imitation coffering are rare. The most striking of these relics are the eight surviving coffers, most skilfully pieced together out of many fragments, from the ceiling of an elaborate hall of Constantinian date which came to light below the present cathedral of Trier (Augusta Trevirorum).[67] In four of these coffers are a pair of dancing Cupids on a blue ground. Each of the four other coffers contains a draped female bust, again with a blue background. In three instances nearly the entire bust could be restored, but only small portions of the fourth were retrieved. All are nimbate: two are heavily bejewelled and probably portray ladies of Constantine's family; the third, who is crowned with flowers and holds a plectrum, might represent a personification. Portions of an earlier, but still provincial, example belonged to a corridor surrounding the courtyard of a second-century house at Verulamium in Hertfordshire.[68] The largest piece, found in fragments on the floor, bears a design carried out on a purple ground and consisting of a series of interlacing octagons outlined in ornamental yellow lines and arranged symmetrically in rows. The centre of each octagon contains a rectangular panel and in each of the surviving sixteen panels is either the naturalistic figure of a bird or, in two cases, the frontal mask of a feline. These octagons and panels were clearly meant to imitate coffering; and the fact that the birds are set at different angles to one another must imply that the painting was meant to be viewed from below.

Portrait Painting and Painting in the Minor Arts

PORTRAIT PAINTING

APART FROM THE MUMMY PORTRAITS from Egypt (*cf.* pp. 131–2), relatively few painted portraits of the Roman age survive. Of paintings from the walls of Pompeii that we can reckon as genuine likenesses of contemporary people the most famous is that from the House of the Terentii, which depicts the busts of a married pair. The husband has been identified as Terentius Neo, one of the owners of the house and described in an inscription found on the site as a 'studiosus'.[1] Both man and wife are shown as fairly young, with highly individualised and unidealised bourgeois features. The slight moustache and beard of the man and the woman's hair-style, with a fringe of small curls above the brow, indicate a Neronian date for the painting. Terentius' garment is white and he holds a scroll, as befits his learned calling. The wife wears a dark dress and holds in her right hand a *stilus* to her lips and writing-tablets in her left hand: she must have helped her husband in his literary or legal pursuits. The gesture and attributes of Terentius' lady have a close counterpart in what is possibly another Pompeian mural portrait, the well-known roundel with the bust of a young and pretty girl, again with the coiffure of Nero's time, who holds in her right hand a *stilus* to her lips and in her left hand tablets—the so-called 'poetess'.[2]

An example of a non-mummy portrait painting on wood is the roundel, found in Egypt and now in Berlin, which depicts Septimius Severus with his empress Julia Domna and their two sons Caracalla, in front of his father, and Geta, in front of his mother.[3] Seeing that the elder boy, Caracalla, who was born in 188, is shown at about twelve years of age the painting

Plate 74

can hardly have been executed later than 199–200, when the imperial family toured Egypt. Septimius and Caracalla, the latter proclaimed Augustus in 197–8, wear bejewelled laurel wreaths and hold sceptres. Julia Domna has her characteristic coiffure, very stiffly waved and covering both ears, and wears pearls round her throat and in her hair. Geta, raised to the rank of Caesar in 197–8, is also sceptred; but his face has been painted out, presumably at the time of his murder and *damnatio memoriae* in 212. The background is buff, the eyes and hair are dark brown, and the wreaths and garments are mainly gold. The whole group is rendered in complete frontality. That painted portrait-bust medallions of this type on wood were not uncommon is suggested by the scene on a painted wooden sarcophagus found at Kertch in the Crimea, on which is depicted a painter in his studio with two completed portrait roundels hanging on its wall.[4]

A delightful fourth-century series of miniature portraits are those on glass medallions, painted in gold leaf, with details added mainly in brown and white against a dark blue background. Probably the best-known of these is the family group, now in the Museo Civico at Brescia, of an aristocratic Roman lady with her boy and girl.[5] All three have the same colouring of hair and eyes and resemble one another strikingly in features. All wear *tunica* and *pallium* (over-mantle), the boy's being white, those of mother and daughter gold, and into the girl's *pallium* elaborate patterns have been woven. Among the other vividly realistic portraits of this type, all with delicate brown shading and occasional touches of polychrome on the gold, the finest are the married pair, the man Eusebius, the group of father, mother, and baby, and the boy Simplicius in the Vatican;[6] the man in the Pamphilus Catacomb;[7] the man in the Museo Civico at Arezzo;[8] and the mother with her little son in the Metropolitan Museum of Art, New York.[9] The persons here portrayed must surely have sat to the miniaturists. Nothing could offer stronger proof than do these exquisite paintings of the persistence of technical skill of the highest order, and of the naturalistic tradition inherited from Hellenistic and early- and mid-imperial times, in the minor arts of the late-antique period—and that in an age in which the trends of monumental portrait sculpture were very different (*cf.* pp. 40–2).

For a more or less continuous series of painted portrait busts running from the first to the fourth century we turn to Roman Egypt, to the mummy portraits executed either in encaustic or in tempera, mostly on a thin wooden panel laid in the mummy case on the head of the corpse, less often on the linen shroud in which the body was wrapped.[10] The painting was done either directly on the wood or linen or on a prepared ground of gypsum plaster, the pigments being mixed in water, with some kind of glue or gum added (tempera), or with wax (encaustic), producing colours of the rich and luminous quality which is the special feature of these portraits. The chief implement used was the brush, the butt end of which may have served for working the wax while it was still in a soft and pasty state.

What strikes us most about these paintings is their remarkable resemblance to modern portraits in oils. They can be approxi-mately dated by the hair- and beard-styles of the men and by the coiffures of the women; and those that were painted in the first, second, and early third centuries display a quite extraordinary plasticity and three-dimensional effect with their brilliant high-lights and contrasting shadows.[11] This impression of depth is enhanced by the slightly oblique turn of the bust to left or right, while the head is virtually full-face. The facial features are intensely individualised, so that we feel that real living people, with whom we can establish contact, are looking at us; and this is even true of some of the fourth-century portraits,[12] belonging to a time when both the face and the bust tended to assume a more rigid frontality, when all the forms were flattened and the features schematised.[13] It would seem to be rather

Plate 76

unlikely that the subjects of these paintings sat for their funerary portraits while they were still alive. Perhaps in small communities the local painters would have been familiar with their faces in life or they may have hastily copied the features of the deceased and then worked up the sketches into vivid, living likenesses. It is true that the same general facial types recur and that old age is seldom rendered. But the details are often so personal and intimate that it is hard to believe that these painters produced nothing but stock, generalised pieces, only roughly suited to the men and women whom they purported to portray.

The people for whom these mummy portraits were painted were members of comfortably-off Hellenised families which had settled in Egypt either in Ptolemaic times or after the country's incorporation into the Roman Empire under Augustus. They had become Egyptianised to the extent of adopting local burial custom and, presumably, the notions of the after-life that this careful preservation of the corpse implied. But their taste for a realistic, and even veristic, iconographic style was completely Graeco-Roman and in most of the cases in which names are inscribed they are in Greek. Examples are the early-second-century youth Artemidorus,[14] the girl Irene, daughter of Silanos, who sports a Neronian hair-style,[15] and the young woman Hermione, styled *grammatike* (grammar-school mistress), whose date is somewhat uncertain. The complete exposure of her ears suggests the second quarter of the third century, whereas the absence of any trace of a pad of hair turned up behind, as in all third-century coiffures, would seem to indicate the gathering of the locks into a bun on the nape of the neck in accordance with late-second-century fashion.[16]

ILLUSTRATED MANUSCRIPTS

Here we shall include only those illustrated manuscripts (codices) whose miniatures and text are generally agreed to have been painted and written not later than *c.* 500. In view of the lower date/limit set for Roman art in this book (*cf.* p. 15), we cannot take into account such sixth/century Christian manu/ scripts as the Vienna Genesis and the Rossano and Sinope (now in Paris) Gospel codices, the illustrations of which are still Graeco/Roman in their style and may have been modelled on earlier book illuminations, or any illustrated Carolingian, medieval, and Renaissance manuscripts of ancient authors and compilations, such as the Vatican Terence, the Calendar of 354, and the Notitia Dignitatum, with miniatures that were clearly based on classical prototypes.

A tiny fraction of the total number of known papyri shows illustrations in the shape of diagrams or outline drawings. But true pictures in polychrome are always associated with the parchment codex, whose leaves were obviously far better suited to the painter's art than were paper rolls. The history of the ancient codex as a book form begins towards the end of the first century AD.[17] Yet of the five surviving illustrated codices (two of the Old Testament, two of Virgil, one of the Iliad) that come within our survey none has been convincingly dated before the late fourth or early fifth century. Of earlier codices with minia/ tures illustrating the texts of biblical or pagan writers we have no direct evidence. Nevertheless, the fact that in the Iliad of *c.* 500, now in the Ambrosian Library at Milan (*cf.* pp. 139– 141), Books I and II are illustrated episode by episode, with close adherence to the text, whereas the illustrations of the other books follow the text only in a general way, might suggest that an illustrated text of that part, at least, of Homer was already in existence and was used by this miniaturist either directly or through the medium of a copy/book. Since the Ambrosian miniatures for Books I and II are strongly Hellenistic in their style, this presumed earlier codex could have been of third/ or even second/century AD date. This is, however, only guess/ work; and there would seem to be no reason why the pictures of the rest of the Ambrosian Iliad and of the other three manu⁄scripts of our late⁄antique group should necessarily be straight reproductions of previously existing book illuminations. Some, indeed, certainly were not. For on the earliest manuscript of our series, the so⁄called Itala of Quedlinburg fragment of an illus⁄trated Old Testament (see below), there can be read, where the paint has flaked off, written instructions as to what was to be shown, presumably from the person commissioning the codex or from the head of the workshop to the miniaturist, who must himself have composed the pictures *ad hoc*, doubtless with the aid of copy⁄books compiled from various sources and giving him ideas on grouping, on individual figures, and on architec⁄tural and landscape details. It is true that these book illustrators were not painters of the first flight, but artisans, sometimes, although not always, highly skilled and clever artisans. Yet it has been calculated[18] that the cost of illustrated codices of this kind must have been a very heavy one that only a relatively few wealthy and cultivated persons could afford; and direct access to manuscripts by copyists may not always have been easy. It seems likely that in most cases the miniaturists worked from copy⁄books containing sketches made from wall and easel paintings, from marble and stucco reliefs, and from statuary in the round; and there have come down to us a number of large⁄scale paintings, mosaics, carvings, etc., with Homeric and Virgilian scenes dating from the first century BC onwards.

The Itala of Quedlinburg, now in Berlin,[19] consists of five leaves of a codex with an illustrated text of parts of I Samuel 10, 15, II Samuel 2, and I Kings 5, the text being according to the Itala or pre⁄Vulgate Latin version of the Scriptures. It is usually reckoned as the earliest of our group, as dating from the second half of the fourth or the early fifth century. The minia⁄tures, which depict episodes from the history of Samuel, Abner, and Solomon, are realistic and naturalistic in their style and show figures widely spaced⁄out against a simple background.

Gestures are vivid and the colouring is rich. One picture, for instance, shows Saul arrayed in golden armour and a purple cloak. There are a few landscape details and the artist has succeeded in conveying some effect of depth and atmosphere. Other Old Testament and perhaps New Testament illumin-ated codices, of which all trace has vanished, may have been produced at this period. But good as these Itala pictures are, there is nothing in them to support the oft-repeated notion that illustrated bibles supplied the models of such monumental and highly complex mural paintings as those in the third-century Dura-Europos synagogue (*cf.* pp. 126 f.) and in the fourth-century Via Latina catacomb (*cf.* p. 121). These wall painters, if not consummate artists, coped with more exacting and ambi-tious programmes than any attempted by the ancient (including sixth-century) biblical miniaturists whose work is known to us. Only very occasionally do the fragmentary miniatures in the fifth-century Greek 'Cotton Genesis', probably produced in Egypt and now in the British Museum, show scenes of crowded figures reminiscent of those in the mural pictures.[20] It is not in any case easy to envisage such mural painters making enlargements of small book illuminations for their own purposes. No one has, to my knowledge, yet suggested that the large-scale mythological paintings and reliefs of the second and third centuries AD were based on illustrations in the codices of pagan writers.

The illustrated Virgil *Codex Vaticanus Latinus 3225* is generally dated to the early fifth century on account of certain details of its miniatures that show affinities with works of art that were certainly made at that time.[21] The surviving text runs from Georgics iii, 1 to Aeneid xi, 895 and with this go fifty miniatures of which six fill the whole page, including one that is composed of six small, individually framed landscape scenes, while the rest of the miniatures have writing above or below them. At the end of the text of Aeneid vi is the scar of a medallion that may once have held a painted portrait of Virgil.

The pictures fall into three groups according to the nature of their frames, a white line dividing the outer red and inner blue bands of which the frames consist in pictures 1–10 (group 1) and 26–50 (group 3), whereas in pictures 11–25 (group 2) the white line is absent. This difference in the frames appears to correspond to a difference in the treatment of the paintings. For example, those of group 2 show a bluish wash, which is not found in those of groups 1 and 3; and the group 2 pictures diverge from the rest in the positioning in the field of human figures, animals, and objects and in the generally more impressionistic handling of the bodily forms that they display. Two miniaturists would seem to have been at work upon the codex, one executing the pictures of groups 1 and 3, the other those of group 2.

But in spite of these small variations, all the miniatures of Codex 3225 are alike in being genuine little paintings, with strong, sometimes quite hard colours worked with compact pigments: they are not just coloured drawings, which is what most of the Ambrosian Iliad illustrations give the impression of being (*cf.* pp. 139–41). Common to the pictures of all three groups with an outdoor context is the use of a strip of pink colour between the blue of the sky and the dark of the foreground, a feature also found in some of the Itala of Quedlinburg miniatures. All have an architectural or landscape setting, the elements of which are no mere adjuncts, but integral parts of the scene. None show much sense of naturalistic perspective or of space and depth. But several pictures reveal a very bold and effective use of vertical perspective—for instance, the building of Carthage (no. 10), the Greeks emerging from the Wooden Horse (no. 14), the view of Pergamea in Crete (no. 19), the map of Sicily (no. 21), the view of Carthage (no. 23), the scene on Circe's isle (no. 39), the ships changed into maidens (no. 47), and the council of the Trojans (no. 49). Some of the landscape features are almost Pompeian in treatment: other elements, such as some costumes, are of the fourth century; and the views of cities just cited have their nearest parallels in the late-antique. Clearly the motifs incorporated by the miniaturists in their paintings were of various times and styles; and these miniatures cannot have been copied slavishly from a single earlier codex or from a single earlier cycle of Virgilian pictures. They must have been freely composed for this particular codex, the size and position of each picture having been determined by consultation between the artists and the writer, or writers, of the text. This would not preclude the influence on the miniatures of sketches of pre-existing complete Virgilian scenes derived from reliefs, paintings or mosaics—if, indeed, such scenes did not sometimes originate with the draftsmen who compiled the copy-books.

The second Virgilian manuscript of our period, *Codex Vaticanus Latinus 3867 'Romanus'*,[22] is the most enigmatic of our group as regards both its date and its place of origin. The miniatures of the Itala fragment and of the Vatican Codex 3225 are good, competent work and both are likely to have been executed in Italian workshops. But those of the 'Romanus', while for the most part richly and brightly painted and ambitious in design, show a crude and even childish style of draftsmanship which harmonizes ill with the excellence of the script and the generally *de luxe* appearance of the codex. C. Nordenfalk's attempt to date the manuscript in the early fourth century on account of an alleged resemblance between some of the figures in its pictures and those in works of Constantinian art[23] does not carry great conviction. A fifth-century date is the one most usually proposed; and it may be that the person who commissioned the manuscript was a wealthy provincial who could only command the services of a local miniaturist.

Nineteen pictures in this codex have survived, of which seven illustrate the Eclogues, two the Georgics, and ten the

Aeneid, those belonging to the Eclogues being carried out in softer tones than the rest and occupying part only of their folios, whereas the others are full-page illustrations. Three of the pictures in the Eclogues text are portraits of Virgil seated facing and flanked by a reading-desk and a box of scrolls. These are not too badly done and may be copies of some well-known type. The four other Eclogues scenes show musical contests between shepherds, many of the elements of which are somewhat monotonously repeated, but with landscape features that are fairly naturalistic. The two Georgics miniatures are characterised by the total absence of any horizon: the figures of shepherds, dogs, sheep, and other animals and the very stylised trees, shrubs, and flowers are strewn all over the field. The Aeneid pictures, for all their crudity of execution, illustrate the text in a detailed and vivacious way. Among the most vivid are the scenes of Aeneas, Acestis, and Helymus seated on thrones as they preside over Anchises' funeral games, while Ascanius sacrifices at Anchises' tomb (no. 11); of the Trojan fleet caught in the storm at sea (no. 12); of Dido and Aeneas banqueting (no. 13); of Priam and the Wooden Horse below the walls of Troy (no. 14); and of Dido and Aeneas sheltering in the cave (no. 15). The most complex pictures portray the incident of Ascanius' unintentional shooting of Silvia's pet stag (no. 15) and the battle between six Trojans and six Rutulians, where the combatants confront each other in two distinct groups and vertical perspective is used to produce the effect of crowds (no. 17). The two last pictures (nos. 18 and 19) present somewhat wooden groups of the gods seated in council. In these miniatures the Trojans all wear Phrygian caps, including Aeneas, who is never shown with it in Codex 3225; and here, too, the gods, the leading Trojans, and Dido are often nimbate, which they never are in the other illustrated Virgil. So far as the pictures of 3225 and 3867 survive, of only one episode in the Aeneid, the wounding of the pet stag, are illustrations found in both, but within that episode each minia⁄ turist has chosen a different incident. We can, indeed, be pretty confident that there was no connection whatsoever between these two illuminated Virgil codices.

The Ambrosian Iliad[24] is probably the latest in our series of illustrated manuscripts and it certainly originated in the eastern half of the Roman world. Some features in a number of its miniatures, which seem to have been the artist's own con⁄ tributions, underived from earlier sources, link it with works of art produced at Constantinople *c.* 500. The codex as we now have it consists of loose fragments, since at some time the pictures were cut out of the book; and all that survives of the text of Homer are the portions that are written on the backs of the pictures. Fifty⁄eight miniatures, illustrating Books I, II, IV–XVII, and XXI–XXIV, have been preserved. But the original text must have contained the whole poem and many more pictures. All the miniatures are of identical width, but they vary in height. All are framed by an inner blue and an outer red band, and occasionally two separate, superimposed scenes are contained within the same frame, the upper one being normally shallower than the lower one. The names of the characters and the summaries of the revelant passages in the text now seen on the pictures were added at a later date.

R. Bianchi Bandinelli's verdict on these Iliad miniatures, that they are a corpus of Homeric illustrations derived from the iconographic and stylistic traditions of various periods and collected and painted by a single miniaturist, is, to my mind at least, mainly convincing. The preparatory drawings made rapidly in pen and pencil and revealed where the colours have flaked off are of the same character throughout; so also are the human figure types and facial features. Again, the polychromy is of a uniform kind in all the pictures. The background is always of a light buff wash, to which the paint was applied in tempera. The whole effect is very gay; and, since the colouring is conventional rather than naturalistic, a balance of contrasting shades is normally maintained over the whole area of a picture. The tones are clear and bright, but never gaudy: the prevailing ones are vermilion, orange, crimson, purple, dark and light green, dark and light blue, yellow, and mauve. Shading is sparingly used and is always carried out in a darker variant of the colour of the object shaded.

The marked divergencies between the pictures in composition, in the number and size of the figures introduced, and in the presence or absence of architectural and landscape details is to be explained partly by the simple fact that their subjects are of different characters and partly by the wide variety of models that the artist followed. For Books I and II he does, as we have seen (*cf.* p. 133), appear to have had before him a single illustrated codex or copies of its miniatures. But for the rest, where the pictures follow the text less faithfully he must have used copy-books compiled from many sources. Bianchi Bandinelli certainly implies that the miniaturist's models were exclusively Homeric illustrations. On the other hand, there would seem to be no reason why some copy-book sketches should not have been groups of figures or scenes illustrating other subjects and adapted by the artist to a Homeric context. In the preparatory drawings on the parchment there are numerous corrections, particularly in the case of scenes of a complicated nature, as though he were changing and even compressing models to suit his own requirements as a miniaturist. Why should he have made such corrections if those models depicted the Homeric subjects that he had to illustrate? The most successful and interesting of the Ambrosian Iliad's complex pictures are the splendidly spontaneous battle and siege scenes with crowded *mêlées* of figures climbing, in the boldest vertical perspective, up the surface of the miniatures. According to Bianchi Bandinelli, scenes of this type were ultimately derived from monumental paintings of the late second and third centuries that have not survived. As he points out, the extant works of art nearest to the Iliad scenes are the very pictorial Roman battle and mythological sarcophagi of that period (*cf.* pp. 101–2). But most of these present, not scenes from the Iliad, but episodes from other sagas or battles of Greeks and Amazons or, most frequently, battles of Romans and barbarians. Some of the correspondences between those western reliefs and our eastern miniatures are, indeed, so close that it is difficult not to con-clude that the Ambrosian Iliad was inspired by sketches of them (or even by the sketches made for them) handed down to the miniaturist of this codex through the generations in copy-books. At any rate, he was a skilful and vivid draftsman and colourist and his work provides what is perhaps the largest and most remarkable single body of evidence for the persistence of the influence of late-Hellenistic and early- and mid-imperial art into the late-antique, or even proto-Byzantine, period.

PAINTING ON GLASS (OTHER THAN PORTRAITS)

The subjects other than portraits (*cf.* pp. 130–1) of the painted gold-glass vessels of the fourth century are mainly Christian in their content—figures of Christ and of saints, biblical scenes, etc.—and properly belong to the story of the early Christians. A few, on the other hand, show mythological and *genre* subjects of a pagan or 'neutral' character, such as Hercules and the Eryman-thian boar, Achilles among the daughters of Lycomedes, Venus, personifications of Roma and Constantinopolis, a Nereid on a sea-horse, the Tres Monetae, Cupid, Cupid and Psyche, Minerva superintending a carpenter's workshop, boxers, hunters, animals, etc.[25]

The most important group of Roman-age painted glasses are those with mythological, battle, gladiatorial, hunting, *genre*, and animal scenes worked in polychrome and mainly assign-able to the third century, although some could be of later date.

The most spectacular of them is a very well-preserved bowl in the Ray Smith Collection in America, depicting the Judgment of Paris.[26] Paris, Hermes, and the three goddesses are skilfully deployed on a rocky platform with water and two of Paris' sheep in the foreground, and the human and animal figures are painted in shades of grey-blue, buff, brown, and mauve against a deep red background. The forms of the letters of the inscriptions on this bowl are pronounced to be not later than the first half of the third century; and a glass fragment with the head of Thetis found at Dura-Europos must have been painted before that city fell to the Persians in *c.* 257.[27] Less easy to date precisely is the series of painted glasses found in the famous hoard at Begram in Afghanistan,[28] since the date, *c.* 250-3, that has been proposed for the 'closure' of the cache is only conjectural; and one glass vessel found in it, a *diatreton* or 'cage-cup', with open-work figure scenes carved on its exterior was almost certainly made in the late third or fourth century. The most complete of the Begram painted vessels are four conical beakers, one with two women plaiting garlands and two men assisting,

Plate 75

two with gladiatorial combats, and one with a zone of hunting above and of fishing below. The considerable fragment of another beaker shows the chariot battle between Achilles and Hector, painted in bright blue, yellow, green, dark red, etc., the figures being strewn all over the field in the late-antique manner. Three other fragments present spirited battle scenes, with some bold foreshortening of men and horses, possibly derived ultimately from large-scale paintings or reliefs. On two further sherds, both from the same vessel, is a blue panther with black spots attacking a gazelle. Two pieces of painted glass found in Egypt clearly belong to the same types as those in the Begram series: one is from a beaker with a gladiatorial fight in its upper zone and a beast fight in its lower zone, the other carries the portion of a beast fight.[29] A one-handled flagon from Kertch in the Crimea shows Daphne being changed into a tree and accompanied by Pothos (Desire), Phoebus (Apollo), and Ladon (her father).[30] Painting on glass was obviously a prized and pleasing Roman minor art, of which all too few examples have survived.

PAINTED POTTERY

The pottery wares with painted decoration of the Roman period that are known to us were mainly produced on the south-eastern outskirts of the Empire or in its peripheral northern and western provinces. The least classical of these is the Nabataean ware found at Petra and on other sites in the Nabataean Arab sphere and running from the first century BC to the third century AD. Its bowls and plates show abstract patterns or floral motifs of varying degrees of stylisation painted in dark brown on a deep pink ground.[31] Jars from Nubia dating from early imperial times carry very crude figure scenes worked in coloured outlines;[32] while glazed plates from Egypt have better drawn, but conventionalised, animal and plant designs in brown and turquoise blue.[33]

The most attractive of these painted provincial Roman-age wares is that which was produced in the Rhineland potteries during the second and third centuries AD and imitated in Britain in the Nene Valley district where the most important and extensive of the local British pottery industries was located. On pots of this type the decoration is carried out in thick, opaque white paint, with occasional touches of polychrome, on a glossy slip that is generally black or very dark brown, much more seldom red. The designs, often accompanied by painted mottoes, are mostly either of an abstract character or in the form of stylised floral motifs, running scrolls, of Graeco-Roman parentage, with clusters of berries and slender leaves and tendrils being particularly favoured.[34] Some pots from the Trier area have paintings of a more elaborate kind—busts of gods and

143

personifications,[35] figures of the Seasons,[36] or animals.[37] The ambitious attempts made by British potters to emulate the Rhenish figure-painting met with varying success. The best surviving instance of their work is on a sherd found at Wroxeter (Viroconium) in Shropshire. A running horse of quite out-standing quality is rendered in a paste of thick, white, opaque paint trailed on the pot's black coat. The animal's trumpet-shaped muzzle, its round eye, and its flattened back ear are strongly stylised in the Celtic fashion, while the neck and body are more naturalistic in their lines.[38] Nothing so gaily orna-mental as these Rhineland and Nene Valley painted pieces had been produced by ancient potters since the 'West Slope' (Attic) and 'Gnathian' (South Italian) Hellenistic wares with their floral and—in the case of 'Gnathian'—figured decoration executed mainly in white and yellow paint on a dark back-ground.[39]

PAINTED ARMOUR

Of this class of painting the surviving examples are very rare, the principal pieces being five wooden shields, richly adorned with abstract designs and figure scenes painted in brilliant polychrome, which came to light at Dura-Europos.[40] Brightly painted shields are mentioned by Arrian (*Tactica* 34 ff.) as used by the riders in cavalry sports and exercises in the Roman army; and it seems very likely that the Dura shields all served that purpose. One of these is oblong, 'door-shaped', as Arrian calls these sports shields. The central boss is surrounded by bands of geometric patterns: at the top are two flying Victories crowning an eagle, below is a striding lion. Here the painting is worked on a thin, red-dyed layer of parchment covering the wood. Three of the other shields are of the more usual oval cavalry shape and their painting is done on a layer of plaster spread on the wood. On two of them complex figure scenes occupy the broad frieze round the central boss—a battle of Greeks and Amazons in the one instance, in the other, episodes from the Trojan War, including the appearance of the Wooden Horse below the walls of Troy. The field of the third oval shield is filled by the statuesque, frontal, standing figure of a warrior god wearing a species of Roman military dress and with a yellow nimbus behind his helmeted head. The fourth oval shield is represented by a parchment fragment on which a map is painted—a sea with ships sailing over it and by the shore a series of walled towns inscribed with their names in Greek and depicting the various stages on an itinerary, possibly one that the owner of the shield had himself followed. If so, he must have got a Greek-speaking craftsman to copy, none too accurately, an official map, on which the names would have been in Latin.

CHAPTER IX

Mosaics

FLOOR MOSAICS

O F THE WORKS OF ART with which the structural features of Roman buildings were adorned floor mosaics are probably the best known, since a far larger number of these than of wall and vault mosaics and of paintings and stucco reliefs on walls and ceilings have, for obvious reasons, managed to survive the ravages of time. A mosaic pavement may be found virtually intact in a room of whose walls only a foot or even less remains. Such pavements are, in fact, often extremely well preserved. They are sometimes highly spectacular and of very great interest as regards both their content and their style. They are, moreover, found in almost every quarter of the ancient Roman world. Here we can only survey the subject in its broadest outlines, citing outstanding examples, but not attempt' ing any detailed description or discussion of them.

The history of ancient floor mosaics with both geometric, or abstract, and representational designs begins in the late fifth or early fourth century BC with the pavements laid in natural pebbles, mainly black and white, with a few coloured ones here and there, in private houses at Olynthus in northern Greece.[1] (In this chapter the term 'representational' is taken to cover figures and groups of humans and animals, objects of all kinds, and floral motifs whether stylised or naturalistic.) In these Greek mosaics, which include such mythological scenes as Bellerophon slaying the Chimaera shown two-dimension' ally in panels framed by abstract and floral borders, the influence of floor textiles is clear. Some are laid like rugs in the centres of living-rooms, others appear at doors like mats, while a few are 'carpets' running right up to the walls of the chambers. The same is true of the later, more plastically worked, and partially coloured pebble mosaics found at Pella in Macedonia and dating from the late fourth and early third centuries BC, where the panel pictures, or *emblemata*, similarly framed and showing mythological, hunting, and beast-fight themes, are normally placed in the centres of the floors.[2] And these rug-like and occasionally more carpet-like effects are in evidence in Hellenistic mosaics worked in a very different technique, in which natural pebbles have been abandoned and their place has been taken by *tesserae*, that is, small fragments of black and white and coloured stones and marbles, whether of local or of foreign origin. In the now largely three-dimensional representational *emblemata* rendered by this method the *tesserae* are often tiny and subtly shaped (*opus vermiculatum*), the purpose being to imitate painting as closely as the different medium allows. The earliest surviving *emblema* of this kind is in a mid-third-century BC house at Morgantina in Sicily and shows Ganymede and the eagle.[3] Examples dating from the second century BC have come to light at Palermo in Sicily,[4] on the island of Delos (in the 'House of the Masks', in particular[5]), at Pergamon in Asia Minor,[6] at Alexandria,[7] etc. It may well be that the whole idea of mosaics laid in *tesserae* originated in Hellenistic Sicily and spread thence to other Hellenistic centres.

Such, then, is the Hellenic and Hellenistic ancestry of Roman floor mosaics, throughout whose history the different and sometimes conflicting principles of 'rug' and 'carpet' were at work. We still find the 'rug' and 'mat' effects in Roman times both when representational and abstract panels are centred in surrounds of plain *tesserae* and when representational *emblemata* are set in the middle of surrounds of geometric patterns. But increasingly under the Empire it was the notion of the pavement as a 'carpet' running right up to the walls of a room that was paramount; and in the Roman world a tension arose between the view of the floor as a single, unified, integral space to be completely, and as far as possible evenly, covered with an 'all-over' design—a view for whose specifically Roman or at any rate western origin a good case has recently been made[8]—and the prevailing Hellenistic attitude to the floor as a kind of 'easel' or 'wall' on which to 'hang' a central and wholly dominating panel picture. This latter attitude was the natural extension of the originally Hellenic 'rug' idea, as the figured panels grew, from the second century BC onwards, more elaborate and complicated, often with landscape and architectural settings and three-dimensional perspective producing an illusion of space, recession in depth, and atmosphere. Such pictures were obviously intended to be seen by the spectator from one viewpoint only and to be the focus of his attention, while he could almost ignore the rest of the pavement.

Emblemata of this type have, as we have seen, come to light on Hellenistic sites, where they sometimes bear the signatures of Greek mosaicists.[9] The Elder Pliny tells us that Sosos of Pergamon made a mosaic panel of doves drinking from, or perching on, a goblet.[10] Two small mosaic *emblemata* found at Pompeii are signed by Dioscurides of Samos.[11] And since, as we shall find, the vast majority of figured pavements unearthed in Italy were designed on very different lines, we may conclude, not unreasonably, that such pictures represent an importation into the peninsula of the work of mosaicists from Greek lands. The whole art of mosaics made with *tesserae*, of those with geometric and floral, no less than of those with figured, compositions, was, of course, borrowed by Italy from the Hellenistic world. But whereas the 'all-over' mainly black-and-white, less often coloured, abstract patterns and floral motifs, such as rosettes and running scrolls (sometimes inhabited by birds and animals), were eagerly adopted by Italian craftsmen, who developed them continuously from the second century BC until the fourth century AD[12] and initiated in the late first century their diffusion through the northern and western provinces (where polychrome and complex versions were immensely popular),[13] three/dimensional *emblemata* found in Italy date chiefly from the last two centuries BC, after which they fell out of favour.[14] The Dioscurides panels are mounted on marble trays; and these and a number of other small *emblemata* from Pompeii and elsewhere were probably imported ready worked from Hellenistic workshops in east/Mediterranean lands.[15] Large mosaic *emblemata* of this early period, such as the famous Alexander and Darius piece from the 'House of the Faun' at Pompeii[16] and the great panoramic Nilotic mosaic from the temple of Fortuna at Praeneste (Palestrina) in central Italy, with its bird's/eye view and high horizon,[17] were doubtless worked on the spot by foreign artists. The only significant group of three/dimensional polychrome *emblemata* from Italy dating from a later age that has come down to us is the quartet of mytholo/gical and landscape scenes found in Hadrian's Villa at Tivoli.[18] Of these the Centaur fight, now in Berlin, is by far the best: it and two of the other three scenes, all now in the Vatican, are probably the work of an east/Mediterranean mosaicist; the fourth scene, a bull/fight, which shows little sense of perspective and depth, may be by the hand of a local pupil of the foreign master.

Plate 77

It is, indeed, in an eastern province, at Antioch on the Orontes in Syria, where a continuous sequence of mosaic pavements, running from *c.* AD 100 to the sixth century, has been uncovered, that the Hellenistic three/dimensional *emblema* tradition has survived most conspicuously.[19] There, throughout the second and third centuries, we find a series of *emblemata* with mythological, marine, and theatrical scenes often composed of a number of figures in elaborate architectural and landscape settings in which depth and atmosphere are rendered no less effectively than in the panel pictures of the late Republic found in Italy. To such a picture the whole of the rest of a floor at Antioch is strictly subordinated; and the same is the case with panels in which a single figure or bust, plastically modelled as in painting, is represented. Not until the time of Constantine do there appear the first beginnings of the western attitude to a mosaic floor as an entity over which the interest of its figure scenes and groups should be evenly distributed, no emphatic stress being laid on a dominating panel or set of panels. No other site in the eastern half of the Empire has yet produced anything that can compare with these Antiochene three-dimensional *emblemata*. Yet it seems unlikely that they were quite unique in this region of the Roman world. In the western provinces such pictures of the mid-imperial period are extremely rare. Well-known examples from Tripolitania, possibly the work of eastern craftsmen, are the originally nine square panels with scenes from agricultural life, rendered with recession in depth and naturalistic perspective, from the villa at Zliten and the four similarly treated oblong panels, two with mythological and two with marine subjects, from the 'Villa del Nilo' near Lepcis Magna.[20] But these are not centred in their pavements, as are their counterparts at Antioch; each set is arranged over its floor in a grid, which thus preserves its unity and creates a diffused interest. A three-dimensional *emblema* from Ampurias in Spain depicting the sacrifice of Iphigenia[21] has close affinities with an Antiochene theatrical panel representing Iphigenia in Aulis[22] and might also be by the hand of an easterner.

Plate 78

In Italy during the second century AD the prevailing style for figured pavements was the black silhouette with interior lines in white worked completely two-dimensionally on a flat white ground. This style had its beginnings in first-century AD Pompeii, in a series of threshold mosaic panels adorned with the figures of boars, watch-dogs, etc.;[23] and it appears again on a late-first-century pavement at Ostia showing the heads of Wind Gods and personifications of provinces.[24] But its fullest development was in the second century; and it is in the Ostia of that and later times that its best and most numerous examples

have survived.[25] The favourite themes are marine, athletic, and
hunting scenes, and other scenes with animals. An out/
standingly fine instance is the pavement depicting Neptune and
his train in the 'Neptune Baths' at Ostia. There, as so often
with these silhouette pictures, the drawing is extremely good—
vigorous and naturalistic. No attempt is made to ape painting.
The technique is admirably suited to the mosaic medium; and
the composition, eschewing all rendering of space, covers the
whole floor most satisfactorily as with an 'all/over' carpet
pattern. Less accomplished artistically, but full of liveliness and
interest, are the figures and groups on the floors of the offices of
business firms in the Piazzale delle Corporazioni and on the
principal pavement of the 'Drivers' Baths', both at Ostia and
dating respectively from the late and early second century.
The silhouette style did, indeed, survive at Ostia, with rather
less ambitious subjects, until quite late into the third century,
in the 'House of the Gorgons', for example, as it also did, more
sporadically, in Rome and on other Italian sites.[26] But from the
end of the second century a distinct falling/off in draftsmanship
is evident. The most attractive black/and/white pieces of this
later period are those in which figures are contained in floral
scrolls or framed by arabesques.

Plate 79

Plate 80

Second/century figured polychrome mosaics from Italian
sites, other than the three/dimensional *emblemata* already men/
tioned (*cf.* p. 149), are relatively rare.[27] Panels with single figures,
human and animal or with spaceless groups of men and beasts,
occasionally mythological in content, sometimes occur. When
such pseudo/*emblemata* appear as centre/pieces, care is taken
not to focus all attention on them but to give the elaborate
surrounds of geometric patterns an equal share of interest. In
other instances figured panels of this kind are spread in a grid
over the floor's entire surface. Another method is to inset a
number of busts or full/length figures into 'medallions' formed
by the twists of wreaths or ribbons, or into a series of octagons,

in a dominating, 'all-over' geometric composition. This reduction of single figures and even of scenes to the role of subsidiary adornments in a carpet-like abstract design, or as a means of securing equal importance for all parts of a floor, we shall find again as a characteristic of many polychrome provincial figured pavements running from the second to the fourth century (*cf.* pp. 152–5). Italian polychrome pavements of the third century carry on the same devices. One large room in the fourth-century 'House of the Dioscuri' at Ostia contains a great 'all-over' marine mosaic of Venus, Nereids, Tritons, etc.,[28] a coloured counterpart of the second-century silhouette marine pieces, but far less well drawn and far less skilfully composed than are those. This later type of scene has also its provincial coloured parallels, for instance, the roughly contemporary 'Triumph of Neptune' pavement, now in the Louvre, from Cirta (Constantine) in Numidia.[29]

The second-century figured silhouette pavements of Italy form, as we have seen (pp. 150–1), a distinctive and attractive group. Apart from those, the real mosaic interest of the second, third, and fourth centuries lies outside Italy, in the great polychrome figured series of the Roman provinces, where, in the west, the tendencies that we have observed in the second- and third-century coloured pavements found on Italian sites were developed on an enormous scale. The somewhat different story of our one large eastern series of mosaics has been already very briefly sketched (*cf.* pp. 149–50) and must be studied in detail in Levi's monumental publication.[30] Of the pavements of some of the western provinces there exist detailed catalogues and discussions, which can be consulted.[31] In these works and in others to be cited later, publications will be found of most of the examples mentioned in the following pages. In this chapter we shall have to confine ourselves to a very rapid glance at the principal styles and main types of composition displayed by the surviving wealth of provincial material.

Of all the western areas of the Empire, Roman Africa, from Algeria on the west to Cyrenaica on the east, is undoubtedly the richest in its yield of figured pavements.[32] These are, for the most part, difficult to date precisely. But the majority would seem to fall between the first half of the second and the latter part of the third century, with some notable fourth-century pieces. Apart from the few with true *emblemata* of Hellenistic type (*cf.* p. 150), many African mosaics present framed rect-angular or circular panel pictures, often with quite complex figure scenes from mythology, the hunting field, and agricultural life. But even when the individual figures in such pictures have a three-dimensional and naturalistic quality, the compositions are totally lacking in spatial effects. The figures and groups tend to be strewn all over the field without true perspective or to be arranged in superimposed registers, sometimes on either side of a central figure, so as to produce an 'all-over', tapestry-like look. And when such pictures are seen in relation to the whole pavements of which they form the centre-pieces, we find that they are sometimes almost smothered by large and elaborate floral surrounds; or that they have to share the spectator's atten-tion with figures or trees set diagonally at the corners and with outward- or inward-facing scenes along the sides of the rect-angle or square in which they are centred. Gaulish examples of the latter scheme come from Lillebonne and Villelaure;[33] and the well-known waggoner from Orbe in Switzerland is part of one of a set of similar scenes surrounding a central picture that is now lost.[34] Occasionally, as on a floor with agricultural and hunting episodes from Oudna in Africa, no emphasising frame of any kind separates the central picture from the outward-facing lateral ones that enclose it. In the 'Ocean Baths' at Sabratha in Tripolitania the mask of Oceanus in a central octagon resembles in the fineness of its technique and three-dimensional style a true Hellenistic *emblema*. But its very rich and highly complicated geometric setting disputes its predominance.[35] Similarly, the central roundel with its excellently modelled figures of Theseus and the Minotaur on the pavement from Cormerod in Switzerland, another *emblema*-like picture, is almost in danger of being squeezed out of existence by the boldly drawn, black-and-white labyrinth that girdles it on every side.[36]

Plate 81 Striking instances of pavements composed of grids of square figured panels are the Seasons pavement and the pavement with fishes, both from Zliten in Tripolitania, the latter being framed by four friezes of inward-facing scenes of gladiatorial and other contests,[37] and the Muses pavement from Trier in Germany.[38] The Virgil mosaic from Low Ham in Somerset, a piece very crude in drawing but in content of no small importance, shows a form of grid on which the pictures are contained in one square and two long and two short rectangular panels, all closely juxtaposed and all given equal weight of interest.[39] The Orbe Gods of the Week,[40] the Nennig (Germany) gladiators,[41] and the Cologne Dionysiac[42] mosaics are excellent examples of pavements with figure scenes in squares, octagons, and spaces of other shapes 'reserved' in a rich, 'all-over', geometric 'carpet'. Another type of mosaic with figure insets is illustrated by the pavement from the Johann-Philipp Strasse in Trier.[43] Here the whole rectangle is occupied along its long sides by two rows each composed of three roundels alternating with two ovals, the end roundel and the centre roundels in each row being linked by a transverse oval. In each oval is a full-length figure and in each roundel is a bust, all set at a variety of different angles; and the two cruciform spaces left on either side of the central transverse oval are filled with figure groups—the hatching from an egg of Castor, Pollux, and Helen, in the presence of Leda and Agamemnon (each figure is inscribed with its name, 'Agamemnon' being clearly an error for 'Tyndareus'), and an enigmatic ritual scene in which an egg again features.

A further scheme of 'all-over' composition is that which suggests the projection on to a floor of a design first intended for a painted ceiling. This is exemplified by the square eastern portion of the new Romano-Christian mosaic pavement from Hinton St Mary in Dorset,[44] where the central roundel, enclosing a male bust with the Chi-Rho monogram behind the head, represents the apex of a cupola, the four half-circles surrounding the roundel represent lunettes, the four quarter-circles, in the corners of the square, squinches, and the transverse panels linking the roundel with the quarter-circles, the groins of a vault. An Orpheus composition, found chiefly in Britain, very occasionally elsewhere, in which the birds and animals pass in procession, clockwise or anti-clockwise, in concentric circles, whether divided up into sections or uninterrupted, round the centrally placed figure of their enchanter, reflects a desire to fill the whole floor with a unified design that can be viewed from any angle.[45]

Probably the outstanding mosaic contribution of the fourth and fifth centuries is the great undivided picture spreading right up to the walls of the room whose floor it adorns and uninhibited by any striving to produce an illusion of depth or of naturalistic perspective and horizon. Unrivalled examples of this style have been yielded by the vast country villa near Piazza Armerina in central Sicily, a villa whose pavements form the largest single area of floor mosaics yet discovered in the Roman world and have been assigned to various dates within the fourth century.[46] Brilliantly coloured and often revealing a notable understanding of drawing, modelling, and design, these Sicilian pavements may be said to represent the acme of the late-antique mosaicist's achievement. The subjects and the types of composition found in this collection are extremely varied. They include one of the most spectacular mosaic circus scenes so far known; and here, as always in such cases, the long oblong space is admirably filled by providing a complete view of the racing chariots on both sides of the *spina*, as from the viewpoint of an onlooker from above. There are female athletes, sporting children, and groups of singers and reciters in superimposed registers that are firmly parted by horizontal lines. There are floral scrolls inhabited by living creatures and grids of squares each containing the head of a bird or beast inset in a wreath. In each of the three apses of a great *triclinium* is a single monumental mythological picture of which the details are plastic and naturalistic, while the whole is completely innocent of any rendering of space and depth. There are bath scenes and a mythological scene in which members of the villa owner's family are featured, and many other themes that enrich the repertory. But it is the large, expanding figure compositions that interest us chiefly in the present context. These are the scene of Orpheus and the Beasts, the crowded Arion marine scene, the Labours of Hercules in the central area of the three-apsed *triclinium*, the 'Little Hunt' and, most impressive of all, the 'Great Hunt' in the long corridor. In the last, on either side of a group of three static figures, of whom the leading one will be the villa's proprietor, is deployed a great moving picture of the hunting and capturing in Africa or some eastern land and the shipping overseas of wild beasts and birds for display in the arenas of the west. In all of these five Piazza Armerina pavements the figures and groups tend to rise in tiers from the bottom to the top of the field, without any lines of demarcation between the registers. In the 'Great Hunt' there are three such registers; and in this respect the Sicilian piece is analogous to the pavement of the ambulatory round the peristyle of the Great Palace of the Emperors at Constantinople. That splendid polychrome mosaic, assigned by some to the fifth, by others to the sixth, century shows figures and groups of men and animals, of a mythological and *genre* character, excellently drawn and modelled in the full Hellenistic tradition and accompanied by

Plate 82

Plate 83

landscape accessories all strewn loosely across the floor in three superimposed tiers against a white background.[47] On this floor, the last to fall within our period (if, indeed, it does not fall just outside it), the delicate draftsmanship and shading of the figures and other motifs, and of the lovely running floral scroll inhabited by birds and human masks which borders it along one side, almost recall the *emblemata* of Morgantina and Delos. Yet its general composition, like that of the fifth- and sixth-century Antiochene pieces, is typically late-antique and western.

WALL AND VAULT MOSAICS

It goes without saying that wall and vault mosaics surviving from the Roman age are relatively few. At Pompeii some have been found on the niches and walls of domestic fountains, worked in *tesserae* of glass-paste as well as of marble and often showing framing lines of natural shells. The designs are mainly geometric with some small figure motifs included.[48] Occasionally we meet with full panel pictures from the walls of rooms, such as the scene of Apollo on Scyros from the 'House of Apollo' at Pompeii[49] and the group of Neptune and Amphitrite from the 'House of Poseidon and Amphitrite' at Herculaneum, where the altar niche of a *nymphaeum* in the *atrium* is flanked by walls richly adorned with brightly coloured vertical vine scrolls, hunting scenes, floral swags, etc. on a mainly blue ground.[50] Here again borders of natural shells appear throughout and all present the illusion of painting with naturalistic modelling and shading. A niche of Hadrianic date in the 'Baths of the Seven Sages' at Ostia carries delicately coloured floral scrolls on its semidome and soffit.[51] Another niche from Ostia of rather later second-century date contains a full-length figure of Silvanus depicted with his dog in a setting of trees against a deep blue background.[52] The semidome of the east plunge-bath in the *frigidarium* of the 'Hunting Baths' at Lepcis

Plate 85

157

Magna (*cf.* p. 124) holds the remnants of one of the most varied
and extensive pre-Christian figured vault mosaics yet discovered
in the Roman world.[53] Three main scenes—Dionysiac,
marine, and Nilotic—can be distinguished. The earliest
Christian vault and wall mosaics so far known are those,
dating from about the middle of the third century, in the small
mausoleum of the Julii family in the Vatican necropolis under
St Peter's. On the vault against a golden background is
Christus-Helios driving in a chariot amid a spreading green
vine design; on the walls are the Angler, Jonah, and the Good
Shepherd.[54] These pictures are characteristic of a time in which
Christian iconography was still more symbolic than narrative.
The best-preserved vault mosaics of the early fourth century are
the panels in the ambulatory of Santa Costanza in Rome, a
building whose origin, whether pagan or Christian, is still in
dispute. The 'all-over' compositions are at any rate 'neutral' in
their content. They consist of purely abstract patterns, of series
of circles and octagons each framing a single figure, of birds,
branches, shells, and metal vessels intermingled and strewn
haphazardly across the field, and of spreading vine scrolls in
which are incorporated vintage scenes and portrait busts.[55]
Fragmentary, but of great interest, are the three mosaic friezes,
showing hunting scenes, Christian scenes, and figures of the
Seasons, etc., in the dome of the mausoleum at Centcelles in
north-east Spain.[56] The fifth-century biblical mosaic pictures
from the Old and New Testaments on the nave walls and
triumphal arch of Santa Maria Maggiore in Rome and the
fifth-century wall and vault mosaics in Ravenna's baptisteries
and churches properly belong, with those of other church
mosaics of the same period,[57] to the story of the early Christians.
Here it must suffice to note that some of the most complex Old
Testament scenes in Santa Maria Maggiore show the spaceless
type of composition, with figures in tiers or registers, that is typical
of panel pictures on provincial pavements (*cf.* p. 153).

Plate 84

Pavements and wall decorations of *opus sectile* are worked, not in *tesserae*, but in comparatively large fragments of coloured marbles (*intarsia*). The use of this technique in floors began as early as the second century BC and reached its peak in the fourth century. The designs are nearly always abstract, as on the pavement from the Diocletianic restoration of the Curia in the Roman Forum.[58] The finest series comes from the fourth-century aristocratic private houses at Ostia.[59] Wall panelling in *opus sectile* is mainly of the late-antique period and often displays elaborate figured pictures. From the Basilica of Junius Bassus in Rome we have, among other subjects, the full-face scene of a consular procession (Palazzo del Drago) and two groups of a tigress despatching a calf (Palazzo dei Conservatori).[60] A panel with the hind-parts of a lion was found at Ostia near the Porta Marina;[61] and in the same area of the city there has recently come to light a building of yet undetermined character with many fragments of *opus sectile* wall veneering. These include a group similar to those in the Conservatori, some handsome floral scrolls, a young, male, beardless bust, and the bust of Christ, moustached, bearded, and with a nimbus, shown in the act of blessing.[62]

CHAPTER X

Epilogue

(*a*) *Figured Metal Relief Work.* (1) Decorated armour used in cavalry sports and for ceremonial and parade purposes in the Roman army: helmets with or without face-mask visors, greaves, knee-guards, shields, horse chamfrons, scabbards, inlaid sword-blades. (2) Silver table-ware, etc.: the great silver hoards, e.g. Boscoreale (Paris), Hildesheim (Berlin), Pompeii, 'House of Menander' (Naples), Hoby (Copenhagen), Berthouville (Paris), Graincourt-lès-Havrincourt (Paris), Esquiline, including four silver figurines (British Museum), Mildenhall (British Museum), Traprain Law (Edinburgh), Kaiseraugst (Augst); single pieces, e.g., Corbridge *lanx* (Alnwick Castle), Parabiago *patera* (Milan), Cesena dish (Cesena). (3) Bronze table-ware: jugs with figured handles; skillets with figured handles, figured 'medallions' in the centres of the interiors, or figured designs (often enamelled) on the exterior walls; bowls with figured handles. (4) Pewter table-ware with incised designs in 'negative' relief. (5) Votive plaques in silver and bronze. (6) Bronze mounts for articles of furniture, caskets, etc. (7) Bronze box-lids and mirror-cases. (8) Bronze lamps with figured handles, etc. (9) Silver and bronze *phalerae* ('medallions' worn on the person), bronze crowns, armlets, buckles, brooches, etc. with figure work.

(*b*) *Coin- and Medallion-types.* Gold, silver, and bronze: for obverse portraits *cf*. Chapter II; reverse types show single figures, groups of figures, complicated figure scenes, birds and animals, objects, etc., often of high artistic quality and of great interest from the political, social, and religious points of view.

Plate 86

Plate 87

Plate 88

(*c*) *Stucco Work.* (1) Reliefs on walls and ceilings. (2) Figures modelled in the round.

Plate 89

(*d*) *Lead Figured Relief Work.* (1) Sarcophagi and cists, found chiefly in Syria, Palestine, Gaul, and Britain. (2) Caskets and tanks. (3) Sealings.

(*e*) *Miscellaneous Figured Carving.* (1) *Wood:* e.g., Gallo-Roman figures; fifth-century doors of Santa Sabina, Rome. (2) *Ivory:* figurines, caskets, plaques, diptychs (fourth and fifth centuries). (3) *Bone:* figurines, knife-handles, hairpin-heads, plaques, mounts. (4) *Shale:* table-legs, in Britain. (5) *Jet:* figurines, plaques, pendants, knife-handles, hairpin-heads, mainly found in the Rhineland and in Britain.

Plate 90

(*f*) *Figured Carving in Precious Stones.* (1) Cameos, including large pieces with political scenes and imperial portraits, e.g., Blacas Augustus (British Museum), Gemma Augustea (Vienna), Grand Camée de France (Paris), apotheosis of Germanicus (Paris), portraits of Claudius (Windsor Castle and British Museum), triumph of Claudius (The Hague), Claudian imperial group (Vienna), imperial group (Trier). (2) Gems with intaglio designs, including portraits, mythological figures, birds, animals, objects, etc. (3) *Phalerae* with mythological figures, etc.

Plate 91

(*g*) *Glass with Figured Work.* (1) Mould-blown, in relief and in the round. (2) Cut and engraved. (3) Medallions on glass vessels. (4) *Phalerae* with portraits, mythological figures, etc. (5) Cameo glass. (6) Cage-cups (*diatreta*).

(*h*) *Pottery with Figured Relief Work.* (1) First-century BC and AD Italian red-gloss moulded wares. (2) First- and second-century Gaulish red-gloss and black-gloss wares with moulded, *appliqué*, and incised ('negative' relief) decoration. (3) Second- and third-century Gaulish and British wares with *en barbotine* decoration. (4) Fourth- and fifth-century red-gloss wares from

Mediterranean lands with moulded and *appliqué* decoration. (5) Pots from Gaul and Britain with human faces and masks in *appliqué*. (6) Pots in Gaul and Britain in the shape of human heads and animals.

(*i*) *Terracotta and Pipeclay Figurines.*

(*j*) *Miscellaneous Pottery Relief Work.* (1) Cake moulds. (2) Plaques. (3) Antefixes. (4) Lamps.

(*k*) *Figured Textiles from Egypt:* Fifth century AD.

Notes on the Text

CHAPTER I

1 Livy, v, 22; vi, 29.
2 Pliny, *Naturalis Historia*, xxxv, 154.
3 *Ibid.*, xxxiv, 21.
4 *Ibid.*, xxxiv, 32.
5 *Ibid.*, xxxiv, 26.
6 For Roman republican coin types in general, see E. A. Sydenham, *The Roman Republican Coinage*, 1952.
7 Pliny, *op. cit.*, xxxiv, 34.
8 Valerius Maximus, viii, 14, 6.
9 Villa Giulia, Rome: M. H. Swindler, *Ancient Painting*, 1929, fig. 372.
10 Pliny, *op. cit.*, xxxv, 22.
11 *Ibid.*, xxxv, 135.
12 Diodorus Siculus, xxxi, 18, 2.
13 *Op. cit.*, xxxv, 110.
14 National Museum, Naples: B. Andreae, *Das Alexandermosaik*, 1959.
15 Torlonia Museum, Rome: M. Pallottino, *Etruscan Painting*, 1952, pp. 115–24.
16 Ehemals Staatliche Museen, Berlin: I. S. Ryberg, *Rites of the State Religion in Rome*, 1955, pp. 20–22, plate 6, fig. 13.
17 New Capitoline Museum, Rome: D. Mustilli, *Il Museo Mussolini*, 1939, pp. 15–16, plate 12.
18 G. Becatti, *L'arte romana*, 1962, plates 4–5.
19 Delphi Museum: *Fouilles de Delphes*, iv, 1927, pp. 40–41, plate 78.
20 National Museum, Budapest: A. Hekler, *Die Sammlung antiken Skulpturen in Budapest*, 1929, pp. 100–2, no. 92.
21 Palazzo dei Conservatori (Braccio Nuovo), Rome: A. Andrén, *Architectural Terracottas from Etrusco-Italic Temples*, 1940, pp. 350–60, plates 110–12.
22 J. Babelon, *Le portrait dans l'antiquité d'après les monnaies*, 1942, plates 4–10; *Journal of Roman Studies*, xlv, 1955, plates 6–7.
23 Billienus: *Délos*, v, 1912, pp. 41–45, fig. 60–61; Ferus: *Délos*, xiii,

1932, p. 21, fig. 13; unknown Italian (now in the National Museum, Athens): *ibid.*, pp. 17–22, plates 14–19. For artists at work on Delos in general, see W. A. Laidlaw, *A History of Delos*, 1933, pp. 288–9; W. F. Ferguson, *Hellenistic Athens*, 1911, pp. 409–12; P. Roussel, *Délos, colonie athénienne*, 1916, pp. 287–9.

24 *Op. cit.*, xxxiv, 30.

25 Archaeological Museum, Florence: R. West, *Römische Porträt-Plastik*, i, 1933, plates 8, no. 24; 9, no. 25.

26 vi, 53.

27 *Op. cit.*, xxxv, 6.

28 Although *imagines* carried at funerals were in origin an aristocratic preserve, there are passages in Latin literature which indicate that by the first century BC some leading plebeian families had also acquired the right—unofficially, perhaps.

29 These references, covering the history of Roman art from the sixth century BC to *c.* 30 BC are collected and discussed by O. Vessberg in *Studien zur Kunstgeschichte der römischen Republik*, 1941, pp. 5–114.

30 *Cf.* G. C. Picard, *L'art romain*, 1962.

CHAPTER II

1 A. Hekler, *Greek and Roman Portraits*, 1912, plate 127a.

2 We must leave out of account here the highly problematic bronze head in the Palazzo dei Conservatori in Rome, the so-called 'Brutus', which has been variously assigned to the late fourth, third, second, and early first centuries BC, while other scholars see in it a sixteenth-century artist's conception of a Roman republican notable.

3 B. Schweitzer, *Die Bildniskunst der römischen Republik*, 1948, fig. 89, 96. See also this work for the coin portraits of the first century BC.

4 *Ibid.*, fig. 85–86, 91.

5 *Ibid.*, fig. 117, 124–5.

6 *Ibid.*, fig. 146.

7 *Ibid.*, fig. 147.

8 E.g., Vessberg, *op. cit.*, plates 6, no. 1–4; 7, no. 4–5.

9 Schweitzer, *op. cit.*, fig. 161.

10 J. Charbonneaux, *L'art au siècle d'Auguste*, 1948, plate 52.

11 Hekler, *op. cit.*, plates 167–8.

12 Charbonneaux, *op. cit.*, plates 50–51, 73; H. Kähler, *Die Augustus‚ statue von Prima Porta*, 1959.

13 L. Polacco, *Il volto di Tiberio*, 1955.

14 G. Lippold, *Die Skulpturen des vaticanischen Museums*, iii, 1, 1936, no. 550, plates 40–41.

15 Museo Nazionale Romano delle Terme: H. P. L'Orange, *Apotheosis in Ancient Portraiture*, 1947, p. 56, fig. 31.

16 *Ibid.*, p. 57, fig. 32; *cf.* note on plate 8.

17 B. M. Felletti Maj, *Museo Nazionale Romano: i ritratti*, 1953, p. 79, no. 141.

18 E.g., statue in the Vatican: P. Ducati, *L'arte in Roma*, 1938, plate 104, fig. 2.

19 *Ibid.*, plate 105, fig. 1.

20 E.g., bust in the Vatican: *ibid.*, plate 129, fig. 1.

21 E.g., bust in the Museo Nazionale Romano delle Terme: B. M. Felletti Maj, *Museo Nazionale Romano: i ritratti*, 1953, pp. 52–53, no. 82.

22 Archaeological Museum, Madrid: P. Arnt, *Photographische Einzelauf‚ nahmen antike Sculpturen*, no. 1765–70. For Livia's iconography in general, see W. H. Gross, *Iulia Augusta: Untersuchungen zur Grund‚ legung einer Livia‚Ikonographie*, 1962.

23 E.g., the basalt head in the Louvre identified by some as Octavia, by others as Livia: *Cambridge Ancient History*, vol. of plates iv, 1934, plate 166a.

24 For Julio‚Claudian female hair‚styles, see R. West, *Römische Porträt‚ Plastik*, i, 1933, plates 44, 46, 59–60.

25 For Flavian female hair‚style, see L. Goldschneider, *Roman Portraits*, 1940, plate 46; Ducati, *op. cit.*, plate 107, fig. 1: for Trajanic female hair‚styles, see M. Wegner, *Hadrian, etc.*, 1956, plates 38–40; 41b; 42.

26 Wegner, *op. cit.*, plates 41a; 43–47.

27 For Hadrianic and Antonine portraits, male and female, see Wegner, *op. cit.*, and *Die Herrscherbildnisse in antoninischer Zeit*, 1939.

28 E.g., L'Orange, *op. cit.*, p. 76, fig. 50.

29 J. J. Bernoulli, *Römische Ikonographie*, ii, 3, 1894, plates 15–19.

30 For third‚century portraits, male and female, see B. M. Felletti Maj, *Iconografia romana imperiale da Severo Alessandro a M. Aurelio Carino (222–285 d.c.)*, 1958.

31 Bernoulli, *op. cit.*, plates 20a, b; *cf.* note on plate 18.

32 *Cambridge Ancient History*, vol. of plates v, 1939, plate 114a; E. Harrison, *The Athenian Agora i: Portrait Sculpture*, 1953, pp. 88, note 1; 97, note 44.

33 H. P. L'Orange, *Studien zur Geschichte des spätantiken Porträts*, 1933, plates 32–35, 42.

34 For fourth- and fifth-century portraiture in general, male and female, see *ibid.* and R. Delbrueck, *Spätantike Kaiserporträts*, 1933.

35 M. F. Squarciapino, *La Scuola di Afrodisia*, 1943, plates P, 23, 25.

36 For some of the remarkable new portraits of late-antique and earlier imperial times recently brought to light at Aphrodisias, see *Illustrated London News*, 5 January, 1963; 21 December, 1963; 28 December, 1963; 27 February, 1965.

37 E. Rosenbaum, *Roman Portraits from Asia Minor*, 1965.

38 For portrait sculpture of the Roman age in mainland Greece, see, for instance, Harrison, *op. cit.*, and the references there cited.

39 L'Orange, *op. cit.*, plates 221, 223.

40 *Ibid.*, plates 216–18.

CHAPTER III

1 For examples from Gaul and Roman Germany, see O. Brogan, *Roman Gaul*, 1953, fig. 46a; H. Schoppa, *Die Kunst der Römerzeit in Gallien, Germanien und Britannien*, 1957, plates 68, 91; M. Pobé and J. Roubier, *The Art of Roman Gaul*, 1961, plate 159: for examples from Britain, see J. M. C. Toynbee, *Art in Roman Britain*, 1963, plates 13–19, 21–24, 27, 29, 36–37: for examples from Roman Africa, see G. C. Picard, *Les religions de l'Afrique antique*, 1954, plates 3–4, 8.

2 E.g., Toynbee, *op. cit.*, pp. 143–5, no. 38, plate 43.

3 E.g., bronze and stone figures in the British Museum (no. 36062, 51100, 36051).

4 P. Merlat, *Répertoire des inscriptions et monuments figurés du culte de Jupiter Dolichenus*, 1951; *Jupiter Dolichenus: essai d'interprétation et de synthèse*, 1960.

5 For Mithraism and its art in general, see M. J. Vermaseren, *Corpus Inscriptionum et Monumentorum Religionis Mithriacae*, i, 1956, ii, 1960; *Mithras, the Secret God*, 1963.

6 For examples, see Pobé and Roubier, *op. cit.*, plates 172, 180, 184–5, 190; Toynbee, *op. cit.*, frontispiece, plates 44–48.

7 New Capitoline Museum, Rome: D. Mustilli, *Il Museo Mussolini*, 1939, pp. 10–11, plate 13. A comparable mythological group from Arles in southern Gaul, a work of remarkable feeling and power, probably shows Medea about to slay her children: Schoppa, *op. cit.*, plate 108.

8 *Cambridge Ancient History*, vol. of plates iii, 1930, plate 120c.

9 P. Ducati, *L'arte in Roma*, 1938, plate 127.

10 E. Strong, *Art in Ancient Rome*, 1929, ii, fig. 352–3, 355.

11 Capitoline Museum, Rome: M. Squarciapino, *La scuola di Afrodisia*, 1943, plates 6–7. *Cf.* A. W. Lawrence, *Later Greek Sculpture*, 1927, p. 113.

12 *Mittheilungen des Kaiserlichen Deutschen Archäologischen Instituts: Athenische Abteilung*, xiv, 1889, pp. 160–9, plate 5.

13 *Hesperia*, xix, 1950, pp. 103–9, plates 61–71.

14 *Studies Presented to David Moore Robinson*, i, 1951, pp. 705–12, plates 75–80.

15 *Jahrbuch für Antike und Christentum*, i, 1958, pp. 20–51, plates 1–5.

16 M. Wegner, *Die Herrscherbildnisse in antoninischer Zeit*, 1939, pp. 190–1, plates 22–23.

17 *Fasti Archaeologici*, iv, 1951, no. 3344, fig. 53.

18 Vatican Museum (Sala degli Animali): W. Amelung, *Die Skulp-turen des Vatikanischen Museums*, ii, 1908, no. 116, plate 31; British Museum: A. H. Smith, *Catalogue of Sculpture in the Department of Greek and Roman Antiquities in the British Museum*, iii, 1904, no. 2131; Photo Mansell no. 1250.

19 National Museum, Naples: Photo Alinari Napoli no. 34193.

20 National Museum, Athens: Photo B. Ashmole.

21 Historical Museum, Berne: W. Lamb, *Greek and Roman Bronzes*, 1929, plate 92.

22 Historical Museum, Berne: Pobé and Roubier, *op. cit.*, plate 195.

23 Lydney Park, Gloucestershire: R. E. M. and T. V. Wheeler, *Report on the Excavation of the Prehistoric, Roman, and Post-Roman Site in Lydney Park, Gloucestershire*, 1932, plate 25.

24 Stratfield Saye House, Hampshire: Toynbee, *op. cit.*, p. 150, no. 60, plate 61.

The Art of the Romans

CHAPTER IV

1 Palazzo dei Conservatori (Braccio Nuovo), Rome: *Mélanges d'Archéo-logie et d'Histoire*, lxxi, 1959, pp. 263–79, plate 1; D. E. Strong, *Roman Imperial Sculpture*, 1961, plates 17–18.

2 *Ibid.*, plates 22–23.

3 *Arti Figurative*, i, 1945, pp. 181–96.

4 Antiquario Forense, Rome: *Bollettino d'Arte*, xxxv, 1950, pp. 289–294; *Opuscula Romana*, iii, 1961, pp. 139–55; *Rivista dell' Istituto Nazionale d'Archeologia e Storia dell' Arte,* xix, 1961, pp. 55–78.

5 D. E. Strong, *op. cit.*, plate 37.

6 From the abundant literature of the Ara Pacis Augustae the following items may be cited: G. Moretti, *Ara Pacis Augustae*, 1948; J. M. C. Toynbee, *The Ara Pacis Reconsidered and Historical Art in Roman Italy,* 1953; T. Kraus, *Die Ranken der Ara Pacis,* 1953; K. Hanell, 'Das Opfer des Augustus an der Ara Pacis' (*Opuscula Romana*, ii, 1960, pp. 33–120). The sculptured remains of the Ara Pacis have been removed from their original site and from the museums of Italy and re-erected in their original order on a reconstruction of the altar put up some distance to the north of its find-spot.

7 Tacitus, *Historiae*, iv, 53.

8 Vatican Museum: D. E. Strong, *op. cit.*, plate 51.

9 Pergamon: H. Kähler, *Pergamon*, 1949, plate 40; Orange: D. E. Strong, *op. cit.*, plate 54: for the reliefs as a whole, see R. Amy, etc., *L'arc d'Orange*, 1962.

10 *Mélanges d'Archéologie et d'Histoire*, lvi, 1939, pp. 81–120; D. E. Strong, *op. cit.*, plates 47–49.

11 *Ibid.*, plate 46; H. Kähler, *Rome and her Empire* ('Art of the World' Series), 1963, plates on pp. 93, 95.

12 D. E. Strong, *op. cit.*, plates 59–60.

13 Vatican Museum: F. Magi, *I rilievi flavi del Palazzo della Cancelleria*, 1945; J. M. C. Toynbee, *The Flavian Reliefs from the Palazzo della Cancelleria in Rome*, 1957.

14 P. H. von Blanckenhagen, *Flavische Architektur und ihre Dekoration*, 1940, pp. 116–33, plates 38–42.

15 D. E. Strong, *op. cit.*, plate 52.

16 C. Cichorius, *Die Reliefs der Trajanssäule*, 1896–1900; K. Lehmann-Hartleben, *Die Trajanssäule*, 1926; I. A. Richmond, 'Trajan's Army

on Trajan's Column' (*Papers of the British School at Rome*, xiii, 1935, pp. 1–40); P. Romanelli, *La colonna Traiana*, 1942; G. Becatti, *La colonna coclide istoriata*, 1960.

17 For examples, see *Altertümer von Pergamon*, iii, 2, 1910, plate 34, fig. 1; K. Weitzmann, *Illustrations in Roll and Codex*, 1947, fig. 6–7, 11–12, 13a, b.

18 E.g., a relief from the Flavian funerary monument of the Haterii in the Lateran Museum: E. Strong, *La scultura romana*, i, 1923, fig. 83.

19 E.g., the Neronian column at Mainz: *Germania Romana*, 2nd ed., iv, 1928, plates 1–5.

20 M. Pallottino, *Il grande fregio di Traiano*, 1938.

21 C. Pietrangeli, *L'arco di Traiano a Benevento* (Documento fotografico Athenaeum), 1943. For the sculptured panels on the great trophy of Trajan at Adamklissi in Rumania, dedicated in AD 109, see F. B. Florescu, *Monumentul de la Adamklissi: Tropaeum Traiani*, 1960. These reliefs show scenes from the Dacian wars and are very crudely carved, perhaps by army craftsmen of provincial origin.

22 In the Curia (Senate House): *Mélanges d'Archéologie et d'Histoire*, xliv, 1927, pp. 154–83; *Memoirs of the American Academy in Rome*, xxi, 1953, pp. 127–83.

23 E. Stong, *op. cit.*, ii, 1926, fig. 125.

24 *Ibid.*, fig. 122, 126–7.

25 *Ibid.*, fig. 131–8.

26 *Kunstgeschichte in Bildern i; das Altertum 13: Römische Skulptur*, new ed., p. 416, fig. 1–6; *Mitteilungen des Deutschen Archäologischen Instituts: Römische Abteilung*, xlviii, 1933, pp. 309–10, plate 50.

27 E. Strong, *op. cit.*, ii, 1926, plate 50.

28 J. M. C. Toynbee, *The Hadrianic School*, 1934, plates 34–35.

29 D. E. Strong, *op. cit.*, plate 91.

30 *Ibid.*, plate 92.

31 E. Strong, *op. cit.*, ii, 1926, fig. 153–63.

32 A. von Domaszewski, E. Petersen, and G. Calderini, *Die Marcus-Säule*, 1896; P. Romanelli, *La colonna Antonina*, 1942; J. Morris, 'The Dating of the Column of Marcus Aurelius' (*Journal of the Warburg and Courtauld Institutes*, xv, 1952, pp. 33–47); C. Caprino, etc., *La colonna di Marco Aurelio*, 1955; G. Becatti, *La colonna di Marco Aurelio* 1957.

33 E. Nash, *Pictorial Dictionary of Ancient Rome*, i, 1961, pp. 126–30. These reliefs have never as yet been published *in extenso*.

34 III, 9, 12.

35 D. E. Strong, *op. cit.*, plate 111.

36 D. E. L. Haynes and P. E. D. Hirst, *Porta Argentariorum*, 1939; M. Pallottino, *L'arco degli argentari*, 1946.

37 *Africa Italiana*, iv, 1931, pp. 32–152; *Journal of Roman Studies*, xxxviii, 1948, pp. 72–80.

38 M. Squarciapino, *La scuola di Afrodisia*, 1943, pp. 80–96.

39 Nash, *op. cit.*, pp. 115–17.

40 *Ibid.*, pp. 120–5.

41 The inscribed formula on the piece with the two fragmentary figures, VOTIS X ET XX, is found on coins of Gallienus.

42 E. Strong, *op. cit.*, ii, 1926, plates 65–66.

43 K. F. Kinch, *L'arc de triomphe de Salonique*, 1890; Kähler, *op. cit.*, plate on p. 183; D. E. Strong, *op. cit.*, plates 134–5.

44 H. P. L'Orange and A. von Gerkan, *Der spätantike Bildschmuck des Konstantinsbogens*, 1939; A. Giuliano, *L'arco di Costantino*, 1955.

45 G. Bruns, *Obelisk und seine Basis auf dem Hippodrom zu Konstantinopel*, 1935.

46 *Archaeologia*, lxxii, 1922, pp. 87–104, plates 15–23.

CHAPTER V

1 *Cambridge Ancient History*, vol. of plates iv, 1934, plate 80a.

2 E. Strong, *La scultura romana*, i, 1923, plates 13–15; ii, 1926, fig. 149–150.

3 *Ibid.*, ii, 1926, plates 42–43.

4 *Ibid.*, i, 1923, fig. 49–51.

5 Villa Torlonia, Avezzano: D. E. Strong, *Roman Imperial Sculpture*, 1961, plate 50.

6 Palazzo dei Conservatori, Rome: E. Strong, *op. cit.*, i, 1923, fig. 33–34; Lateran Museum, Rome: *ibid.*, fig. 36–37; Uffizi Gallery, Florence: *ibid.*, fig. 35.

7 Bardo Museum, Tunis: P. Poinssot, *L'autel de la Gens Augusta à Carthage*, 1929.

8 J. M. C. Toynbee, *The Hadrianic School*, 1934, pp. 231–4, plate 57.

9 E. Strong, *op. cit.*, ii, 1926, plate 44.

10 *Bollettino della Commissione Archeologica Comunale di Roma*, lxiii, 1935 (1936), plates 2, 4 between pp. 159 and 165.

11 For examples, see the bibliography cited in note 5 to Chapter III.

12 E.g., *Cambridge Ancient History*, vol. of plates v, 1939, plate 120; D. M. Robinson and Hoyningen Heune, *Baalbek and Palmyra*, 1946, plates 118–19.

13 E.g., G. I. Kazarow, *Die Denkmäler des thrakischen Reitergottes in Bulgarien*, 1938.

14 H. Schoppa, *Die Kunst der Römerzeit in Gallien, Germanien und Britannien*, 1957, plates 74, 82–83, 90, 109.

15 For temple pediments under the Empire in general, see P. Hommel, *Studien zu den römischen Figurengiebeln der Kaiserzeit*, 1954.

16 H. Mattingly, *Coins of the Roman Empire in the British Museum*, ii, 1930, plate 29, no. 5–6.

17 F. Fremersdorf, *Die Denkmäler des römischen Köln*, ii, 1950, plate 10.

18 Roman Baths Museum, Bath: J. M. C. Toynbee, *Art in Roman Britain*, 1963, pp. 161–4, no. 90–91, plate 96.

19 E. von Mercklin, *Antike Figuralkapitelle*, 1962.

20 *Ibid.*, fig. 737–58.

21 Corinium Museum, Cirencester: Toynbee, *op. cit.*, plates 97–100.

22 *Germania Romana*, 2nd ed., part iv, 1928, plates 1–12.

23 E. Strong, *op. cit.*, i, 1923, fig. 27.

24 *Ibid.*, fig. 29.

25 J. M. C. Toynbee, *The Hadrianic School*, 1934, plate 44, fig. 2.

26 E. Strong, *op. cit.*, i, 1923, fig. 76.

27 P. H. von Blanckenhage, *Flavische Architektur und ihre Dekoration*, 1940, plate 36, fig. 97–98.

28 *Ibid.*, plate 29, fig. 80; 34, fig. 94. For 'peopled scrolls' in general, see *Papers of the British School at Rome*, xviii, 1950, pp. 1–43, plates 1–26.

CHAPTER VI

1 *Germania Romana*, 2nd ed., part iii, 1926, plates 26, fig. 1–2.

2 *Ibid.*, plates 34, fig. 1–2; 37, fig. 2–5; H. Dragendorff and E. Krüger, *Das Grabmal von Igel*, 1924.

3 *Germania Romana*, 2nd ed., part iii, 1926, plates 38–40.

4 M. Rostovtzeff, *The Social and Economic History of the Roman Empire*, 2nd ed., 1957, p. 32, plate 4.

5 *Mitteilungen des Deutschen Archäologischen Instituts: Römische Abteilung*, lii, 1937, pp. 1–43, plates 1–13.

6 *Monumenti Antichi*, xix, 1908, pp. 540–614.

7 E. Strong, *La scultura romana*, i, 1923, fig. 83.

8 E. Strong, *Art in Ancient Rome*, 1929, i, fig. 207–11.

9 J. M. C. Toynbee and J. B. Ward Perkins, *The Shrine of St Peter and the Vatican Excavations*, 1956.

10 G. Calza, *La necropoli del porto di Roma nell' Isola Sacra*, 1940.

11 Rostovtzeff, *op. cit.*, p. 218, plate 38 (Sens); p. 217, plate 37 (Sens and Arlon).

12 J. Klemenc, *Rimske Izkopanine v Šempetru*, 1961.

13 *Illustrated London News*, 22 January, 1955, pp. 138–42; 29 January, 1955, pp. 182–5.

14 E. Strong, *La scultura romana*, i, 1923, fig. 39.

15 *Ibid.*, fig. 79.

16 *Le Arti*, iv, 1, 1941, pp. 163–9, plates 51–52, fig. 4–6.

17 G. Brusin, *Il Reale Museo Archeologico di Aquileia*, 1936, fig. 88.

18 *Ibid.*, fig. 32–33, 42.

19 J. M. C. Toynbee, *The Hadrianic School*, 1934, plate 49, fig. 3–4.

20 Hamdy Bey and T. Reinach, *Une nécropole royale à Sidon*, 1892.

21 R. Herbig, *Die jüngeretruskischen Steinsarkophage*, 1952.

22 E. Nash, *Pictorial Dictionary of Ancient Rome*, ii, 1962, p. 355, fig. 1131.

23 G. Rodenwaldt, *Der Sakophag Caffarelli*, 1925.

24 E. Strong, *La scultura romana*, i, 1923, fig. 83; D. E. Strong, *Roman Imperial Sculpture*, 1961, plate 66.

25 Ed. H. Stuart Jones, *The Sculptures of the Museo Capitolino*, 1912, plate 23, no. 65.

26 E. Strong, *op. cit.*, plate 23.

27 F. Cumont, *Recherches sur le symbolisme funéraire des Romains*, 1942, plate 41, fig. 3.

28 *Ibid.*, p. 401, fig. 80.

29 W. Amelung, *Die Sculpturen des Vatikanischen Museums*, ii, 1908, plate 1, no. 1. *Cf.* a relief of the same period in the Museo Nazionale Romano, Aula vi, no. 115174.

30 Cumont, *op. cit.*, plate 41, fig 1.

31 *Journal of Roman Studies*, xviii, 1928, pp. 215–16, plates 24–25.

32 J. M. C. Toynbee, *The Hadrianic School*, 1934, plate 43, fig. 1.

33 *Ibid.*, plate 37, fig 1–2.

34 E.g., *ibid.*, plates 37, fig. 3–4; 38, fig. 1–2; 39, fig. 2–3; 40, fig. 1–4; 42, fig. 1–4.

35 E.g., E. Strong, *op. cit.*, ii, 1926, plate 52.

36 P. G. Hamberg, *Studies in Roman Imperial Art*, 1945, plates 39 (Palermo: Museo Nazionale); 41 (Rome: Galleria Borghese).

37 *Ibid.*, plate 40.

38 *Ibid.*, plate 44; *Mitteilungen des Deutschen Archäologischen Instituts: Römische Abteilung*, lxiv, 1957, pp. 69–91.

39 Hamberg, *op. cit.*, plate 43.

40 D. E. Strong, *op. cit.*, plate 98.

41 *Ibid.*, plate 119.

42 *Bollettino d'Arte*, xxxix, 1954, pp. 200–20, fig. 1–20 (Acilia); *Atti della Pontificia Accademia*, serie iii: *Memorie*, iv, 2, 1938, pp. 49–85, plates 10–14 (Praetextatus Catacomb).

43 Metropolitan Museum of Art, New York; F. Matz, *Ein römisches Meisterwerk: der Jahreszeitensarkophag Badminton–New York*, 1958.

44 G. M. A. Hanfmann, *The Season Sarcophagus in Dumbarton Oaks*, 1951.

45 E.g., Toynbee, *op. cit.*, plate 51, fig. 2.

46 E.g., examples in the courtyard of the Salonika Museum.

47 E.g., examples at Eleusis and Delphi.

48 Toynbee, *op. cit.*, plates 51, fig. 1; 52, fig. 1–3; 53, fig. 3.

49 *Journal of Roman Studies*, xlvi, 1956, pp. 10–16, plates 1–3.

50 For Attic *Kline* (couch-) sarcophagi in general, see *Jahrbuch des Deutschen Archäologischen Instituts*, xlv, 1930, pp. 116–89.

51 For Asiatic sarcophagi in general, see C. R. Morey, *The Sarcophagus of Claudia Antonia Sabina and the Asiatic Sarcophagi* (= *Sardis*, v, i), 1924.

52 *Ibid.*, fig. 3–14.

53 *Ibid.*, fig. 61–64 (Selefkeh); 65–67 (Sidamara).

54 *Ibid.*, fig. 72–74 (Athens, National Museum); fig. 75–77 (Rome, Palazzo Borghese: from Torrenuova).

55 *Ibid.*, fig. 56–57, 83–89.

56 *Ibid.*, fig. 39–41.

57 *Ibid.*, fig. 99 (Florence); *Rivista dell' Istituto Nazionale d'Archeologia e Storia d'Arte*, n.s. vii, 1958, pp. 129–214; B. Andreae, *Studien zur römischen Grabkunst*, 1963, plates 1–29 (Velletri); *Illustrated London News*, 6 April, 1963, pp. 500–1 (Via Cassia).

58 J. B. Ward Perkins, *Roman Garland Sarcophagi from the Quarries of Proconnesus (Marmara) (Smithsonian Report for 1957)*, 1958.

59 M. Gough, *The Early Christians*, 1961.

60 For Christian sarcophagi in general, see J. Wilpert, *I sarcofagi cristiani antichi*, 1929–36.

61 F. Gerke, *Die christlichen Sarkophage des vorkonstantinischen Zeit*, 1940.

62 M. Lawrence, *The Sarcophagi of Ravenna*, 1945.

CHAPTER VII

1 M. H. Swindler, *Ancient Painting*, 1929, fig. 525–6.

2 *Ibid.*, fig. 527.

3 E. Nash, *Pictorial Dictionary of Ancient Rome*, i, 1961, p. 329; G. E. Rizzo, *Le pitture della 'Casa dei Grifi'*, 1936.

4 L. Curtius, *Die Wandmalerei Pompejis*, 1929, fig. 54.

5 A. Maiuri, *La Villa dei Misteri*, 1931; M. Bieber, *Jahrbuch des Deutschen Archäologischen Instituts*, xliii, 1928 (1929), pp. 298–330; J. M. C. Toynbee, *Journal of Roman Studies*, xix, 1929, pp. 67–87; G. Zuntz, *Proceedings of the British Academy*, xlix, 1963 (1964), pp. 177–201.

6 M. M. Gabriel, *Livia's Garden Room at Prima Porta*, 1955.

7 P. W. Lehmann, *Roman Wall Paintings from Boscoreale in the Metropolitan Museum of Art*, 1953.

8 Vitruvius, *De Architectura*, v, 6, 8; vii, 5, 2.

9 K. Woermann, *Die antiken Odyseelandschaften*, 1876; P. H. von Blanckenhagen, *Mitteilungen des Deutschen Archäologischen Instituts: Römische Abteilung*, lxx, 1963, pp. 100–46; A. Gallina, *Le pitture con paesaggi dell' Odissea dall' Esquilino*, 1964.

10 Curtius, *op. cit.*, fig. 54.

11 E. Brizio, *Pitture e sepolcri scoperti sull' Esquilino*, 1874; M. Borda, *Capitolium*, xxxiv, 1959.

12 A. Frova, *L'arte di Roma e del mondo romano*, 1961, p. 387, fig. 357.

13 Curtius, *op. cit.*, fig. 62.

14 *Ibid.*, fig. 65.

15 W. Technau, *Die Kunst der Römer*, 1940, p. 140, fig. 110.

16 *Ibid.*, p. 141, fig. 111; H. Kähler, *Rome and her Empire* ('Art of the World' series), 1963, plate on p. 84.

17 *De Architectura*, vii, 5, 3–4.

18 C. M. Dawson, *Romano-Campanian Mythological Landscape Painting*, 1944.

19 *Ibid.*, plate 22, no. 59.

20 *Ibid.*, plate 6, no. 18.

21 Curtius, *op. cit.*, fig. 213.

22 Dawson, *op. cit.*, plate 14, no. 39.

23 G. M. A. Richter, *Scriti in onore di Bartolomeo Nogara*, 1937, pp. 381–8.

24 Technau, *op. cit.*, p. 145, fig. 114; Kähler, *op. cit.*, plate on p. 109. For a quite extravagantly elaborate version of one of these lateral architec- tural vistas, see *ibid.*, plate on p. 111.

25 M. Borda, *La pittura romana*, 1958, plate 5 and figures on p. 227.

26 G. E. Rizzo, *La pittura ellenistico-romana*, 1929, plate 25; Borda, *op. cit.*, plate 6.

27 *Ibid.*, figure on p. 221; G. Lugli, *La zona archeologica di Roma*, 1931, fig. 70.

28 Borda, *op. cit.*, figures on pp. 223–5.

29 Nash, *op. cit.*, i, 1961, pp. 343–5.

30 J. M. C. Toynbee and J. B. Ward Perkins, *The Shrine of St Peter and the Vatican Excavations*, 1956, plates 3, 5–6.

31 E.g., Borda, *op. cit.*, figures on pp. 124, 127, 129, 132–6, 138.

32 *Ibid.*, plate 9 and figure on p. 130.

33 *Ibid.*, figure on p. 131; J. Carcopino, *De Pythagore aux Apôtres*, 1956, plates 11, 13–14.

34 A. Ferrua, *Le pitture della nuova catacomba di Via Latina*, 1960, plates 23, 28, 37, 85, 105, 109, 115.

35 Borda, *op. cit.*, figures on pp. 126, 331.

36 *Ibid.*, figure on p. 366.

37 S. Aurigemma, *Tripolitania*, i, 2: *Le pitture d'età romana*, 1962, pp. 95–98, plates 84–90.

38 *Illustrated London News*, 21 April, 1934, pp. 598–9, fig. 6–7; S. Gabra and E. Drioton, *Peintures à fresque et scènes peintes à Hermoupolis-Ouest* (Service des Antiquités de l'Égypte), 1954, plates 15–17.

39 A. Frova, *Pittura romana in Bulgaria*, 1943.

40 F. Wirth, *Römische Wandmalerei*, 1934, plates 17, 21. Attempts have been made to date the Villa of the Quintilii landscape, despite its find-spot, to the first century AD.

41 For an excellent general account of Ostian wall paintings, see R. Meiggs, *Roman Ostia*, 1960, pp. 436–46.

42 Borda, *op. cit.*, figures on pp. 105, 108, 112.

43 *Ibid.*, figure on p. 103.

44 *Ibid.*, figures on p. 305.

45 Meiggs, *op. cit.*, plate 29b.

46 Borda, *op. cit.*, figure on p. 111.

47 Meiggs, *op. cit.*, p. 443.

48 Borda, *op. cit.*, p. 21 and figure on p. 320; Nash, *op. cit.*, p. 360, no. 436.

49 Borda, *op. cit.*, figure on p. 120; Nash, *op. cit.*, p. 360, no. 437.

50 Palatine Museum: *ibid.*, p. 338, no. 405.

51 *Monumenti Antichi*, xxxix, 1943, pp. 2–166, plates 3–12.

52 *Archaeologia*, xciii, 1949, p. 181, plates 42–43.

53 Borda, *op. cit.*, figure on p. 365.

54 *Ibid.*, upper figure on p. 364.

55 *Ibid.*, figure on p. 137, plate 23.

56 M. Rostovtzeff, *Caravan Cities*, 1932, plate 33, fig. 1–2.

57 *Ibid.*, plate 34.

58 M. Rostovtzeff, *Dura-Europos and its Art*, 1938, plate 13.

59 Ed. M. Rostovtzeff, etc., *The Excavations at Dura-Europos: Preliminary Report on the Fifth Season of Work, 1931–32*, 1934, pp. 238–88, plates 39–51.

60 C. H. Kraeling, *The Excavations at Dura-Europos: Final Report, viii, 1, the Synagogue*, 1956.

61 M. J. Vermaseren, *Corpus Inscriptionum et Monumentorum Religionis Mithriacae*, i, 1956, no. 42–45, 48–52, fig. 13, 16–24.

62 *Ibid.*, no. 390, fig. 112.

63 *Ibid.*, no. 180–5, 187–97, fig. 50–55, 57–61.

64 *Illustrated London News*, 23 February, 1963, pp. 262–3.

65 Vermaseren, *op. cit.*, no. 480–4, fig. 134–41.

66 Borda, *op. cit.*, plate 7.

67 *Aus der Schatzkammer des antiken Trier*, 1951, pp. 45–51, plates 5–6,

Beilage 1–5; *Historia*, iv, 1955, pp. 131–50; *Archeologia Classica*, x, 1958, pp. 60–63; *Jahrbuch für Numismatik und Geldgeschichte*, x, 1959–1960, pp. 79–90.

68 *Antiquaries Journal*, xxxix, 1959, pp. 17–18, plate 1; J. M. C. Toynbee, *Art in Roman Britain*, 2nd ed., 1963, p. 194, no. 170, plates 196, 198.

CHAPTER VIII

1 National Museum, Naples: *Journal of Roman Studies*, xvi, 1926, pp. 145–54, plate 16.

2 M. Borda, *La pittura romana*, 1958, figure on p. 264.

3 *Die Antike*, xii, 1936, pp. 155–72, plates 10–11.

4 *Ibid.*, p. 162, fig. 6.

5 W. F. Volbach, *Early Christian Art*, 1961, plate 61.

6 C. R. Morey (ed. G. Ferrari), *The Gold-Glass Collection of the Vatican Library*, 1959, no. 1, 3, 5–6, plate 1.

7 *Ibid.*, no. 222, plate 24.

8 *Ibid.*, no. 234, plate 25.

9 *Ibid.*, no. 452, plate 36.

10 For an excellent general survey of painted mummy portraits, see A. F. Shore, *Portrait Painting from Roman Egypt* (British Museum), 1962.

11 E.g., Shore, *op. cit.*, plates 1–2, 6, 8–9, 11–12, 16.

12 E.g., *ibid.*, plate 3.

13 E.g., *ibid.*, plates 4, 17–18.

14 *Ibid.*, plate 19.

15 Stuttgart Museum: Borda, *op. cit.*, figure on plate 218.

16 Girton College, Cambridge: W. M. Flinders Petrie, *Roman Portraits and Memphis* (iv), 1911, plate 13.

17 C. H. Roberts, 'The Codex' (*Proceedings of the British Academy*, 1954, pp. 169–204).

18 R. Bianchi Bandinelli, *Hellenistic-Byzantine Miniatures of the Iliad* (*Ilias Ambrosiana*), 1955, pp. 162–3.

19 H. Degering and A. Boekler, *Die Quedlinburger Itala Fragmente*, 1932; A. W. Byvanck, 'Die Datierung der Berliner Itala' (*Mnemosyne*, ser.

3, vi, 1938, pp. 241–51). Byvanck thinks that the instructions to the miniaturist found on this manuscript (*cf.* p. 134) were written by the writer of the text, who had before him an illustrated codex containing the originals of the Itala pictures. But if he had, why could not the miniaturist have copied such models directly?

20 E. Kitzinger, *Early Medieval Art in the British Museum*, 1940, plate 12 (lower figure).

21 *Fragmenta et picturae Vergiliana Codicis Vaticani Latini 3225*, 3rd ed., 1945; J. de Wit, *Die Miniaturen des Vergilius Vaticanus*, 1959.

22 *Picturae Ornamenta Complura Scripturae Specimina Codicis Vaticani, 3867*, 1902.

23 *Der Kalender vom Jahre 354, etc.*, 1936, pp. 31–36.

24 A. Calderini, A. M. Ceriani, and A. Mai, *Ilias Ambrosiana*, 1953 (facsimile edition in colour); Bianchi Bandinelli, *op. cit.* (see note 18).

25 See note 6.

26 *Burlington Magazine*, June 1953, pp. 180–7, fig. 1–4.

27 Ed. M. Rostovtzeff, *The Excavations at Dura-Europos: Report on the Fourth Season of Work, 1930–31*, 1933, pp. 252–4, plate 7, fig. 4. For a third-century glass bottle of Rhenish manufacture with a chariot race painted in brilliant polychrome on a dark purple-blue ground, see *Aus Rheinischer Kunst und Kultur: Auswahlkatalog des Rheinischen Landesmuseums Bonn*, 1963, p. 99, no. 52, colour plate opposite p. 96.

28 J. Hackin, *Recherches archéologique à Begram*, 1939, pp. 30, 36–42, 119, no. 163, 197, 199, 201–2, 364, fig. 29–36; *Nouvelles recherches archéologiques à Begram*, 1954, pp. 254–9, no. 27, 54, 59–60, fig. 257–269, 369, 371–2; F. Coarelli in *Studi Miscellanei*, i, 1961, plates 13, fig. 1–4; 14, fig. 1–3; 15, fig. 1–2; 16, fig. 1; 17, fig. 2–4; 18, fig. 2, 4.

29 *Bulletin of the Metropolitan Museum of Art, New York*, xxxii, 1937, pp. 176–7, fig. 3–4.

30 *Mitteilungen des Deutschen Archäologischen Instituts: Römische Abteilung*, xliv, 1929, pp. 63–64, fig. 5, plates 12–13.

31 E.g. R. J. Charleston, *Roman Pottery*, 1955, plates 82A, 83B.

32 *Ibid.*, plate 80.

33 *Ibid.*, plate 42A.

34 *Ibid.*, plates 70–75; *Germania Romana*, 2nd ed., v, 1930, plates 29, fig. 5; 30, fig. 1–2.

35 *Trierer Zeitschrift*, i, 1926, pp. 1–17, fig. 3a, 8d–10, plates 1–2.
36 *Ibid.*, p. 8, fig. 8c, plate 3, fig. 3.
37 *Ibid.*, p. 8, fig. 8a, plate 3, fig. 2.
38 *Journal of Roman Studies*, lii, 1962, p. 170, plate 24, fig. 4.
39 R. M. Cook, *Greek Painted Pottery*, 1960, pp. 204–7, 352–3, plate 56A, B.
40 F. Cumont, *Fouilles de Doura-Europos (1922–23)*, 1926, pp. 323–37, plates 109–10; ed. M. Rostovtzeff, *The Excavations at Dura-Europos: Report on the Sixth Season of Work, 1932–33*, 1936, pp. 456–66, frontispiece and plates 25, 25a; *ibid., Report on the Seventh and Eighth Seasons of Work, 1933–34 and 1934–45*, 1939, pp. 326–69, plates 41–46.

CHAPTER IX

1 D. M. Robinson, *Excavations at Olynthus*, ii, 1930, pp. 80–88, fig. 205; v, 1933, plates 1–17; viii, 1938, plates 16, fig. 1–2; 51, fig. 2; 84; 85, fig. 2; 87.
2 *Archaeology*, xi, 1958, pp. 251–3, with figures; xvii, 1964, pp. 78–81, fig. 4–10.
3 *Art Bulletin*, xlii, 1960, pp. 243–62.
4 *Monumenti Antichi*, xxvii, 1921, plates 1, 3–4.
5 *Délos*, xiv, 1933, 'Les mosaïques de la Maison des Masques', plates 1–3, 7–9, fig. 10 on p. 37.
6 M. Rostovtzeff, *The Social and Economic History of the Hellenistic World*, 1941, ii, p. 660, plate 74 (signed by Hephaistion).
7 *Ibid.*, i, p. 254, plate 35 (signed by Sophilos).
8 I. Lavin, 'The Hunting Mosaics of Antioch and their Sources', *Dumbarton Oaks Papers*, xvii, 1963, pp. 181–286, fig. 1–142.
9 See notes 6–7.
10 *Naturalis Historia*, xxxvi, 184; *cf.* E. Pfuhl, *Masterpieces of Greek Drawing and Painting*, 1955, plate 121, fig. 155.
11 *Ibid.*, plates 116–17, fig. 150–1.
12 E.g., M. E. Blake in *Memoirs of the American Academy in Rome*, viii, 1930 (=Blake I); xiii, 1936 (=Blake II); xvii, 1940 (=Blake III) (*passim*); G. Becatti, *Scavi di Ostia: Mosaici e pavimenti marmorei*, 1961 (*passim*).

13 E.g., Gaul: *Inventaire des mosaïques de la Gaul et de l'Afrique: i, Narbonnaise et Aquitaine*, 1909, 1911; *i, 2, Lugdunese, Belgique, et Germanie*, 1909, 1922 (*passim*); H. Stern, *Recueil général des mosaïques de la Gaule: Gaule-Belgique*, i, 1, 1957; i, 2, 1960; i, 3, 1963 (*passim*); Germany: K. Parlasca, *Die römischen Mosaiken in Deutschland*, 1959 (*passim*); Switzerland: V. von Gonzenbach, *Die römischen Mosaiken der Schweiz*, 1961 (*passim*); Britain: J. M. C. Toynbee, *Art in Britain under the Romans*, 1964, pp. 232–8, plate 56; Spain: J. de C. Serra Ráfols, *La Vida en España en le Época Romana*, 1944, plates 31, 35; Africa: *Inventaire, etc.*: ii, *Tunisie*, 1910, 1913; *Afrique Proconsulaire, Numidie, Maurétaine*, 1911, 1925 (*passim*); S. Aurigemma, *Tripolitania i, 1: I mosaici*, 1960 (*passim*).

14 For a study of these early *emblemata* in general, see Blake I, pp. 125–45.

15 The mosaic *emblemata* mounted on terracotta trays in the Ostia Museum (R. Calza and M. F. Squarciapino, *Museo Ostiense*, 1962, pp. 106–7, 112–13, 121, fig. 55) come from the necropolis at Isola Sacra and could have been affixed to walls, not inset in floors: *cf.* the Death of Pentheus wall-panel mosaic on the outside of the tomb of the Marcii in the Vatican necropolis under St Peter's (J. M. C. Toynbee and J. B. Ward Perkins, *The Shrine of St Peter, etc.*, 1956, plate 19.

16 *See* note 14 to Chapter I.

17 G. Gullini, *I mosaici di Palestrina*, 1956, plate 1.

18 Pfuhl, *op. cit.*, plate 119, fig. 153; *Malerei und Zeichnung der Griechen*, 1923, iii, plate 307, no. 695; E. Rizzo, *La pittura ellenistico-romana*, 1929, plates 184–5.

19 D. Levi, *Antioch Mosaic Pavements*, 1947.

20 Aurigemma, *op. cit.*, plates 83–97, 123–5.

21 R. M. Pidal, *España Romana*, 1935, plate 706, fig. 536.

22 Levi, *op. cit.*, plate 22.

23 Blake I, pp. 121–3, plate 48, fig. 2–3; E. Strong, *Art in Ancient Rome*, 1929, i, p. 65, fig. 55.

24 Becatti, *op. cit.*, plates 122–3.

25 Blake II, pp. 138–71, plates 33–39; R. Meiggs, *Roman Ostia*, 1960, pp. 446–52, plates 24b, 25a, c; Becatti, *op. cit.*, plates 72, 80–101, 105–121, 124–48, 154–68, 170–88.

26 Blake III, pp. 93–98, plates 11, fig. 5; 12, fig. 1; 13, fig. 3; 14, fig. 2;

15, fig. 2–3; 17, fig. 1, 3; 18; Becatti, *op. cit.*, plate 72 ('House of the Gorgons').

27 Blake II, pp. 172–84, plates 40–46.

28 Becatti, *op. cit.*, plates 149–53, 214–16, 223.

29 G. C. Picard, *L'art romain*, 1962, plate 30.

30 See note 19.

31 See note 13.

32 A good selection of these will be found in the work of I. Lavin cited in note 8.

33 Lavin, *op. cit.*, fig. 129–30.

34 Von Gonzenbach, *op. cit.*, plate 49.

35 Aurigemma, *op. cit.*, plates 2–5.

36 Von Gonzenbach, *op. cit.*, plates 34–35.

37 Aurigemma, *op. cit.*, plates 126–59. Parts of both of these pavements are in *opus sectile* (see p. 159).

38 Parlasca, *op. cit.*, plates 31–33.

39 J. M. C. Toynbee, *Art in Roman Britain*, 1963, plate 235.

40 Von Gonzenbach, *op. cit.*, plates 60–63.

41 Parlasca, *op. cit.*, plates 36–39.

42 *Ibid.*, plates 66–79.

43 *Ibid.*, plates 54–55.

44 *Proceedings of the Dorset Natural History and Archaeological Society*, lxxxv, 1964, fig. 2 opposite p. 118; *Journal of Roman Studies*, liv, 1964, pp. 7–14.

45 E.g., Woodchester and Cirencester in Gloucestershire: Toynbee, *op. cit.*, plates 221–2.

46 E.g., G. V. Gentili, *La villa erculia di Piazza Armerina*, 1962; A. Ragona, *Il proprietario della villa romana di Piazza Armerina*, 1962; A. Carandini in *Studi Miscellanei*, 7, 1961–62.

47 G. Brett, W. J. Macaulay, and R. B. K. Stevenson, *The Great Palace of the Byzantine Emperors*, 1947.

48 E.g., Anderson photos: Pompei no. 26447, 24829.

49 Anderson photo: Pompei no. 26395.

50 Alinari photos: Ercolano no. 43125, 43927; E. Kusch, *Herculaneum*, 1960, plates 41–43.

51 Becatti, *op. cit.*, plates 169, no. 269; 219, no. 269.

52 Lateran Museum: *ibid.*, plate 211.

53 *Archaeologia*, xciii, 1949, pp. 179–80, plates 34, 41.

54 O. Perler, *Die Mosaiken der Juliergruft im Vatikan*, 1953.

55 Anderson photos: Roma no. 83–88, 6235, 3256–7.

56 *Madrider Mitteilungen*, ii, 1961, pp. 119–82.

57 E.g., San Lorenzo, Milan (5th cent.); St George, Salonika (4th cent.); Santa Pudenziana, Rome (*c.* 400).

58 E. Nash, *Pictorial Dictionary of Ancient Rome*, i, 1961, p. 301, fig. 357.

59 Becatti, *op. cit.*, plates 204–9, 217, no. 49.

60 Nash, *op. cit.*, pp. 193–5, fig. 216–20.

61 Calza and Squarciapino, *op. cit.*, p. 107, fig. 56.

62 Unpublished.

Select Bibliography

General Art and General Sculpture

E. Strong, *Art in Ancient Rome*, 1929.

P. Ducati, *L'arte in Roma dalle origini al sec. viii*, 1938.

W. Technau, *Die Kunst der Römer*, 1940.

D. Levi, 'L'arte romana' (*Annuario della Scuola Archeologica di Atene*, xxiv–xxvi, 1950, pp. 229–303).

O. Brendel, 'Prolegomena to a Book on Roman Art' (*Memoirs of the American Academy in Rome*, xxi, 1953, pp. 9–73).

B. Sarne (Lübke‑Pernice), *Die Kunst der Römer*, 1958.

A. Frova, *L'arte di Roma e del mondo romano*, 1961.

G. M. A. Hanfmann, *Roman Art*, 1964.

R. E. M. Wheeler, *Roman Art and Architecture*, 1964.

J. Charbonneaux, *L'art au siècle d'Auguste*, 1948.

J. M. C. Toynbee, *The Hadrianic School*, 1934.

E. Strong, *Roman Sculpture*, 1907.

E. Strong, *La scultura romana*, 1923, 1926.

D. E. Strong, *Roman Imperial Sculpture*, 1961.

M. F. Squarciapino, *La scuola di Afrodisia*, 1943.

E. Espérandieu, R. Lantier, *Recueil général des bas‑reliefs, statues et bustes de la Gaule romaine*, 1907–55, with an additional volume on *La Germanie romaine*, 1931.

M. Pobé, J. Roubier, *The Art of Roman Gaul*, 1961.

H. P. Eydoux, *La France antique*, 1962.

H. Schoppa, *Die Kunst der Römerzeit in Gallien, Germanien und Britannien*, 1957.

S. Ferri, *Arte romana sul Reno*, 1931.

S. Ferri, *Arte romana sul Danubio*, 1933.

W. Deonna, *L'art romain en Suisse*, 1943.

Ars Hispaniae, ii, 1947.

The Art of the Romans

J. M. C. Toynbee, *Art in Roman Britain*, 2nd ed., 1963.
J. M. C. Toynbee, *Art in Britain under the Romans*, 1964.

Portraiture

A. N. Zadoks-Josephus Jitta, *Ancestral Portraiture in Rome*, 1932.
O. Vessberg, *Studien zur Kunstgeschichte der römischen Republik*, 1941.
B. Schweitzer, *Die Bildniskunst der römischen Republik*, 1948.
R. West, *Römische Porträt-Plastik*, 1933, 1941.
O. Brendel, *Ikonographie des Kaisers Augustus*, 1931.
W. H. Gross, *Iulia Augusta: Untersuchungen zur Grundlegung einer Livia Ikonographie*, 1962.
L. Polacco, *Il volto di Tiberio*, 1955.
W. H. Gross, *Bildnisse Traians*, 1940.
M. Wegner, *Das römische Herrscherbild: Hadrian, etc.*, 1956.
M. Wegner, *Die Herrscherbildnisse in antoninischer Zeit*, 1939.
B. M. F. Maj, *Iconografia romana imperiale da Severo Alessandro a M. Aurelio Carino*, 1958.
H. P. L'Orange, *Studien zur Geschichte des spätantiken Porträts*, 1933.
R. Delbrueck, *Spätantike Kaiserporträts*, 1933.
H. P. L'Orange, *Apotheosis in Ancient Portraiture*, 1947.
E. Rosenbaum, *Cyrenaican Portrait Sculpture*, 1960.
E. Rosenbaum, *Roman Portraits in Asia Minor*, 1965.

Historical Reliefs

P. G. Hamberg, *Studies in Roman Imperial Sculpture, with special reference to the State Reliefs of the Second Century*, 1945.
I. S. Ryberg, *Rites of the State Religion in Roman Art*, 1955.
(For monographs on individual monuments, see notes to Chapter III.)

Funerary Reliefs

W. Altmann, *Die Grabaltäre der römischen Kaiserzeit*, 1900.
C. Robert, *Die antiken Sarkophag-Reliefs*, 1890–1952.

F. Cumont, *Recherches sur le symbolisme funéraire des Romains*, 1942.
F. Gerke, *Die christlichen Sarcophage der vorkonstantinischen Zeit*, 1940.
K. Lehmann-Hartleben, E. C. Olsen, *Dionysiac Sarcophagi in Baltimore*, 1942
G. M. A. Hanfmann, *The Season Sarcophagus in Dumbarton Oaks*, 1951.
F. Matz, *Ein römisches Meisterwerk: der Jahreszeiten Sarkophag Badminton*, New York, 1958.

Painting

P. Herrmann, *Denkmäler der Malerei des Altertums*, 1904–50.
G. L. Rizzo, *La pittura ellenistico-romana*, 1929.
L. Curtius, *Die Wandmalerei Pompejis*, 1929.
R. P. Hinks, *Catalogue of Greek, Etruscan, and Roman Paintings and Mosaics in the British Museum*, 1933.
G. Wirth, *Römische Wandmalerei*, 1934.
H. G. Beyen, *Die Pompejanische Wanddekoration vom zweiten bis zum vierten Stil*, 1938, 1960.
C. M. Dawson, *Romano-Campanian Mythological Landscape Painting*, 1944.
K. Weitzmann, *Illustrations in Roll and Codex*, 1947.
K. Schefold, *Pompejanische Malerei: Sinn und Ideengeschichte*, 1952.
A. Maiuri, *Roman Painting*, 1953.
O. Elia, *Pitture di Stabia*, 1957.
M. Borda, *La pittura romana*, 1958.
W. J. T. Peters, *Landscape in Romano-Campanian Painting*, 1963.

Mosaics

Hinks, *op. cit.*
M. E. Blake, 'The Pavements of the Roman Buildings of the Republic and Early Empire' (*Memoirs of the American Academy in Rome*, viii, 1930, pp. 9–159, plates 1–50); 'Roman Mosaics of the Second Century in Italy' (*ibid.*, xiii, 1936, pp. 69–214, plates 8–46); 'Mosaics of the Late Empire in Rome and Vicinity' (*ibid.*, xvii, 1940, pp. 81–130, plates 11–34).
(For further bibliography, see notes to Chapter IX.)

Minor Arts

A FIGURED METAL RELIEF WORK

1 Decorated Armour

J. Keim and H. Clumbach, *Der römische Schatzfund von Straubing*, 1951.

J. M. C. Toynbee, *Art in Britain under the Romans*, 1964, pp. 290–300.

2 Silver Table-ware, etc.

H. de Villefosse, 'Le trésor de Boscoreale' (*Monuments Piot*, v, 1899, pp. 7–279, plates 1–36).

E. Pernice, F. Winter, *Der Hildesheimer Silberfund*, 1901.

K. F. Johansen, 'Hoby-Fundet' (*Nordiske Fortidsminder*, ii, 1911–35, pp. 119–64, plates 8–9).

S. Reinach, 'Les Vases d'argent de Cheirisophos en musée de Copen-hagne' (*Gazette des Beaux Arts*, 1923, 2, pp. 129–34, with 2 plates (Hoby Cups).

A. Maiuri, *La casa del Menandro e il suo tesoro di argenteria*, 1933.

E. Babelon, *Le trésor d'argenterie de Berthouville près Bernay*, 1916.

Trésor d'argenterie romaine: Gallerie Charpentier 10 Juin 1958 = Graincourt-les-Havrincourt.

H. B. Walters, *Catalogue of the Silver Plate (Greek, Etruscan, and Roman) in the British Museum*, 1921.

O. M. Dalton, *Catalogue of Early Christian Antiquities in the British Museum*, 1901 (Esquiline Treasure).

J. W. Brailsford, *The Mildenhall Treasure: A Handbook*, 2nd ed., 1955.

A. O. Curle, *The Treasure of Traprain*, 1923.

R. Laur-Belart, *Der spätrömische Silberschatz von Kaiseraugst: Katalog*, 1963.

O. Brendell, 'The Corbridge *Lanx*' (*Journal of Roman Studies*, xxxi, 1941, pp. 100–27).

A. Alföldi, 'Die Silberschale von Parabiago' (*Atlantis*, ii, 1949, pp. 68–73).

P. E. Arias, 'Il piatto argento di Cesena' (*Annuario della Scuola Archeo-logico di Atene*, xxiv–xxvi, 1950, pp. 309–44).

3–9 Bronze Table-ware, etc.

E. Pernice, *Gefässe und Geräte aus Bronze in Pompeji*, 1925.

M. H. P. den Boesterd, *The Bronze Vessels in the Rijksmuseum G. M. Kam at Nijmegen*, 1956.

Toynbee, *op. cit.*, pp. 317–44 (for material from Britain and further references).

B COIN⁄ AND MEDALLION⁄TYPES

E. A. Sydenham, *The Roman Republican Coinage*, 1952.
H. Mattingly *et al.*, *Coins of the Roman Empire in the British Museum*, 1922–1962.
H. Mattingly, E. A. Sydenham, *et al.*, *The Roman Imperial Coinage*, 1923–1949.
K. Regling, *Die antike Münze als Kunstwerk*, 1924.
L. M. Lanckoroński, *Das römische Bildnis in Meisterwerken der Münzkunst*, 1944.
F. Gnecchi, *I medaglioni romani*, 1912.
J. M. C. Toynbee, *Roman Medallions*, 1944.

C STUCCO WORK

1 Reliefs on Walls and Ceilings
2 Figures in the Round
E. L. Wadsworth, 'Stucco Reliefs of the First and Second Centuries still Extant in Rome' (*Memoirs of the American Academy in Rome*, iv, 1924, pp. 9–102, plates 1–49).
E. Rizzo, *Le pitture della 'Casa dei Grifi' (Palatino)*, 1936.
V. Spinazzola, *Pompei alla luce degli scavi nuovi di Via dell' Abbondanza (anni 1910–23)*, ii, 1953, pp. 871–901, fig. 869–900, plates 33–35 ('Casa Omerica').
G. Calza, *La necropoli del Porto di Roma nell' Isola Sacra*, 1940, pp. 108–13, fig. 43–47.
J. M. C. Toynbee and J. B. Ward Perkins, *The Shrine of St Peter, etc.*, 1956, pp. 80–88, plates 12–15, 31.

D LEAD FIGURED RELIEF WORK

1, 2, 3
J. M. C. Toynbee, *Art in Britain under the Romans*, 1964, pp. 345–57 (for material from Britain and further references).

E MISCELLANEOUS FIGURED CARVING

1 Wood

P. Martin, 'Sculptures en bois découvertes aux sources de la Seine' (*Revue Archéologique de l'Est et du Centre-Est*, xiv, 1963, pp. 7–35, plates 1–10).

J. Wiegand, *Das altchristliche Hauptportal an der Kirche der hl. Sabina auf dem aventinischen Hügel in Rom*, 1900.

R. Delbrueck, 'Notes on the Wooden Doors of Santa Sabina' (*Art Bulletin*, xxxiv, 1952, pp. 139–45, fig. 1–9).

J. Darsy, 'Les portes de Sainte-Sabine' (*Rivista di Archeologia Cristiana*, xxxvii, 1961, pp. 5–49).

2 Ivory

J. Natanson, *Early Christian Ivories*, 1953.

R. Delbrueck, *Die Consulardiptychen*, 1929.

J. Kollwitz, *Die Lipsanothek von Brescia*, 1933.

R. Delbrueck, *Probleme der Lipsanothek in Brescia*, 1952.

Toynbee, *op. cit.*, pp. 358–9 (for miscellaneous material from Britain).

3–5 Bone, Shale, Jet

Toynbee, *op. cit.*, pp. 360–71 (for material from Britain and further references).

F FIGURED CARVING IN PRECIOUS STONES

1 Cameos

A. Furtwängler, *Die antiken Gemmen*, 1900.

G. Bruns, *Staatskameen des 4 Jahrhunderts nach Christi Geburt* (*104 Winckelmannsprogramm*), 1948

Journal of Roman Studies, xxix, 1939, plate 16=Windsor Claudius.

British Museum Quarterly, xiii, 3, 1939, pp. 79–81, plate 33b=British Museum Claudius.

H. B. Walters, *Catalogue of the Engraved Gems and Cameos, Greek, Etruscan, and Roman, in the British Museum*, 1926, no. 3577, plate 38=Blacas Augustus.

G. C. Picard, *L'art romain*, 1962, plate 10=Paris Germanicus.

2 Gems

Furtwängler, *op. cit.*

H. B. Walters, *Catalogue of the Engraved Gems and Cameos, Greek, Etruscan, and Roman, in the British Museum,* 1926.

G. M. A. Richter, *Catalogue of Engraved Gems, Greek, Etruscan and Roman, in the Metropolitan Museum of Art, New York,* 1956.

G GLASS
General
A. Kisa, *Das Glas im Altertume,* 1908.

1–4
Toynbee, *op. cit.,* pp. 375–83 (for material from Britain and further references).

Cameo Glass
D. E. L. Haynes, *The Portland Vase,* 1964.

Cage-cups
D. B. Harden and J. M. C. Toynbee, 'The Rothschild Lycurgus Cup' (*Archaeologia,* xcvii, 1959, pp. 179–212, plates 59–75) (and for *diatreta* in general).

H POTTERY
R. J. Charleston, *Roman Pottery,* 1955.
H. B. Walters, *Catalogue of the Roman Pottery in the Department of Antiquities, British Museum,* 1908.
F. Oswald and T. D. Pryce, *An Introduction to the Study of Terra Sigillata,* 1920.
Toynbee, *op. cit.,* pp. 384–415 (for material from British and further references).
A. J. B. Wace, 'Late Roman Pottery and Plate' (*Bulletin de la Société Royale d'Archéologie d'Alexandrie,* xxxvii, 1948, pp. 47–59).
J. W. Salomonson, 'Late-Roman Earthenware with Relief Decoration found in Northern-Africa and Egypt' (*Oudheidkundige Mededelingen uit het Rijksmuseum van Oudheden te Leiden,* xliii, 1962, pp. 53–95, plates 11–32).

J TERRACOTTA AND PIPECLAY FIGURINES
K MISCELLANEOUS POTTERY RELIEF WORK
Toynbee, *op. cit.,* pp. 419–36 (for material from Britain and further references).

THE PLATES

1

2

3a

3b

4

5

6

7

8

9

10

11

12

13

14

15

16

17

18

19

20

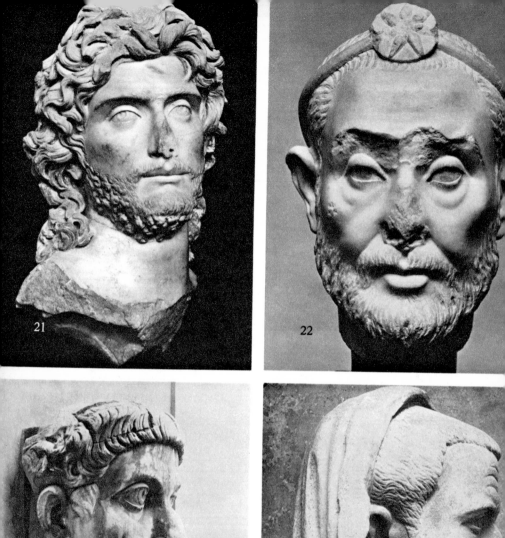

21

22

23

24

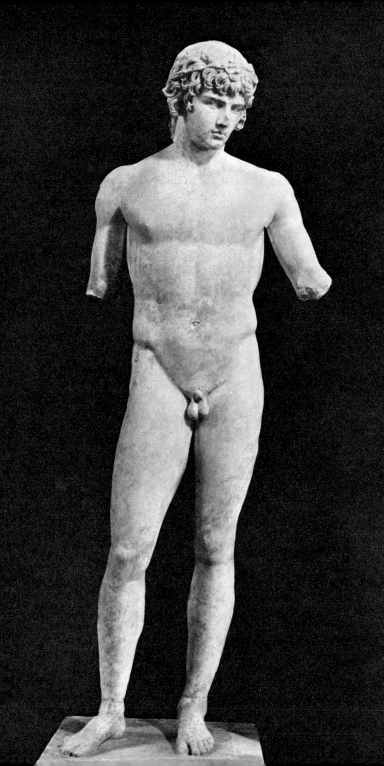

26

27

28

29

30

31

32

DEAL ARTIONI
LICINIA SABINILLA

33

34

35

36

37

38

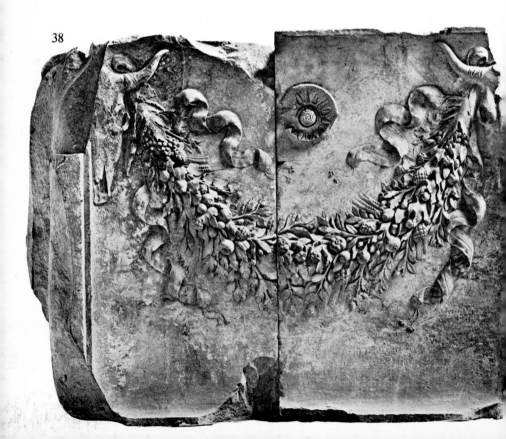

41

42

45

46

47

48

49

50

MATRONIS
AVFANIABVS
QVETTIVS SEVERVS
QVAESTOR C C A A
VOTVM SOLVIT L M
MACRINO ET CELSO CO

51

52

53

54

55

56

57

58

61

62

63

64

65

66

70

74

75

77

78

ΑΓΑΘΗ
ΤΥΧΗ

79

80

84

85

86

87a

87b

91

Notes on the Plates

(Where references to publications of the works illustrated have been already cited in the Notes on the Text, they are not repeated here. All photographs are by courtesy of Museums, Institutes, etc., and private and commercial photo/ graphers.)

1   Part of the marble frieze from the victory monument of Lucius Aemilius Paullus at Delphi, depicting the battle of Pynda (168 BC), in which the Romans defeated the Macedonians under king Perseus. The horseman on the left wears a typical Hellenistic cuirass; and the elaborately decorated, round bronze shields of the Macedonians and the long, oval shields of the Romans are carefully differentiated. The horse turning its head and seen from behind has an almost exact counterpart on a frieze from Lecce in southern Italy. Height of frieze: 54·20 cm. Second century BC. Delphi Museum. See pp. 21–2.

2   Terracotta figure of a seated goddess belonging to a pedimental group found on the Caelian Hill, Rome. The other figures of the group include an armed Mars (?), a standing goddess, a cloaked man, and two sacri/ ficial attendants. Height of figure: 1·46 m. Late second century BC. Palazzo dei Conservatori (Braccio Nuovo), Rome. Photo German Archaeological Institute in Rome. See p. 22.

3   Marble head of an elderly man, probably a priest, in view of his shaven
a,b head and rolled diadem, from the Athenian Agora. Found in a Greek city and undoubtedly the work of a Greek sculptor, this likeness illustrates a strong taste among late Hellenistic artists for that 'veristic' treatment of all facial details which became the hall/mark, partly under Hellenistic influence, of Roman republican portraiture. Height of head: 23 cm. Mid second to mid first century BC. Agora Museum. Photo Agora Excava/ tions, Athens. E. Harrison, *The Athenian Agora i: Portrait Sculpture*, 1953, pp. 12–14, no. 3, plate 3. See p. 30.

4   Marble grave relief from Ostia in the form of a niche with rounded top, showing a husband and wife clasping right hands. The man, who stands

facing the spectator, wears a tunic and a toga and has the hair and beard style of Antoninus Pius: he holds in his left hand the scroll of destiny or of his will. The woman, who stands with her legs crossed and turns her head towards her husband, rests her left hand on his right shoulder and holds a pomegranate, emblem of immortality: she wears a long tunic and a mantle and has the hair style of Faustina I. Both have distinctly portrait like features. Total height of relief: 1·30 m. AD 138–161. Ostia Museum. Photo Gabinetto Fotografico Nazionale, Rome. R. Calza and M. F. Squarciapino, *Museo Ostiense*, 1962, p. 68, no. 1. See p. 29.

5 Marble bust of an elderly man with hard, rugged features. The find spot is unknown. The surface of the face has been cleaned and slightly worked over. The shape of the bust suggests that this is a first century AD copy of a republican 'veristic' portrait of the middle of the first century BC. Height of bust: 36·50 cm. Metropolitan Museum of Art, New York. Photo Metropolitan Museum (courtesy Metropolitan Museum, Rogers Fund, 12.233). O. Vessberg, *Studien zur Kunstgeschichte der römischen Republik*, 1941, pp. 224–5, plate 61, fig. 4. See p. 31.

6 Marble head either of Julius Caesar or of a middle aged man of his time. The find spot is unknown. The head is bald, with a few wisps of hair above the brow. The expression is determined. The features and the folds and wrinkles in the flesh are realistically treated, but the modelling is plastic and there is a classicising strain that is lacking in No. 5. Height of head and neck: 28 cm. Fitzwilliam Museum, Cambridge. Photo Fitzwilliam Museum (reproduced by permission of the Syndics). L. Budde and R. Nicholls, *A Catalogue of the Greek and Roman Sculptures in the Fitzwilliam Museum, Cambridge*, 1964, pp. 49–50, no. 82, plate 26. See p. 32.

7 Marble head of Augustus, found at Chiusi. The emperor is veiled for some priestly function. The portrait belongs to the 'Prima Porta' type of the late first century BC, with a three pronged fork of locks above the brow and individual, but idealised, features. Museo Etrusco, Chiusi. Photo Alinari. *Cambridge Ancient History*, vol. of plates iv, 1934, plate 44b. See p. 33.

8   Marble head of Nero. The find-spot is unknown. The emperor has deep-set eyes that gaze slightly upwards and tiers of trim, curving locks above the brow—the *coma in gradus formata* of Suetonius, *Nero*, 51. The modelling is rich and plastic and the treatment recalls the 'baroque' Hellenistic manner. Height of head and neck: 37·50 cm. AD 64–68. Art Museum, Worcester (Mass.). Photo Worcester Art Museum. M. Milkovich, *Roman Portraits* (Worcester Art Museum), 1961, no. 10, pp. 28–29. See p. 34.

9   Marble head of Vespasian, found at Ostia. The head is square, the hair is sparse, and the neck is wrinkled. The modelling is plastic, but the face, with its heavy folds of flesh, is highly naturalistic. This is the unidealised likeness of the strong-willed and shrewd, but homely, bourgeois emperor. Height of head and neck: 40 cm. AD 69–79. Museo Nazionale Romano delle Terme. Photo Anderson. See pp. 34–5.

10 Marble head of a young woman. The find-spot is unknown. The hair is parted in the centre and worn in two tiers of horizontal curls above the temples, with a single row of tight, round curls framing the brow and two stiff ringlets hanging down on either side of the neck. This was the coiffure affected by Messalina and Agrippina II, Claudius' empresses, and the diadem suggests membership of the imperial House. But the young woman does not resemble either of those two ladies very closely and she could be either Octavia, Claudius' ill-fated daughter and Nero's first wife, or Poppaea, Nero's second wife. Height of head and neck: 35·50 cm. Mid first century AD. Museo Nazionale Romano delle Terme. Photo German Archaeological Institute in Rome. B. M. Felletti Maj, *Museo Nazionale Romano: i ritratti*, 1953, p. 76, no. 131. See p. 36.

11 Colossal marble head of Trajan, found at Ostia. The face is modelled with great mastery and the individual locks of hair are carefully and delicately worked. The eyes are deep-set and the mouth determined. Height of head: 35 cm. AD 98–117. Ostia Museum. Photo Ostia Museum. W. H. Gross, *Bildnisse Trajans*, 1940, p. 132, no. 74, plates 33–35. See p. 35.

12 Marble bust of an elderly lady, found at Palombara Sabina, in central Italy. The features, while plastically modelled, are realistic and in-

dividualised. The hair is scraped back on either side of the head and gathered into a bun set high on the back of the head; and into this bun is also caught a long strand of hair looped to form a prominent puff (*nodus*) above the brow. Height of bust: 32 cm. Late first century BC. Museo Nazionale Romano delle Terme. See p. 35.

13 Marble funerary or honorific statue of a woman, found at Aphrodisias, in Caria. The figure wears a long tunic and a mantle, which is drawn over the head to form a veil and caught tightly round the right elbow. As the corn-ears and poppy held in the left hand indicate, the woman is represented, so far as her body is concerned, in the guise of Ceres. But the face is individual and in front the hair is worn over a high frame in a mountain of high corkscrew curls, after the Flavian fashion. Female fashions in coiffure seem to have spread rapidly from Rome even to distant provinces. Height of figure without plinth: 1·98 m. Late first century AD. Museum of Antiquities, Istanbul. Photo Museum of Antiquities. M. Squarciapino, *La scuola di Afrodisia*, 1943, pp. 53–54, plate 17. See p. 36.

14 Red porphyry head of Hadrian. The find-spot is unknown, but the material suggests that it was carved in Egypt. This is one of the earliest instances of the use of porphyry for an imperial portrait. The hair is richly curled above the brow and there is a short, neat beard. As in the earlier portraits of Hadrian, the pupils and irises of the eyes are not marked in. The smooth polish of the face is in effective contrast to the rough surfaces of the hair and beard. Height of head and neck: 38 cm. AD 117–138. British Museum. Photo British Museum (courtesy Trustees of the British Museum). M. Wegner, *Hadrian, etc.*, 1956, pp. 64, 101; *Fasti Archaeologici*, v, 1952, p. 312, no. 3638, fig. 80. See p. 36.

15 Head of Marcus Aurelius from the famous bronze equestrian statue on the Capitol. The find-spot is unknown. The emperor wears a tunic and a cloak and has a long, thin face, a thick mop of curly hair, and a luxuriant, flowing beard. Photo Anderson. See p. 37.

16 Marble bust of Septimius Severus. The head and body do not belong, but have been cut to fit together. The find-spot is believed to be the

Palatine, Rome. The emperor's luxuriant and curly hair and beard are heavily drilled, which gives to both a very pictorial effect with black and white sharply contrasted. The four locks dangling over the emperor's brow were copied from his patron, the Graeco-Egyptian god Serapis, one of whose art-types shows three, four, or occasionally five such forelocks. Height of bust: 67 cm. AD 197–211. British Museum. Photo British Museum (courtesy Trustees of the British Museum). R. P. Hinks, *Greek and Roman Portrait Sculpture*, 1935, p. 32, plate 44a. See p. 37.

17 Marble head of a woman of the time of Julia Domna, empress of Septimius Severus. The find-spot is unknown. The wig-like hair, which covers the ears completely and is turned up behind to form a pad at the back of the head, as in Julia Domna's portraits, is of onyx and made separately. The features are realistic and flexible in modelling. Height of head: 29 cm. AD 193–211 (or a little later). Ny Carlsberg Glyptotek, Copenhagen. Photo Ny Carlsberg Glyptotek. V. Poulsen, *Romersk Kunst*, 1948, p. 182 and fig. 96. See pp. 37–8.

18 Marble bust of Philip I (the Arabian), found at Porcigliano, in central Italy. The toga is worn in a manner that came into vogue during the third century, with a hard, broad, board-like transverse fold across the chest, known as the *trabea*. The emperor has skull-cap-like hair and a sheath-like beard, both pecked with short chisel-strokes. The facial planes are simplified, but the frowning brows and the schematic gashes on the forehead and the cheeks enhance the portrait's air of strain and apprehension. Height of bust: 71 cm. AD 244–249. Vatican Museum (Braccio Nuovo). Photo Anderson. B. M. Felletti Maj, *Iconografia romana imperiale da Severo Alessandro a M. Aurelio Carino*, 1958, pp. 170–1, no. 193, plate 23, fig. 75. See p. 39.

19 Marble bust of Caracalla, found in Rome. The hair and beard are thick and curly, but shorter and less heavily drilled than are those of his father, Septimius Severus. The scowling brows and sinister expression betray the emperor's character. Height of bust: 57 cm. AD 212–217. Former Berlin State Museum. Photo Berlin Museum. C. Blümel, *Staatliche Museen zu Berlin: Römische Bildnisse*, 1933, pp. 39–40, no. R. 96, plates 59–60. See p. 38.

20   Head of a more than life-size marble statue of Balbinus, found in the
      Piraeus, Attica. The emperor wears a plain diadem. The hair and beard
      are close-cropped and rendered by light chisel-strokes. The features are
      schematic, but there is a hint of realism in the lines on the brow and
      between the eyes. The pitting of the surface is due to the action of the
      water. Height of head: 28 cm. AD 238. Piraeus Museum. Photo German
      Archaeological Institute in Athens. *Jahreshefte des Österreichischen Archäo-
      logischen Instituts*, xxix, 1935, pp. 97–108, plates 4–6. See pp. 38–9.

21   Marble head of a man, from the Theatre of Dionysus, Athens. The
      treatment of the eyebrows, eyes, moustache, and short, curly beard
      strongly recalls portraits of the emperor Gallienus, under whom there was
      a revival of the Antonine 'baroque' style. Hence the Antonine date to
      which this head is sometimes assigned. The long, luxuriant, wig-like
      hair gives a leonine effect; and the head could conceivably be a portrait of
      Gallienus himself in the guise of Alexander the Great. Height of head and
      neck: 48 cm. *c.* AD 260–268. National Museum, Athens. Photo German
      Archaeological Institute in Athens. See p. 39.

22   Marble head of a man, found in Egypt. The diadem with a central
      medallion decorated with a seven-pointed star suggests that this man was a
      priest, possibly of some mystery-cult such as that of Serapis. The beard is
      straight and silky, but the hair, the moustache, and the rich, flexible
      modelling of the face recall Gallienic portraiture. The features are
      decidedly oriental in appearance, notably the strongly arched eyebrows, the
      prominent cheekbones, and the thrusting lower lip. The irises of the eyes
      are painted in. Height of head: 28·80 cm. *c.* AD 260–268. Former Berlin
      State Museum. Photo Berlin Museum. C. Blümel, *Staatliche Museen zu
      Berlin: Römische Bildnisse*, 1933, p. 41, no. R. 99, plate 63. See p. 39.

23   Colossal marble head of Constantine I, found in the Basilica of Con-
      stantine, Rome. The way in which the neck is finished off at the base and
      the fact that a colossal right hand, right arm, and right leg were found
      with the head show that this belonged to a probably acrolithic colossal
      statue. The hair is combed forward on to the brow in neat, slightly
      curving locks, the eyes are large and staring, and the chin is clean-shaven.
      Height of head and neck: 2·60 m. *c.* AD 324–337. Palazzo dei Con-

servatori, Rome. Ed. Stuart Jones, *The Sculptures of the Palazzo dei Conservatori*, 1926, pp. 5–6, no. 2; pp. 11–12, no. 13–15. See p. 40.

24 Marble head in high relief of Licinius I or Constantius I, recut from a head of Hadrian, in one of the eight Hadrianic roundels which are re-used on the Arch of Constantine, Rome. This roundel, one of the four on the north side of the Arch, shows the emperor sacrificing to Hercules. Of the other seven Hadrianic heads three are recut as portraits of Licinius I or Constantius I, four as portraits of Constantine I. The skull-cap-like hair is neatly rendered with the chisel and the sheath-like beard is pecked. The features are simplified. Only the furrows on the brow give a realistic touch. *c.* AD 315. Photo German Archaeological Institute in Rome. For publications, see Chapter IV, note 44. See p. 40.

25 Marble statue of a magistrate, from Aphrodisias, in Caria. The figure wears a long-sleeved tunic and an ample cloak. The drapery falls in stiff, patterned folds. The mop of thick, curly hair is heavily drilled. The face is schematised, with large eyes and two vertical gashes above the nose. The proportions of the body are slender, elongated, and spiritualised. Height of figure: 1·75 m. Late fourth or early fifth century AD. Museum of Antiquities, Istanbul. Photo Museum of Antiquities. See p. 42.

26 Marble statue of Antinous, from Delphi. The body is based on classical Greek models, the proportions of the torso being Polycleitan, the pose and the length of the legs, Lysippan. The head, inclined towards the specta-tor's right, has the carefully worked thick, curly hair, the idealised features, and the sensuous expression that characterise the Antinous type. Height of figure: 1·80 m. *c.* AD 130–134. Delphi Museum. Photo Alinari. See p. 44.

27 Marble statuary group of Jupiter Dolichenus, from his temple on the Aventine, Rome. The god, whose head is too large for his body, stands on the back of a bull, below the belly of which is an eagle. He wears a conical Syrian hat, a cuirass, and a sword-belt, and holds a thunderbolt in his left hand and a double axe in his right hand. His abundant and curly hair and beard are heavily drilled. Height of group: 1·60 m. Early third century AD. New Capitoline Museum, Rome. *Bollettino della*

Commissione Archeologica Comunale di Roma, lxiii, 1935 (1936), p. 151, no. 3, plate 3. See pp. 44-5.

28 Marble head of a barbarian, from Amman (Philadelphia), in Trans-jordania. The head belongs to the figure of a barbarian, naked save for a cloak, who is shown carrying a child and running as from a pursuer. The tumbled, flame-like hair, the anguished expression, and the strained, twisted pose of the body all recall Pergamene work of the first half of the second century BC. But the deep drilling and undercutting of the hair and beard and the highly polished flesh-surfaces are characteristic of the late second century AD. Height of head: 27 cm. Amman Museum. Photo Department of Antiquities of Palestine. See pp. 46-7.

29 Marble head of a Triton, from the Athenian Agora. It belongs to one of the figures (Tritons and Giants), virtually in the round, which are applied to the shafts of the pilasters of the portico added in the mid second century to the Odeion of Agrippa. The rendering of the features is classicising, but the heavily drilled and deeply undercut and wind-blown hair and flowing beard are distinctively Antonine. Mid second century AD. Height of head and neck: 70 cm. Agora Museum. Photo Agora Excavations, Athens. See p. 46.

30 Head of a horse from a group of gilt-bronze life-size statues, found at Cartoceto di Pergola, in north-east Italy. The group includes this head, another similar horse's head, a rider whose head, torso, arms, and legs from the knees downwards are preserved, and the almost complete standing figure of a heavily draped and veiled woman. The hair-styles of the rider and of the woman are of the Julio-Claudian period. Both horses, whose harness is adorned with medallions bearing human busts, are rendered with superb naturalism. Ancona Museum. Photo German Archaeo-logical Institute in Rome. See p. 48.

31 Bronze statuette of a sprinting pig, found at Pompeii. National Museum, Naples. Photo Alinari. See p. 48.

32 Bronze group of the goddess Artio and her tame bear, found at Muri, Switzerland. The bear is approaching from the forest, symbolised by a

tree. The goddess, whose throne is lost, is heavily draped and wears a diadem. She holds a bowl in her right hand and has fruit on her lap and a basket of fruit rests on a low stand beside her. On the plinth is an in-scription: *Deae Artioni Licinia Sabinilla* ('Licinia Sabinilla dedicated this to the goddess Artio'). Total height of group (from bottom of plinth to tree-top): 25·90 cm. Second or third century AD. Historical Museum, Berne. Photo Historical Museum. See p. 48.

33 The right-hand end of a carved frieze-block of grey limestone, found between the Piazza della Consolazione and the Via del Mare, Rome. The fragment shows a horse-chamfron decorated with an imitation flowing main. To the left can be seen a portion of the rim of a round shield. To the right, on the adjacent side of the block, is a cuirass. Early first century BC (?). Palazzo dei Conservatori (Braccio Nuovo), Rome. Photo German Archaeological Institute in Rome. See p. 50.

34 Part of the marble frieze from the exterior of the south precinct wall of the Ara Pacis Augustae, found below the Palazzo Fiano on what was the Campus Martius, Rome. The portion illustrated is from the emperor's procession to the site of the Ara on the day of its foundation, 4 July 13 BC. The foreground figures (passing from left to right) can be identified as flamens, the bearer of the ceremonial axe, Agrippa, his son Lucius Caesar, aged four in 13 BC, Agrippa's wife Julia (or Augustus' empress Livia, in which case the woman in the background laying her hand on the child's head would be Julia), Iullus Antonius, the son of Mark Antony and Fulvia and Praetor Urbanus in 13 BC. Height of the precinct wall, including the acanthus dado below the frieze (see plate 36): *c.* 6·30 m. 13–9 BC. On the reconstructed Ara Pacis, near the Ponte Cavour, Rome. Photo Anderson. See p. 52.

35 Part of the marble frieze from the exterior of the north precinct wall of the Ara Pacis Augustae (see plate 34). The portion illustrated is from the procession of the Roman people on 4 July 13 BC. It shows parents with their children, some carrying sprigs of laurel. Louvre, Paris. Photo Ander-son. See p. 52.

36 Part of the marble acanthus dado from the exterior of the precinct wall of the Ara Pacis Augustae (see plate 34). A slender stalk, bearing leaves

and flowers, shoots up vertically from a central calyx, from which sinuous acanthus scrolls, terminating in leaves and flowers, roll away to right and left across the surface of the wall. Tiny birds and insects lurk in the foliage. Reconstructed Ara Pacis. Photo Anderson. See pp. 52–3.

37 Marble panel depicting the *profectio* (departure) for war of the emperor Domitian, found near the Palazzo della Cancelleria, Rome. The figures (passing from right to left) are: a group of praetorian guardsmen, the Genius Populi Romani, the personification of the Roman Senate, Virtus, Domitian (whose head is recut as a portrait of Nerva), Minerva, Mars, a lictor, and Victory, of whom one wing only survives, the remainder of the panel being lost. Length of panel as preserved: 5·083 m. Late first century AD. Vatican Museum. Photo Archivio Fotografico Vaticano, Rome. See p. 56.

38 Marble swag of fruit and foliage from the upper part of the interior of the precinct walls of the Ara Pacis Augustae (see plate 34). The swag is tied to the horns of *bucrania* (ox-skulls) with fluttering ribbons. In the swag are corn-ears, fir-cones, ivy, pomegranates, quinces, grapes, olives, and oak. Reconstructed Ara Pacis. Photo Anderson. See p. 53.

39 Detail from the reliefs on Trajan's Column, showing a Roman legionary crossing a river. See plate 40. Photo (from a cast) Archivio Fotografico Vaticano. See p. 59.

40 Marble spiral relief-bands from the central part of the shaft of Trajan's Column, in Trajan's Forum, Rome. Among the scenes shown (passing from top to bottom) are: Sarmatian horsemen (in scale armour) fleeing from Romans; Dacian cavalry crossing a river and Dacians attacking a Roman stronghold; Roman auxiliaries displaying the heads of Dacians to Trajan and Roman cavalry attacking Dacians on foot; the building of a Roman stronghold. Total height of Column: 100 Roman feet (*c.* 37·50 m.); height of relief-bands: *c.* 1 m. AD 106–113. Photo Alinari. See pp. 57–60.

41 Marble panel from the left-hand side of the attic of Trajan's Arch at Beneventum, in south Italy, on the façade facing the city. The foreground figures (passing from left to right) are: Minerva, Jupiter, who is handing

his thunderbolt to Trajan (depicted with his suite on the corresponding panel on the right-hand side of the attic), and Juno; in the background are: Hercules, Bacchus, Ceres, and Mercury. Height of panel: *c.* 2·30 m. AD 114–118. Photo after *L'arco di Traiano a Benevento*, 1943, plate 12. See p. 62.

42 Marble panel showing an imperial group, found at Ephesus. The panel is one of a number of reliefs from some public monument. The figures (passing from left to right) probably represent: Marcus Aurelius, Antoninus Pius, Lucius Verus, and Hadrian. Probably AD 138. Belvedere, Vienna. See pp. 65–6.

43 Marble relief from one side of the base of the Column of Antoninus Pius, Rome. The scene shows a parade of infantry and cavalry. Height of base: 2·40 m. *c.* AD 161. Vatican Museum (Giardino della Pigna). Photo Archivio Fotografico Vaticano. See pp. 67–8.

44 Detail from the marble spiral relief-bands on the Column of Marcus Aurelius, Piazza Colonna, Rome. The scene shows the Rain-God poised above the prostrate forms of dead men and horses. Total height of Column: 100 Roman feet (*c.* 37·50 m.); height of relief-bands: *c.* 1 m. AD 180–195. Photo Anderson. See p. 71.

45 Marble relief above the northern lateral passage-way on the side facing the Capitol of the Arch of Septimius Severus in the Forum Romanum, Rome. The scenes are taken from the eastern campaigns of Septimius and include (above): an imperial *adlocutio* (harangue) (right), oriental women on the walls of a beleaguered city (centre), and Roman soldiers by a river-bank (left); (below): the siege of an eastern city (centre), a cavalry battle (right), and fleeing oriental horsemen (left). AD 203. Photo Studio Daisy, Rome (courtesy American Academy in Rome). See pp. 71–2.

46 Marble panel from the four-way Arch of Septimius Severus at Lepcis Magna, in Tripolitania. The scene shows part of a sacrifice in honour of the empress Julia Domna. Height of panel: 1·72 m. Early third century AD. Tripoli Museum. Photo J. B. Ward Perkins. See p. 74.

47 Marble reliefs on the north-east face of the south-west pier of the Arch of
Galerius at Salonika. The scenes (passing from top to bottom) show: an
emperor's arrival at an oriental city; a battle between Romans and
Persians; the four emperors in state, the two Augusti seated and the two
Caesars standing, accompanied by attendants and personifications; and
Victories, each in a niche. Total height of pilaster: 7·42 m. AD 297–311.
See pp. 76–7.

48 Marble frieze above the western lateral passage-way on the north side of
the Arch of Constantine, Rome. The scene depicts Constantine I dis-
tributing largesse to the citizens of Rome after his victory at the Milvian
Bridge in AD 312. Length of frieze: 5·38 m. AD 312–315. Photo Anderson. See p. 78.

49 Marble reliefs on the base of the obelisk of Theodosius I in the hippodrome of Constantinople. On the south-west side (left) the emperor and
his family, accompanied by a bodyguard and other attendants, watch a
chariot race in the circus, part of which is visible on the lower plinth. On
the south-east side (right) the emperor, with members of his family and
court, and two serried rows of citizens watch a dancing display for which
two water-organs are being played. Height of upper plinth: 2·36 m. c. AD
390. See p. 79.

50 Marble relief of Mithras Tauroctonos (Bull-Slayer), found in the
Mithraeum under the former Palazzo dei Musei, near the Velabrum,
Rome. Mithras, wearing a Phrygian cap, a cloak, a long-sleeved tunic,
and trousers, kneels on the back of the bull and plunges his knife into its
shoulder. A dog and a snake, symbols of the good dead, drink the bull's
life-giving blood, while a scorpion, a symbol of evil, attacks its vitals.
Corn-ears sprout from the dying bull's tail, a symbol of life through death.
To left and right stand Mithras' torch-bearing companions, Cautes and
Cautopates, representing light and darkness, life and death. In the left-
hand upper corner are Sol and the raven, sent by Sol to order the bull-
slaying; in the right-hand upper corner is Luna. Below Sol is the scene of
Mithras' capture of the bull in a cave. The inscription reads: *Deo Soli
Invicto Mithrae Ti(tus) Cl(audius) Hermes ob votum dei typum d(onum) d(edit).*
('Titus Claudius Hermes gave this representation of the god as a gift to the

god Mithras, the Unconquered Sun, in payment of a vow'). Height of panel: 87 cm. Third century AD. Antiquario Comunale, Rome. Photo Archivio Fotografico delle Antichità e Belle Arti, Rome. M. J. Vermaseren, *Corpus Inscriptionum et Monumentorum Religionis Mithriacae*, i, 1956, p. 184, no. 435–6, fig. 122. See p. 84.

51 Limestone altar dedicated to the Three Mothers, found at Bonn. On the upper part of the front is a relief of the Three Mothers, who are enthroned on a highbacked seat, all heavily draped and holding dishes of fruit on their laps. The two taller and older Mothers to right and left wear enormous, teacosylike headdresses, probably derived from the native headgear of older Rhineland women. The central Mother is younger and bareheaded, apart from a metal band adorning her hairparting, with long curly locks falling on to the shoulders. The three persons looking over the back of the seat may be the donor of the altar and his wife and daughter. On each short side of the altar (not shown here) is the figure of a girl holding a garland of flowers and a dish of fruit. The inscription on the front reads: *Matronis Aufaniabus Q(uintus) Vettius Severus, quaestor C(oloniae) C(laudiae) A(rae) A(grippinensium) votum solvit l(ibens) m(erito) Macrino et Celso co(n)s(ulibus)* ('Quintus Vettius Severus, treasurer of Cologne, paid this vow gladly and duly to the Aufanian Mothers in the consulship of Macrinus and Celsus'). Height of altar: 1·30 m. AD 164. Rheinisches Landesmuseum, Bonn. Photo Rheinisches Landesmuseum. *Aus Rheinischer Kunst und Kultur: Auswahlkatalog des Rheinischen Landesmuseums Bonn*, 1963, pp. 56–57, no. 17, with plate. See p. 85.

52 Marble Corinthian capital, found in the Baths of Caracalla, Rome. In the foliage stands the naked figure of Hercules, with his lion's skin, club, and bow. Height of capital: 1·16 m. Early third century AD. Baths of Caracalla. Photo Archivio Fotografico Vaticano. See p. 86.

53 Marble pilasters in the Severan basilica at Lepcis Magna, in Tripolitania. The pilaster on the left carries an acanthus scroll, in the spirals of which can be discerned a figure of Venus (below) and the foreparts of animals emerging from flowers. The pilaster on the right is adorned with a vine scroll, springing from a chalice, peopled with Bacchic figures, and surmounted by a Victory. Early third century AD. See p. 88.

54 Stone relief from a tomb, found at Neumagen, on the Mosel. It shows a school scene. The master and two pupils, reading from scrolls, are all seated in high-backed chairs. The master looks angrily at the third boy on the right, who is arriving late. Width of panel: 1·90 m. Late second or early third century AD. Provinzialmuseum, Trier. Photo Provinzialmuseum. W. von Massow, *Die Grabmäler von Neumagen*, 1932, pp. 132–42, no. 180, fig. 83–87, plate 27. See p. 90.

55 Marble relief, found in the tomb of the Haterii, Rome. It shows an elaborate mausoleum in the form of a gabled temple, with a portico of four columns and rich relief-work on its walls and *podium* and in its pediment. Above is the deceased woman lying on a couch. On the left is a great windlass with a wheel, pulleys, and ropes, presumably used in the construction of the mausoleum. Height of panel: 1·31 m. Lateran Museum. Late first century AD. Photo Anderson. O. Benndorf and R. Schöne, *Die antiken Bildwerke des Lateranischen Museums*, 1867, pp. 211–19, no. 344. See p. 92.

56 Marble figure, reclining on a bier, of a boy carved partly in the round and partly in high relief, found on the Via Laurentina, near Rome. The half-draping denotes apotheosis and the snake beside the boy's legs symbolises death. Although the child is supposed to be asleep, his eyes are open. First half of the first century AD. Museo Nazionale Romano delle Terme. Photo Anderson. See p. 97.

57 Marble sarcophagus, found in the tomb of the Egyptians in the Roman cemetery under St Peter's, Rome. The scene on the front, which depicts the discovery of the sleeping Ariadne by Bacchus and his train, is an allegory of the soul's awakening to a 'mystic marriage' with the god in paradise. On the lid, in lower relief, is a Bacchic revel-rout. Late second century AD. Vatican cemetery. Photo Sansaini, Rome. J. Toynbee and J. Ward Perkins, *The Shrine of St Peter and the Vatican Excavations*, 1956, pp. 55–56, plate 22. See p. 99.

58 Marble funerary altar. The find-spot is unknown. The principal side shows the *dextrarum iunctio* of bridegroom and bride, here interpreted as the 'mystic marriage' of husband and wife in paradise. The faces of the pair

are portrait-like and both display Julio-Claudian hair-styles. On the two adjacent sides are boy attendants carrying ritual objects—an umbrella, a basket of fruit, flower garlands, a casket, a cock in a cloth, a *patera*, and a jug—for use at a marriage sacrifice, here interpreted as a sacrifice in honour of the deceased pair. On the fourth side two ecstatic Maenads symbolise paradise. Height of altar: 94 cm. Mid first century AD. Museo Nazionale Romano delle Terme. Photo Gabinetto Fotografico Nazionale, Rome. See p. 95.

59 Marble sarcophagus, found in the Catacomb of Praetextatus, near Rome. On the lid, which takes the form of a bier, reclines a married pair, carved partly in relief and partly in the round, with portrait-like faces, who may be the emperor Balbinus and his empress. On the front (passing from right to left) are: the *dextrarum iunctio* of the man and wife; the man in full armour and his wife offering a sacrifice, with Victory poised between them and Mars to the right of the man; Roma (or Virtus) and Abun-dantia between the woman and the left-hand end of the front. The sarco-phagus has been reconstructed from fragments. Height including lid: 2 m. *c*. AD 238. Praetextatus Catacomb. Photo Archivio Fotografico Vaticano. See p. 102.

60 Marble sarcophagus, found on the Via Tiburtina, near Rome. The scene on the front shows a battle between Roman and Germanic cavalry. On the lid are scenes from the life of a Roman general. Height: 1·85 m. Second half of the second century AD. Museo Nazionale Romano delle Terme. Photo Anderson. B. Andreae, *Motivgeschichtliche Untersuchungen zu den römischen Schlachtsarkophagen*, 1956, p. 15, no. 13 (bibliography). See p. 102.

61 Marble sarcophagus. The find-spot is unknown. In the central roundel, framed by the Signs of the Zodiac, are the busts of a married pair. Below the roundel is a small-scale vintage scene. On either side are two figures of the Seasons in the guise of lanky winged boys—on the left, Winter crowned with reeds and sporting high, laced boots, and Spring crowned with flowers; on the right, Summer crowned with corn-ears, and Autumn crowned with branches of vine. Beside Spring is a small group of a man milking a goat, beside Summer, one of a harvester grasping a sheaf of

corn. All the attributes once held in the Seasons' hands are lost. Height: 1·90 m. *c.* AD 330. Dumbarton Oaks Collection, Harvard University. Photo courtesy Dumbarton Oaks Collection, Washington, D.C. See p. 103.

62 Marble column-sarcophagus, made in Asia Minor and found in a brick tomb at Alberi, near Melfi, in south Italy. This is the short side below the feet of the recumbent figure on the lid. The spirally fluted columns carry capitals and an entablature whose deep undercutting gives a lace-like, black-and-white effect. The figures between the columns (passing from left to right) are: Odysseus wearing a conical cap, Helen, and Diomedes. Total height of sarcophagus: 1·66 m. Second half of the second century AD. Palazzo Pubblico, Melfi. Photo German Archaeological Institute in Rome. See p. 105.

63 Part of the great painted frieze in the *triclinium* of the 'Villa of the Mysteries', Pompeii. On the left, a priestess and two attendants perform a rite of *lustratio* (purification). In the centre, a Silenus playing on a lyre and a male and a female Pan represent the Bacchic setting. At the end of the wall, on the right, a girl (the bride-initiate) starts back in alarm at what she has seen at the left end of the adjacent wall, namely the reflection in a wine bowl, held by a Silenus, of a hideous Silenus mask raised aloft by a Satyr. Height of frieze: 1·63 m. Mid first century BC (according to some critics, Augustan). Photo Anderson. See pp. 110–11.

64 Detail of the painting of a wood, from the walls of a room in the Villa of Livia at Prima Porta, north of Rome. Height of the walls from the floor to the beginning of the barrel-vaulted ceiling: 3 m. *c.* 40–25 BC. Museo Nazionale Romano delle Terme. Photo Istituto Nazionale L.U.C.E. See pp. 112–13.

65 Second Style wall painting in a room (*tablinum*) in the House of Augustus on the Palatine, Rome. The picture on the right shows Io, Argus, and Hermes, that on the left, Polyphemus and Galatea. Second half of the first century AD. Photo Anderson. See p. 116.

66 Two panels from the painted Odyssey frieze, found on the walls of a

room in a Roman house on the Esquiline Hill, Rome. The full panel on the left, with light pouring through a rocky arch, shows Odysseus in Hades talking with the ghosts of the deceased, many of whom have their names written beside them in Greek. The half-panel on the right depicts the punishment in Hades of notorious sinners—the Danaids, Sisyphus, and Tityus. Height of frieze: 1·50 m. Mid first century BC. Vatican Museum. Photo Alinari. See pp. 113–15.

67 Third Style painted wall in the House of Marcus Lucretius Fronto, Pompeii. The central picture shows the Triumph of Bacchus. First century AD. Photo Anderson. See p. 117.

68 Fourth Style painted room in the House of the Vettii, Pompeii. The central picture shows Ixion with his wheel, that on the left, Daedalus presenting the wooden cow to Pasiphae, that on the right, Bacchus and Ariadne. Between AD 63 and 79. Photo Anderson. See p. 119.

69 Panel picture on a Third Style wall in the House of Amandus, Pompeii. The scene shows the story of Daedalus and Icarus. Height of panel: 89 cm. First half of the first century AD. Photo Alinari. See p. 118.

70 Detail of a wall painting in a tomb at Ghirgaresh (Gargàresc), in Tripolitania. This is the candle-bearer on the right-hand side wall outside the principal burial niche. In his left hand he holds a flower garland. He wears a white dalmatic adorned with applied red bands and roundels and a white cloak. Fourth century AD. Photo Archivio Fotografico della Libia Occidentale. See p. 121.

71 Detail of a painted seascape or riverscape with boats and fishes on the wall of one of two vaulted chambers found at Pietra Papa (Porto Fluviale di S. Paolo), Rome. The boat, which is rowed by two nude men, while a third nude man steers, is brightly painted: a panel at the prow shows a reclining and a standing figure, one at the stern, a flying Victory. The fish are disproportionately large. Above the boat can be seen faint traces of three human figures on a larger scale than those in the boat, representing an almost obliterated under-painting. Length of boat: 1·20 m. Early second century AD. Photo Gabinetto Fotografico Nazionale, Rome. See p. 124.

72 Painting on the wall of a niche, found in a Roman house on the slopes of the Capitol, Rome. The scene shows Perseus rescuing Andromeda. Perseus wears a Phrygian cap and a cloak and holds a hooked bill for dealing with the sea-monster. Andromeda is half-draped and wears a pearl necklace and plain armlets. Fourth century AD. Antiquario Comun-ale, Rome. Photo S.P.Q.R. See p. 125.

73 Painting on a side wall adjacent to the terminal niche in the Mithraeum at Dura-Europos, on the Euphrates. Mithras wears a Phrygian cap, a tunic, a cloak, and trousers; he aims with his bow at six fleeing animals—two deer, a lion, a boar, and two gazelles. All have arrows sticking into them, except for the lion, for whom the arrow still in Mithras' bow is doubtless intended. Below the horse's hooves is a snake, a symbol of the good dead, accompanying the god. The colours are red, yellow, and ochre. Early third century AD. See p. 127.

74 Circular painting, probably in tempera, on wood, found in Egypt. It shows a family group of Septimius Severus, Julia Domna, Caracalla, and Geta (painted out). Diameter: 30·50 cm. End of the second century AD. Former Berlin State Museum. Photo Berlin Museum. See pp. 129–30.

75 Painted glass beaker, found in the hoard at Begram, in Afghanistan. The figure forms part of a group of gladiators at rest and in combat. This resting gladiator wears a plumed helmet, a cuirass, and greaves; he holds a spear and a small round shield. The colours are matt brown, ochre, yellow, yellow-red, and green. Height of beaker: 13·20 cm. Third century AD. Kabul Museum. Photo after J. Hackin, *Recherches archéo-logiques à Begram*, 1939, pp. 40–41, no. 201, plate 15, fig. 35. See p. 142.

76 Mummy painting in encaustic on a thin wooden board, found in Egypt. The portrait is that of a youngish man with curly hair and a short beard. He wears a white tunic and a purple cloak fastened with a gold brooch. Height of panel: 40 cm. First half of the second century AD. Myers Collection, Eton College. Photo by courtesy of the Provost and Fellows of Eton College. J. Chittenden and C. T. Seltman, *Greek Art*, 1947, no. 324, plate 79. See pp. 131–2.

77 Large mosaic pavement with a Nilotic landscape, worked in polychrome, in the Temple of Fortuna, Praeneste (Palestrina). Some of the details, particularly in the lower portion of the picture, are restorations. The animals in the upper portion have their names inscribed beside them in Greek, which suggests that the mosaicist may have used a copy-book designed for the illustrators of Greek zoological manuals. In its general effect as a panoramic landscape with naturalistically proportioned figures, this mosaic is the closest extant ancient parallel to the Odyssey landscape paintings (plate 66). Probably early first century BC, since it is likely to be the *lithostrotum* made of very small tesserae (*parvulae crustae*) which Pliny (*Nat. Hist.*, xxxvi, 184) says that Sulla had laid in the Praeneste temple. Photo Anderson. See p. 149.

78 Polychrome mosaic panel from a pavement, found in the 'Villa del Nilo', near Lepcis Magna, in Tripolitania. On the left is the Nile God riding on the back of a hippopotamus and accompanied by twelve small boys representing the number of cubits by which the river had to rise in order to fertilise the fields. On the right two Nymphs clash cymbals, a negro plays the trumpet, and another negro beats time. On the extreme right is a nilometer inscribed 'Good Luck'. Length of panel: 3·22 m. Second century AD. Lepcis Museum. Photo Archivio Fotografico della Libia Occidentale. See p. 150.

79 Black-and-white mosaic pavement in the 'Neptune Baths', Ostia. In the centre, Neptune is being drawn along by four sea-horses, but his chariot has been omitted. Swimming round the god are Nereids on the backs of sea-beasts, sea-Centaurs, human male figures, Cupids on dolphins, other dolphins and fish, and sea-animals of various sorts. 18·10 × 10·40 m. *c*. AD 140. Photo Anderson. See p. 151.

80 Black-and-white mosaic pavement in the 'Drivers' Baths', Ostia. In the central square, 'upheld' by four Atlas-like figures, is a grating for draining away water. In the four spaces between the Atlas-like figures are a man driving a mule cart; three men driving in a mule cart; a man leading two mules named *Pude(n)s* ('Bashful') and *Podagrosus* ('Gouty'); a man watering two mules named *Potiscus* ('Thirsty-Fish') and *Barosus* ('Molly-coddle'). Near the margin of the pavement (not shown here) are sea-

Centaurs, swimming men, etc. 8·70 m. square. Early second century AD. Photo Anderson. See p. 151.

81 Polychrome mosaic pavement from the Villa di Dar Buc Ammèra, Zliten, in Tripolitania. In the large central square is a grid of nine small squares, four containing busts of winged girls personifying the Seasons— Winter hooded and crowned with reeds (above), Spring crowned with flowers (left), Summer crowned with corn-ears (right), Autumn crowned with vine (below); the other five small squares are worked in *opus sectile* (see p. 159). The six lateral squares contain birds and animals, fish, and Nilotic scenes. 3·33 × 2·30 m. Beginning of the fourth century AD. Photo Archivio Fotografico della Libia Occidentale. See p. 154.

82 Detail of the polychrome mosaic pavement in the 'Great Hunt' corridor in the Roman villa near Piazza Armerina, in central Sicily. On the left is the group of the proprietor of the villa, who wears a round cap and a tunic and a mantle that are both richly embroidered, watching the progress of the hunt in the company of two shield-bearing attendants. On the right and above are hunters and wild animals. Total height of frieze: 4 m. Probably second half of the fourth century AD. Photo A. Balbo, Piazza Armerina. See p. 156.

83 Detail of the polychrome mosaic pavement in the north-east colonnade of the peristyle of the Great Palace of the Byzantine Emperors in Constantinople. A brown and yellow eagle with a dark blue-grey left wing is fighting a slate-blue and olive-green snake with pink markings. This group is in the central tier of the frieze, which contains three tiers of figures. In the lower left-hand corner of the plate can be seen the figure of a man, armed with a spear and a shield, in the bottom tier. Total height of frieze: 5·38 m. Fifth or sixth century AD. See pp. 156-7.

84 Part of the vault mosaic in the ambulatory of the Church of Santa Costanza, Rome. This panel contains a spreading vine scroll peopled with birds and naked boys. In the centre is a large portrait bust and on each of the long sides is a vintage scene. The border of interlaced circles is typical of fourth-century mosaic work. The panel on the left consists of circles containing busts, standing figures, and rosettes; that on the right consists

of octagons and circles containing Cupids, birds, and floral motifs. Fourth century AD. Photo Anderson. See p. 158.

85 Glass-paste mosaic façade of a *nymphaeum* installed in one wall of the internal courtyard of the 'House of Neptune and Amphitrite' at Herculaneum. On another wall is a mosaic picture of Neptune and Amphitrite, from which the house gets its name. First century AD. Photo Alinari. See p. 157.

86 Bronze mask from a face-mask visor-helmet, found at Straubing, in Bavaria. Such helmets are described in the first half of the second century AD by Arrian (*Tactica*, 34 ff.) as worn by Roman auxiliary cavalrymen in sports and exercises (*hippika gymnasia*), which the Romans borrowed from the Celts and Iberians and which seem to have had, in the Roman army, a quasi-religious and dramatic character. They are made of very thin metal, with openings at the eyes, the nostrils, and the mouth, and were not intended for use in battle. This mask, although of course worn by a man, appears to be female. It has a great wig, or toupet, which envelops the ears, rises to a sharp point high above the brow, and is covered in front with rows of minute round curls. The mask has something of an oriental flavour, but it may have been partly influenced by Roman stage masks. Height: 27·50 cm. Probably second century AD. Straubing Museum. Photo Bayer. Landesamt für Denkmalpflege. See p. 160.

87 Two silver two-handled cups with figured relief work found at Hoby, on the
a, b south coast of the island of Lolland, in Denmark. On one (b) is depicted the coming of Priam to the tent of Achilles to beg for Hector's body. Achilles is seated with his arms beside him and is accompanied by two youths and two women. Priam, wearing oriental dress (Phrygian cap, trousers, etc.) kneels before Achilles and kisses his hand. On the other side of the cup (not shown here) are Priam's chariot and his aged charioteer, seated asleep, and three sleeping Greek heroes, including Odysseus, with a conical cap. The cup is signed in Greek Χειρίσοφος ἐπόει ('Cheirisophos made it'). On the second cup (a) is presented the story of Philoctetes. The youthful Philoctetes is seated naked, while attendants support him and dress the snake-bite on his foot. On a tree to the right hang the bow and quiver given to Philoctetes by Herakles. On the other

side of the cup (not shown here) the aged Philoctetes, leaning on a staff, is seated on a rock on the island of Lemnos. Before him sits Odysseus, wearing his conical cap, accompanied by Diomedes, and explaining to Philoctetes that he must go with him to Troy, which could not be taken without the arms of Herakles. On the right a servant of Philoctetes is preparing a bird for the heroes' supper. This cup is signed in Greek, but in Latin characters, *Chirisophos epoi* ('Cheirisophos made it'). The Priam and Achilles cup is also inscribed with the name *Silius*, probably that of the owner. Height of cups: 10·90 cm. First century BC or AD. National Museum, Copenhagen. Photo National Museum. See p. 160.

88   Central medallion in the interior of a large silver dish, found at Cesena, in north Italy. The figure scenes, for the most part gilded, are engraved in the silver against a dark niello background. In the upper zone five men are dining out of doors among trees and beneath an awning. They recline on a semicircular couch and are waited on by two servants. In the centre is a small round table covered with a cloth on which the eatables are set out. In the lower zone a groom, again in a setting of trees, is leading a horse out of an elaborate stable with a gabled roof. Below are a stream, a trough, and four birds. The upper zone could represent the celestial banquet and the horse in the lower zone the ride to the other world. Diameter of medallion: 25 cm. Late fourth century AD. Biblioteca Malatestiana, Cesena. Photo Villani, Bologna. See p. 160.

89   Stucco panel from a vault in the Roman house found in the grounds of the Farnesina Villa, on the right bank of the Tiber, Rome. The scene shows a rocky landscape, with a stream, spanned by an arched bridge, in the centre. On the bridge are two women carrying water, one of whom gives a drink from her jar to a kneeling man. On either side of the bridge is a group of buildings: on the left, surrounding a sacred tree, is a walled precinct with columned galleries and a columned entrance, topped by an urn; on the right are an urn-bearing sacred pillar and a sacred tree in the centre of an open colonnade. The details of the figures, trees, and buildings in this idyllic picture are treated with an exquisite delicacy. Late first century BC. Museo Nazionale Romano delle Terme. Photo Moscioni. See p. 161.

90 Panel from an ivory consular diptych. The find-spot is unknown. Such diptychs were given by the consuls, when they entered upon office, as mementoes to their friends. The scene in relief is that of an imperial apotheosis. Below, a large seated statue of an emperor in a gabled shrine is being drawn along on a car by four elephants, each of which has a rider. To the left of the statue the naked soul of the emperor is rising heavenward from the funerary pyre in a four-horse chariot, accompanied by two eagles. Above, the emperor, fully clad, is being carried by two winged Genii into heaven, where four persons receive him. On the right is a curved band containing the Signs of the Zodiac and a bust of Sol. The style of the emperor's dress and the triangle of hair above his brow suggest that he is Antoninus Pius, the four-hundreth anniversary of whose birth was in 486, while the three-hundredth anniversary of his consecra- tion was in 461. The diptych could have been carved with a reference to one of those occasions—a pagan revival under the Christian Empire. Height of panel: 30 cm. Fifth century AD. British Museum. Photo British Museum (courtesy Trustees of the British Museum). R. Delbrueck, *Die Consulardiptychen*, 1929, pp. 227–30, no. 59. See p. 161.

91 Sardonyx cameo in brown and white layers, set in a modern frame. The find-spot is unknown. The portrait is that of the emperor Claudius (16 BC–AD 54), in the guise of Jupiter, with a laurel wreath, a sceptre, and an aegis over his cuirass. The features are idealised, but the double chin and thick neck are individual traits. Dimensions of cameo: 19·10 × 14·60 cm. Mid first century AD. Royal Collection, Windsor Castle. Photo reproduced by gracious permission of H.M. the Queen. *Journal of Roman Studies*, xxix, 1939, p. 148, plate 16 (from a cast). See p. 161.

Index

Numbers in brackets refer to illustrations and notes on them.

264